Ancient Scepticism

Ancient Philosophies

This series provides fresh and engaging new introductions to the major schools of philosophy of antiquity. Designed for students of philosophy and classics, the books offer clear and rigorous presentation of core ideas and lay the foundation for a thorough understanding of their subjects. Primary texts are handled in translation and the readers are provided with useful glossaries, chronologies and guides to the primary source material.

Published

Ancient Scepticism
Harald Thorsrud

Cynics
William Desmond

Neoplatonism
Pauliina Remes

Presocratics
James Warren

Stoicism
John Sellars

Forthcoming

The Ancient Commentators
on Plato and Aristotle
Miira Tuominen

Aristotle
Vasilis Politis

Classical Islamic Philosophy
Deborah Black

Confucianism
Paul Goldin

Epicureanism
Tim O'Keefe

Plato
Andrew Mason

Socrates
Mark McPherran

Ancient Scepticism

Harald Thorsrud

ACUMEN

First published in 2009 by Acumen

Acumen Publishing Limited
Stocksfield Hall
Stocksfield
NE43 7TN
www.acumenpublishing.co.uk

ISBN: 978-1-84465-130-6 (hardcover)
ISBN: 978-1-84465-131-3 (paperback)

British Library Cataloguing-in-Publication Data
A catalogue record for this book is available
from the British Library.

Typeset in Minion.
Printed and bound by Biddles Ltd., King's Lynn.

For her patience, understanding and love, this book is dedicated to Laura: *amicus certus in re incerta cernitur.*

Contents

Preface

When I was a graduate student a slogan was proposed for a department T-shirt: "Philosophy. We've done less in 2,500 years than most people do in a single day." The slogan was rejected. But it reflects a serious sceptical sentiment. When we consider the remarkable progress made by science in the past 400 years, philosophy appears in an unfavourable light. At a minimum, we would like to know why there is so little agreement among professional academics regarding the solutions to philosophical problems, their proper articulation, and even the methods suitable to resolving them.

My desire to find a satisfactory explanation of pervasive disagreement has sustained my interest in the ancient Sceptics. From their arguments and strategies, we can construct various explanations for why philosophers have not and perhaps will not reach consensus. There are, of course, plenty of non-sceptical solutions as well, and I am not convinced that I have a satisfactory explanation yet. But reflecting on the arguments of the ancient Sceptics has proved to be immensely valuable in getting to grips with the broad issue of the limits of reason.

The Sceptics also have some fascinating things to say about the proper response to our rational limitations. These responses are meant to show how Scepticism is a viable position and not merely a set of arguments confined to the study or the classroom. While I cannot say that I have tried to live without beliefs, as the Sceptics suggest we should, their proposals have inspired me to think more clearly about fundamental problems regarding the nature of rational belief and appearances, and the roles they play in action.

It is my hope that this book will encourage readers interested in these and related issues to further their own enquiries. I have tried not to presuppose familiarity with earlier Greek philosophers or with the Sceptics' contemporaries, instead supplying the details where necessary. I have aimed at producing a coherent historical narrative in which to situate the development and transmission of ancient sceptical arguments and strategies.

Nearly every portion of this account, however, is controversial. This is why I have tried to be thorough in providing references to both primary and secondary sources. The references can always be ignored, but they will be helpful for those interested in pursuing a particular idea, especially given the variety of plausible interpretations that are often available. Similarly, the guide to further reading is probably far more extensive than many readers will require. But as it is arranged in sections corresponding to the major figures and periods of ancient Scepticism, I hope it will prove useful for further study.

I had the good fortune to be introduced to the ancient Sceptics by Jim Hankinson and Paul Woodruff, and to Hellenistic philosophy more generally by Stephen White. They were excellent guides, as well as models, and have given me a great deal of encouragement. I am very grateful to the publisher's anonymous readers who provided many detailed and insightful comments, as well as to Tim O'Keefe, Wilhelm Nightingale and Ralph Anske, all of whom read and commented on the manuscript. Also, my students in a seminar at Agnes Scott College generously offered helpful comments on early drafts of the chapters. Although it is likely that some errors or oversights remain, this book is far better for the revisions I have been able to make in response to this critical attention.

My thanks to Kate Williams for expert copy-editing and to Steven Gerrard at Acumen for seeing this project through and for locating the spectacular painting of Carneades on the cover.

Sources and abbreviations

Anonymous
  In Tht. = *In Theaetetum (Commentary on Plato's Theaetetus)*

Aristotle
  NE = *Nicomachean Ethics*
  Met. = *Metaphysics*
  Rh. = *Rhetoric*

Augustine
  Contra Ac. = *Contra Academicos (Against the Academicians)*

Aulus Gellius
  NA = *Noctes Atticae (Attic Nights)*

Cicero
  Ac. = *Academica (Academic Books)*
  Amic. = *De Amicitia (On Friendship)*
  Att. = *Epistularum ad Atticum (Letters to Atticus)*
  De Or. = *De Oratore (On the Orator)*
  Div. = *De Divinatione (On Divination)*
  Fin. = *De Finibus Bonorum et Malorum (On Moral Ends)*
  Fat. = *De Fato (On Fate)*
  Inv. = *De Inventione (On [Rhetorical] Invention)*
  Leg. = *De Legibus (On the Laws)*
  ND = *De Natura Deorum (On the Nature of the Gods)*
  Off. = *De Officiis (On Duties)*

Orat. = *Orator*
Rep. = *De Republica (On the Republic)*
Top. = *Topica*
Tusc. = *Tusculanae Disputationes (Tusculan Disputations)*

Diogenes Laertius
DL = *Lives and Opinions of Eminent Philosophers in Ten Books*

Eusebius
Praep. Ev. = *Praeparatio Evangelica (Preparation for the Gospels)*

Lactantius
Div. Inst. = *Divinae Institutiones (Divine Institutes)*

Philo of Alexandria
De Ebr. = *De Ebrietate (On Drunkenness)*

Philodemus
Index Ac. = *Index Academicorum (History of the Academy)*

Photius
Bib. = *Bibliotheca (Library)*

Plato
Ap. = *Apology*
Gorg. = *Gorgias*
Prot. = *Protagoras*
Rep. = *Republic*
, *Tht.* = *Theaetetus*

Plutarch
Adv. Col. = *Adversus Colotem (Against Colotes)*
Com. Not. = *De Communibus Notitiis (Against the Stoics on Common Conceptions)*
Prof. Virt. = *De Profectibus in Virtute (On Moral Progress)*
St. Rep. = *De Stoicorum Repugnantiis (On Stoic Self-Contradictions)*
Vit. Alex. = *Vitae Parallelae, Alexander (Parallel Lives, Alexander)*
Vit. Cat. Mai = *Vitae Parallelae, Cato Maior (Parallel Lives, Life of Cato the Elder)*

Sextus Empiricus
M = *Pros Mathēmatikous (Latin: Adversus Mathematicos; Against the Professors)*

PH = Pyrrhoniae Hypotyposes (Outlines of Pyrrhonism)

Many of the passages from these and other relevant sources are excerpted
and translated in:

IG = B. Inwood & L. P. Gerson (eds), *Hellenistic Philosophy: Introductory Readings*, 2nd edn (Indianapolis, IN: Hackett, 1997).

LS = A. A. Long & D. N. Sedley (eds), *The Hellenistic Philosophers*, 2 vols (Cambridge: Cambridge University Press, 1987).

Chronology

Many of the dates below are approximate (see the *Oxford Classical Dictionary* and Dorandi 1999). The dating of events in the Academy in the first century BCE is particularly controversial, as are the dates for the later Pyrrhonists.

BCE

399	Death of Socrates
387	Plato opens the Academy
347	Death of Plato, Speusippus becomes head of the Academy
334–324	Anaxarchus and Pyrrho travel through Asia with Alexander the Great
335	Aristotle opens the Lyceum
300	Zeno opens the Stoa; Timon becomes a student of Pyrrho
298	Arcesilaus comes to Athens, eventually studies at the Academy
275	Death of Pyrrho
268	Arcesilaus becomes head of the Academy, initiating its sceptical phase
241	Death of Arcesilaus
230	Death of Timon
156/5	Carneades goes to Rome as part of an Athenian embassy, having earlier become head of the Academy

137 Carneades retires

128 Death of Carneades, Clitomachus becomes head of the Academy

110 Philo of Larissa becomes head of the Academy

90 Antiochus secedes from Philo's Academy

89/8 Philo flees to Rome from political instability in Athens

early-mid 1st century (?) Aenesidemus revives Pyrrhonism

84 Death of Philo

68 Death of Antiochus

46–44 Cicero writes most of his philosophical dialogues

43 Death of Cicero

1st century Anonymous commentator on Plato's *Theaetetus*
             Philodemus

30–45 CE Philo of Alexandria

CE

1st–2nd century (?) Agrippa (some time between Aenesidemus and Sextus)

46–125 Plutarch

125–180 Aulus Gellius

2nd century Numenius

Aristocles (although he may be as early as the first century BCE)

2nd–3rd century Sextus Empiricus

3rd century Diogenes Laertius

240–320 Lactantius

260–339 Eusebius

354–430 Augustine

9th century Photius

ONE
Introduction

The Greek word *skepsis* means enquiry or investigation. But a sceptic is not merely one who investigates; almost everyone does that. Sceptical investigation is distinctively shaped by the possibility of deception and error; and it is an important corrective to our credulous and sometimes gullible inclinations. In this book we shall examine the two philosophical movements – Pyrrhonian and Academic – that stretch from approximately the third century BCE to the second century CE and together constitute ancient Scepticism.

Both Academic and Pyrrhonian Scepticism develop in complicated ways in response to each other and in response to their common dogmatic opponents. In order to trace these lines of historical influence and development, I present the Sceptics in the following chapters in chronological order (with the exception of Chapters 5 and 6). While it would be misleading to describe the whole of ancient Scepticism as a unified philosophical movement, the ancient Sceptics do share some family resemblances. As a general introduction, I offer a brief characterization of common argumentative strategies and concerns followed by a sketch of the historical narrative to be developed and some remarks about the distinction between Academics and Pyrrhonists.

Suspension of judgement

By the time the Sceptics arrived on the scene there were many competing and incompatible philosophical theories available. One of the central preoccupations of Greek philosophy from the Presocratics onward was to account for the variability and deceptiveness of appearances, and more generally to explain how and why things change. This led to a great deal of speculation and philosophical argument regarding the relation of appearance to reality. But on this important issue, as on virtually everything else, philosophers disagree. This fact adds considerably to the sceptic's impression that we are not up to the task of explaining the variability and deceptiveness of appearances. Philosophers as well as ordinary people disagree with each other about virtually everything; at times we even disagree with ourselves.

The solution, it seems, must be epistemic: we need some nonarbitrary and principled way to resolve these disagreements. But even with regard to the proper method for resolving disagreements, philosophers disagree.

All of this is grist for the sceptical mill. But ancient Scepticism does not develop merely as a rejection of the aspirations and views of earlier philosophers; it also draws on them in a positive way.

Perhaps the most valuable skill the Greek Sophists (fifth and fourth centuries BCE) offered to teach is the ability to argue persuasively for or against any proposition. Protagoras, for example, claims that on every issue there are two opposed accounts (DL 9.51, see also 3.37), and that mastering his rhetorical techniques will lead to sound, practical judgement (*Prot.* 319a). The historian Thucydides, who is strongly influenced by the Sophists, opposes one account of events to another in order to do justice to the complexity of human affairs and to arrive at a properly cautious, and informed, judgement (*History of the Peloponnesian War* 1.22–23). The Sophist Antiphon teaches his students how to oppose arguments for the sake of learning to be an effective legal advocate. For his part, Aristotle counters Plato's worry about the unscrupulous use of rhetorical power by claiming that arguing for and against an issue, and deriving opposed conclusions from the same premises, helps us to discern where the truth lies (*Rh.* 1.1; *Topics* 1.1–2, especially 101a34–36).

In general, the practice of opposing arguments was developed as a valuable means of arriving at philosophical judgements about the truth, deliberative decisions about the best course of action and forensic judgements about innocence and guilt. In many of the Sceptical appropriations of this method, however, the outcome is suspension of judgement (*epochē*), even if the goal is initially the discovery of truth. (However, Cicero's later Academic version of this method marks a reversion to its originally positive employment; see Chapter 5, and further below.)

In so far as the ancient Sceptics promote the suspension of judgement, they are quite unlike other schools or movements. Normally we seek to understand a philosopher in terms of his doctrines, and the arguments he offers in support. For example, a Stoic believes virtue is sufficient for a good life, an Aristotelian believes we need some external goods in addition to virtue to live well, and an Epicurean believes nothing is worthwhile in the absence of pleasure. When studying such philosophers we try to determine what their doctrines amount to and why they believe them to be true.

We employ the same focus whether the doctrines in question are positive or negative. An atheist, for example, argues that God does not exist, or that we cannot know whether God exists. And an anti-realist argues that there are no mind-independent structures in the world, or that we cannot know such structures exist. Even though we sometimes refer to such views as sceptical, we must note that the cognitive attitude expressed is not uncertainty or indecision, but rather a kind of belief: to disbelieve *p* is to believe that not-*p*. From the agnostic's standpoint, both the theist and the atheist are mistaken. And generally speaking, from the standpoint of one who has suspended judgement, those who confidently deny are just as dogmatic as those who confidently affirm. For this reason the former are often referred to as negative dogmatists.

It is controversial whether any ancient Sceptics were negative dogmatists. Whether or not they were (which will be explored case by case in the following chapters) it is easy to see how they might have appeared to be. As far as the sceptic is concerned, no one, so far, has managed to establish a non-arbitrary, principled way of resolving the ubiquitous disputes. Every argument has so far been (or at least could be) refuted or met with an equally compelling counter-argument. If the Sceptics were so successful in refuting all arguments, it is hard to see how they could resist the negatively dogmatic conclusion that knowledge is impossible. At the very least it seems they must have believed something about our cognitive limitations, or about what we should do in light of these limitations.

Inconsistency

This suspicion is evident in the frequently raised objection that it is inconsistent to claim to know that knowledge is impossible or even to believe that we should have no beliefs. More generally, the project of rationally establishing that nothing can be rationally established seems to be a non-starter. Either the sceptic will provide reasons for this conclusion or he will not. But he would not provide reasons if he thought it were futile to do so. So he has to assume that we *can* rationally establish something if he is going to try to rationally establish that we *cannot*. On the other hand, if the sceptic offers no reasons, then it seems we can just ignore him.

We may restate this problem by considering the status of the premises in sceptical arguments. Either the sceptic has adequate justification for his premises or he does not. In either case he is in trouble. If he has adequate justification, scepticism is refuted. If he does not, then we may demand to be persuaded that his premises are true. The only way he can do this is to show that his premises are adequately justified, which again undermines his sceptical conclusion. (For more on this argument see Chapter 7.)

But the sceptic does not need to employ any personal convictions in his arguments. Instead, he may draw all that he needs from his interlocutor. Plato often portrays Socrates arguing in this manner. In his conversation with Euthyphro, for example, Socrates draws out the implications of a definition of piety that he probably does not accept himself. If we say that piety is what is dear to the gods, and we believe that the same thing is dear to Hera but displeasing to Hephaestus, we will have to conclude that the same thing is and is not pious (*Euthyphro* 7a–8a). Whether or not Socrates accepts any of these propositions is beside the point since he is primarily interested in testing Euthyphro. This is why Socrates elsewhere compares himself to a barren midwife who gives birth to no philosophical theses but merely draws them out of others (*Tht.* 148e–149a).

This style of argument is called "*ad hominem*", not in the pejorative sense of an irrelevant attack on someone's character, but because it relies solely on the proponent's own views. It is also called "dialectical", since the argument is essentially part of a dialogue in which one person defends his position against the other's attack. From the sceptic's perspective, the crucial point is that the questioner need not endorse either the premises or the conclusion of the argument. He may even remain agnostic about the standard of justification that he holds his interlocutor to.

The dialectical style of argument is a common sceptical strategy, but it is by no means a necessary feature of ancient Scepticism. Nevertheless, this strategy shows us one of the ways of responding to the inconsistency charge. If the sceptic is able to engage in his characteristic argumentative activity without committing himself to any beliefs about the efficacy of reason, the desirability of truth or some other related matter, then he will not be vulnerable to the charge of inconsistency. Since the sceptic need not believe anything he is asserting, he cannot be charged with inconsistently believing those things.

But the persistence with which the charge of inconsistency is levelled suggests either a persistent misunderstanding or that at least some Sceptics did in fact hold some second-order beliefs about the status of first-order beliefs; in other words, perhaps some of them did believe they knew that knowledge is impossible or that we should hold no beliefs. It is, after all, a short step from the observation that so far no belief has been adequately justified to the dogmatic conclusion that no belief can be justified. Academic Sceptics, in particular, have been thought to be negatively dogmatic in this way. In Chapters

3 and 4 we shall see why this claim is so often repeated and why it is mistaken.

Impracticality

While the charge of inconsistency presupposes that the sceptic has some beliefs, another persistent objection presupposes that the sceptic has no beliefs. Many critics argue that a life without beliefs is impractical, claiming that one must have beliefs either in order to act, or, at least, in order to act well and live a good, moral life (see Striker 1980). This type of objection is aptly described by the Greek term *apraxia* (inaction).

In responding to *apraxia* objections the Sceptics describe various positive attitudes one may take towards appearances without compromising the suspension of judgement. (We should note that in these discussions, intellectual seemings are counted as appearances along with ordinary perceptual seemings – so it may appear that the book is green, and it may appear that two arguments are equally compelling.) There is no standard sceptical account of how life without belief is possible. This is due in part to differences about the scope of *epochē* (how much we are to suspend judgement about) as well as the proper understanding of the sceptically acceptable attitudes that guide the Sceptics' actions.

Despite these differences, the fact that most Sceptics were so keen to respond to *apraxia* objections indicates how important the practicality of scepticism is to them. Unlike most modern and contemporary varieties, the ancient Sceptics offered their scepticism as a way of life. This is in keeping with the general Hellenistic emphasis on philosophy as a set of practices or spiritual exercises (Hadot 1995, 2002). As we shall see in Chapter 2, the earliest official ancient Sceptic, Pyrrho, makes the revolutionary move of substituting the question "What must I know to live well?" with the sceptical question "How can I still live well in the absence of knowledge?"

The insistence on the viability of scepticism is in stark contrast with the way modern and contemporary philosophers often insulate their daily life from their sceptical doubts. For example, after proposing to take seriously the possibility that there is an all-powerful evil demon systematically deceiving him, Descartes calms the fears that might arise from his radical hypothesis: "I know that no danger or error will result from my plan, and that I cannot possibly go too far in my distrustful attitude. This is because the task now in hand does not involve action but merely the acquisition of knowledge" (Cottingham 1986: 15). The point of Descartes' sceptical journey is to establish the reliability of his cognitive equipment, thereby providing a firm and lasting foundation for the sciences. And while he is convinced that scientific progress will improve the human condition, his attempt to establish its philosophical foundation is a purely theoretical matter. His scepticism is a thought experiment. He has no intention of allowing such speculation to influence his actions, and he would be utterly unimpressed by the *apraxia* objection.

None of the ancient Sceptics start out with the view that scepticism is an awful, if rarefied, condition that must be overcome. Ancient Scepticism is not so much a problem or set of objections as an argumentative practice situated in a philosophical way of life. And, at least for Pyrrhonian Sceptics, *epochē* is an accomplishment and the means to tranquility.[1]

The distinction between Academics and Pyrrhonists

Although it is easy enough to classify the Sceptics as Academic or Pyrrhonist (see Figure 1), this sheds little light on any substantive differences between individual Sceptics or between the two camps more generally.

In the second century CE, the Roman author Aulus Gellius refers to the distinction between Academics and Pyrrhonists as an old question treated by many Greek writers (*NA* 11.5.6; see Striker 1981). Gellius uses the following terms to describe both Academics and Pyrrhonists: *skeptikoi* (those who investigate), *ephektikoi* (those who suspend judgement), and *aporētikoi* (those who are puzzled).[2] As to the difference, he reports it in this way:

the Academics apprehend[3] (in some sense) the very fact that nothing can be apprehended, and they determine (in some sense) that nothing can be determined, whereas the Pyrrhonists assert that not even that seems to be true, since nothing seems to be true.   (*NA* 11.5.8)

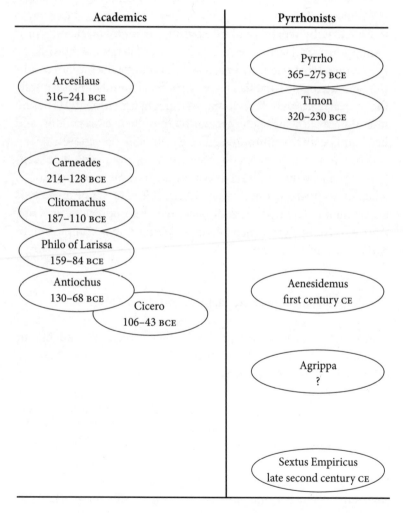

Figure 1. Academics and Pyrrhonists.

The Pyrrhonian Sceptic Sextus Empiricus offers roughly the same distinction in his preliminary division of kinds of philosophy:

> Those who are called Dogmatists ... think they have discovered the truth ... The schools of Clitomachus and Carneades, and other Academics, have asserted that things cannot be apprehended. And the Sceptics are still investigating. Hence the most fundamental kinds of philosophy are reasonably thought to be three: the Dogmatic, the Academic, and the Sceptical. (*PH* 1.3–4)[4]

It is crucial to note that he singles out Clitomachus and Carneades as negatively dogmatic Academics, since we find later that he does not think that all Academics fit this mould.

> There have been, so most people say, three Academies: one – the oldest – was Plato's, a second was the Middle Academy of Arcesilaus ... and the third was the New Academy of Carneades and Clitomachus. Some add a fourth, the Academy of Philo ... and some reckon as a fifth the Academy of Antiochus. (*PH* 1.220)

Sextus goes on to show how his Pyrrhonism differs from each of these Academic positions. At the beginning of the Academy, Plato is clearly dogmatic in so far as he makes assertions about Forms, or providence, or the virtuous life. And at the end of the Academy, Philo and Antiochus are dogmatic in allowing for some form of apprehension (see Chapter 5). It is only the intervening positions of Arcesilaus and Carneades that might plausibly be thought to be the same as Pyrrhonian Scepticism.

But according to Sextus, Carneades makes confident affirmations about things being inapprehensible, while the Pyrrhonian Sceptics do not. Furthermore, Carneades relies on, or goes along with, the way things seem when he has determined they are plausible. Pyrrhonists, by contrast, do not make such distinctions among appearances to which they yield in a more passive sense. (We shall explore

Carneades' plausible appearances in Chapter 4, and Sextus' reliance on appearances in Chapter 9).

The proper understanding of these distinctions is highly controversial. In particular it is unclear whether it is fair to describe Carneades as negatively dogmatic, and permanently closed to the possibility of discovering the truth. Although Carneades does confidently argue and affirm that things are not apprehensible, in Cicero's account he does not claim to have apprehended this (*Ac.* 2.110). Furthermore, his affirmations may have been part of a dialectical strategy, in which case they would not have been affirmed in his own voice. So it is possible to reject Carneades' negative dogmatism while preserving what Sextus says about his reliance on appearances; this interpretation will be developed in Chapter 4.

Sextus sees an even smaller difference between the Pyrrhonist and Arcesilaus. In fact he describes them as "virtually the same" in so far as they make no assertions about reality, prefer no appearances on the basis of greater plausibility, and suspend judgement about everything (*PH* 1.232). The only serious point of distinction is that Arcesilaus thinks suspension of judgement is a good thing and assent a bad thing, whereas the Pyrrhonist will only acknowledge that they appear so. So Sextus thinks Arcesilaus does after all make some assertions about reality. (I explain Arcesilaus' commitment to the real value of *epochē* as a consequence of his Socratic inheritance in Chapter 3.)

The charge of negative dogmatism probably originates in the earliest account of the distinction between Academics and Pyrrhonists. Some time in the first century BCE, a member of the Academy, Aenesidemus, grew dissatisfied with the increasingly dogmatic tendencies of the school and set out to revive a more radical form of scepticism, inspired by the early Sceptic Pyrrho (see Chapter 6 for the revival, Chapter 2 for the origination). In the first book of his *Pyrrhonian Discourses*, he claims that Academics confidently affirm some things and reject others, while the Pyrrhonists consistently doubt everything, and determine nothing; they do not even determine that they determine nothing.

Aenesidemus is right about the increasingly dogmatic tendencies in the Academy of the first century BCE. But it is unlikely that he intends to label as negatively dogmatic the entire sceptical Academy in all of its phases. At one point he says the Academics, *especially the ones now*, appear to be just Stoics fighting against Stoics (Photius, *Bib.* 170a15–16). It is possible that Aenesidemus intends his charge of negative dogmatism to apply only, or at least mostly, to his contemporaries. He probably saw the history of the Academy as a gradual decline from the rigorous scepticism of Arcesilaus to the exhausted dogmatic compromises of Philo and Antiochus. On this view, as the Academics carried on their intense dialectical struggles, especially with the Stoics, they were driven to make more and more concessions. Specifically in response to charges of inconsistency and impracticality they expanded the notion of sceptically acceptable assent, and correspondingly reduced the scope of *epochē*. In the end, Philo is left rejecting only the Stoics' claims to certainty, and Antiochus becomes a Stoic in all but name.

In opposition to this narrative of decline, we may also see the outcome of the Academy's 200 years' worth of dialectical engagement with their opponents in a positive light. In that case, the Academics would have been right to modify the originally radical scepticism of Arcesilaus. Cicero, who counts himself a lifelong Academic, stands at the end of this history. Although his view of Academic philosophy is coloured by his own inclinations and by his goal of disseminating Greek philosophy among the Roman elite, he is our most extensive and sympathetic source. And his view is uncomplicated by any awareness of a Pyrrhonian revival in the first century BCE. So his remarks are probably free of polemical interests with regard to the distinction between Academics and Pyrrhonists.

Cicero provides some very informative accounts of the history of the sceptical Academy. In the *Academica*, for example, he endorses an account that probably reflects Arcesilaus' own view of the Academy's historical development. He asserts that it is the obscurity of things that led Socrates to his confession of ignorance:

> as even before him, it had led Democritus, Anaxagoras, Empedocles, and virtually all the early philosophers to say that nothing could be cognized, apprehended, or known,

because the senses were limited, our minds weak, and the course of our lives brief, while the truth had been submerged in an abyss (as Democritus said), everything was subject to opinion and custom, no room was left for truth, and consequently everything was shrouded in darkness. That's why Arcesilaus used to deny that anything could be known, not even the residual claim that Socrates had allowed himself, i.e. the knowledge that he didn't know anything.

(*Ac.* 1.44–45)[5]

Cicero does not explain further what he means by the "obscurity of things" or how his famous predecessors arrived at it. Whatever the case may be, Arcesilaus ends up suspending judgement about everything; and by arguing against all comers, like Socrates, he is supposed to have convinced most people to do the same.

Cicero does not claim in this passage (or in the parallel passage at *Ac.* 2.72–74) that the Presocratics were fully sceptical. He cites them, as presumably Arcesilaus did, as noteworthy predecessors who rightly despaired of acquiring empirical knowledge (Brittain & Palmer 2001). For Democritus, since our perceptions never reveal the atomic structure of things, they can never reveal the truth. And in so far as Parmenides denies the reality of change, there is no knowledge to be had about natural, physical processes. But the Academics refuse to go along with the negatively dogmatic denial of the existence or accessibility of truth; they merely deny that anything is graspable in the manner defended by the Stoics (*Ac.* 2.73).

Arcesilaus also counts Socrates and Plato as genuine Sceptics since Socrates thought that nothing can be known (with the one important exception of his own ignorance) and Plato argues on both sides of every issue, and affirms nothing in his books (*Ac.* 2.74, 1.46; see Chapter 3).

Cicero extends this historical account, emphasizing, or perhaps constructing, a methodological continuity. Socrates first practised the Academic method of arguing against everything and openly judging nothing. It was then revived by Arcesilaus, confirmed or strengthened by Carneades, and from there it continued to flourish right down to his own age (*ND* 1.11). Cicero clearly understands this method to consist of three components: relieving others from deceptions, concealing one's own views and searching for the most probable solution on every disputed issue (*Tusc.* 5.11; see Chapter 5). Relieving others from deception is compatible with Arcesilaus' insistence on *epochē*. But concealing one's view clearly implies one has something to conceal, on which he apparently has not suspended judgement. And seeking the most probable view leads Cicero to endorse certain positions as more likely to be true than others. In Cicero's philosophical fallibilism, the scope of *epochē* has dramatically contracted; one may now believe all sorts of things as long as one stops short of claiming to know anything.

Cicero considers this method to be among the greatest gifts that Greek philosophy has to offer. So he must have thought that whatever alterations were necessary to produce it were important steps forward. His glossing over the differences between his fallibilism and the scepticism of earlier Academics can be explained by his interest in establishing an authoritative genealogy and perhaps not wanting to appear to be a philosophical innovator, to whatever extent he was. It was not in the least bit necessary that the radical scepticism of Arcesilaus should grow into fallibilism. But that it did develop this way, and that Cicero welcomed the growth, are integral parts of the overall narrative I shall develop in this book.

On a narrower view, Cicero does not belong among the Greek Sceptics: he is a Roman; he is most famous for being a statesman and orator rather than a philosopher; and he endorses a method that leads to the acquisition of fallible, philosophical beliefs.[6] But since he stands at the end of the historical development of Academic Scepticism, and since he is our most extensive source for that history, we must take account of his view of things. This is why I have included such an extensive discussion of Cicero in Chapter 5. I also believe his fallibilist view is worth considering on its own merits. It certainly exerts a great deal of influence in the subsequent history of ideas, spurring on such figures as Augustine, Petrarch, Erasmus and Hume, to name only a few (see § "The legacy of ancient Scepticism" in the Guide to Further Reading for a select bibliography).

Whether we opt for the positive or negative assessment of the Academy's slide into fallibilism, and the dogmatic views of Philo and Antiochus, it is well established that such a slide occurs. This development inspired Aenesidemus' revival of Pyrrhonism. After Aenesidemus another important Sceptic Agrippa, whom we know practically nothing about, developed an even more formidable set of sceptical arguments (Chapter 8). These arguments were then appropriated by Sextus Empiricus along with material from Aenesidemus, other Pyrrhonists now lost to us and a good deal of argumentation from the Sceptical Academics via the writings of Clitomachus and others. So Pyrrhonian Scepticism, in its mature formulation, draws on many strands of the earlier Sceptical tradition, Pyrrhonian and Academic.[7]

Given these facts, the prospect of drawing clear lines between Pyrrhonists and Academics as such is slim. The only uncontroversial point we can make on this topic is that while they are all concerned to show that the sceptical life is viable, the Academics never promise that it will be tranquil, whereas the Pyrrhonists do.

A more promising approach is to differentiate each of the ancient Sceptics on their own terms. The family resemblances we have explored motivate the following questions:

- How does the sceptic arrive at *epochē*?
- How much does he suspend judgement about – what is the scope of – *epochē*?
- How does he respond to charges of inconsistency?
- How does he respond to *apraxia* objections? Does he allow himself some beliefs or not? And more generally, what kind of life would such a sceptic live?

Before turning to these questions and the detailed examination of the various Sceptics, we must first consider some problems in interpreting the fragmentary evidence.

Some problems of interpretation

It is ironically fitting that there should be so much dispute about the ancient Sceptics. This is due, on one hand, to the meagre and fragmentary state of our evidence, which makes it difficult to judge the historical accuracy of views and methods attributed to them. There are many challenges in sorting through the evidence, which is often at one or two removes from the original Sceptic. In addition to problems of translation from Greek and Latin, there are possible distortions to account for, owing perhaps to the reporter's own agenda, a lack of concern with historical accuracy or plain old misunderstanding. The genre of the sources must also be factored in, as they range from polemical treatises, satirical verse and philosophical dialogues to biography and doxography, which is a catch-all description for a kind of reporting and arranging of philosophical doctrines (*doxai* or *dogmata*).[8]

On the other hand, disputes about ancient Scepticism are also fuelled by purely philosophical disagreements as well. Sometimes the evidence can be read in logically incompatible ways, at which point commentators turn for guidance to philosophical considerations and some version of the principle of charity, which in its most general formulation commands us to opt for the most coherent and plausible construal we can find.

In what follows, I have tried as much as possible to let the Sceptics speak for themselves. That is, I have sought first and foremost to provide historically accurate accounts of the development of Academic and Pyrrhonian Scepticism. This approach has the virtue of leaving open the question of whether we should take their positions seriously as live philosophical options. That sort of question, I believe, should be answered only after we have articulated as clearly as possible the historical position in question. To assume in advance that the ancient Sceptics provide us with viable alternatives to our current choices of philosophical methods and positions runs the risk of impoverishing the past by imposing our current conceptions of what is important, interesting and viable. To see our predecessors' views too narrowly in terms of our own also ultimately limits our current array of choices. Studying the history of ideas may lead us to discover (or rediscover) an exciting philosophical approach that is not currently being discussed or practised. Of course, it may also lead to the conclusion that some particular idea is irretrievably foreign to us, a product of radically different times. But this should be as welcome a conclusion as a failed hypothesis in the natural sciences: *should be*, despite the fact that it generally is not. It would be very strange if the standard opening of so many historical studies – "so and so has been unjustly neglected" – were always true.

Nonetheless, I think it is true that until about thirty years ago, the ancient Sceptics had been unjustly neglected. The situation is quite different today. This book would not have been possible if it were not for the fact that so much excellent scholarship has been produced, illuminating both the historical and philosophical aspects of ancient Scepticism; the guide to further reading testifies to this. I have drawn extensively from the secondary literature in arriving at my own views. But it is crucial to note, in concluding this introduction, that on virtually every substantial point of interpretation there are plausible alternatives to those I present. I believe the narrative I develop in this book makes the best sense of the evidence, historically and philosophically, but it should be accepted, if it is accepted, with the same caution with which it is offered.

TWO

Pyrrho and Timon: the origin of Pyrrhonian Scepticism

The history of ancient Scepticism officially begins with the enigmatic character, Pyrrho of Elis (*c*.365–275 BCE). Pyrrho wrote nothing himself, so what little evidence we have regarding him comes mostly from the writings of his pupil Timon and a book by a nearly contemporary biographer, Antigonus of Carystus. Only fragments of these works survive in the accounts of other, later writers. Diogenes Laertius, for example, draws from both in his biography of Pyrrho (DL 9.61–108). These later accounts look at Pyrrho through the lens of what Pyrrhonism had become hundreds of years later, so they must be used with caution.[1]

Nevertheless, in seeking to understand the history of Greek Scepticism it is necessary to reconstruct Pyrrho's position. This is so for two reasons. First, the founder of Academic Scepticism, Arcesilaus, was influenced by Pyrrho. And secondly, the founder of neo-Pyrrhonian Scepticism, Aenesidemus (Chapter 6) looked to Pyrrho as an inspirational model of the sceptical life. Clearly we need some account of Pyrrho's views and his character to make sense of this historical influence.

Two recurrent themes in the evidence are Pyrrho's remarkably tranquil life, and his refusal to make any firm determinations about things. There is nothing unusual about a Greek philosopher promoting tranquillity as the proper goal. And there is nothing unusual about the generally sceptical thrust of his view. A number of philosophers had held, for various reasons, that certain kinds of knowledge are beyond our reach, or that we should remain indifferent and impassive to fortune. Pyrrho's novel contribution, and the justification for his status as father of Greek Scepticism, is the way he combines these: he proposes that tranquillity is won by means of a firmly unopinionated and indifferent attitude. No one before him had suggested that the recognition of our cognitive limitations would lead to such a happy ending. On the contrary, it was widely accepted that knowledge plays an integral role in attaining whatever is claimed to be the proper goal of life.

Aristotle (384–322 BCE), for example, holds that human cognitive and sensory equipment is sufficiently matched with the structure of reality to enable us to satisfy our natural desire for understanding. Nature simply does not endow its creatures with natural desires that cannot, in principle, be satisfied. So acquiring knowledge is part of the proper fulfilment of our natures. Knowledge is thus an essential component in a flourishing life; it is both intrinsically valuable as the satisfaction of a natural desire and instrumentally valuable in establishing the appropriate ends of action. This Aristotelian position is particularly important because it provides the context for our most informative piece of evidence regarding Pyrrho.

Eusebius' report of Aristocles' report of Timon's account of Pyrrho

Some time around the second century CE, an Aristotelian philosopher, Aristocles, wrote a book entitled *On Philosophy* (Chiesara 2001: xvii–xviii). We would know nothing of this book if it were not for Eusebius (*c.*260–339), a Christian bishop, who quotes directly from it in his own work, *Preparation for the Gospel*. Given that Pyrrho's views are reported originally by Timon, who is then quoted by Aristocles, who is then quoted by Eusebius, one might think the text is of questionable historical value. Fortunately, it seems that both Aristocles and Eusebius have in fact preserved the actual words of Timon.

Unfortunately, the passage still contains a crucial ambiguity. On one translation, Timon means to say that Pyrrho thinks things are *indeterminate*; on the other, that they are *indeterminable*. I have inserted alternative translations of the ambiguous sentence below. On the first, labelled [M] for metaphysical, Pyrrho is making a claim primarily regarding the nature of things (they are indeterminate). On the second, labelled [E] for epistemological, Pyrrho is making a claim primarily regarding our knowledge (we are unable to make accurate determinations about things). Here is the passage:

> It is supremely necessary to investigate our own capacity for knowledge. For if we are so constituted that we know nothing, there is no need to continue inquiry into other things. Among the ancients too there have been people who made this pronouncement, and Aristotle has argued against them. Pyrrho of Elis was also a powerful advocate of such a position. He himself has left nothing in writing, but his disciple Timon says that whoever wants to be happy must consider these three questions: first, how are things by nature? Secondly, what attitude should we adopt towards them? Thirdly, what will be the outcome for those who have this attitude? According to Timon,

> [M] Pyrrho declared that things are equally *undifferentiated and unstable and indeterminate; for this reason* neither our sensations nor our opinions tell us truths or falsehoods.

> [E] Pyrrho declared that things are equally *indifferentiable and unmeasurable and undecidable, [since]* neither our sensations nor our opinions *[consistently]* tell us truths or falsehoods.[2]

Therefore, for this reason we should not put our trust in them one bit, but we should be unopinionated, uncommitted and unwavering, saying concerning each individual thing that it no more is than is not, or it both is and is not, or it neither is nor is not. The outcome for those who actually adopt this attitude, says Timon, will be first speechlessness, and then freedom from disturbance...

(*Praep. Ev.* 14.18.1–4 [LS 1F])

The core of Pyrrho's teaching emerges in response to the three related questions: how are things by nature, what attitude should we adopt towards them and what will be the outcome of adopting such an attitude?

Timon offers these as problems that must be resolved by those who wish to be happy. And the second question clearly asks for, and is given, a normative response: we *should* trust neither sensations nor opinions. The ethical significance of this account is confirmed by Aristocles' complaint that if Timon had intended his writing to have some beneficial effect, then it would have to be by means of convincing us of the truth of Pyrrho's statements (*Praep. Ev.* 14.18.16). That is, he assumes that teaching can only improve the student by imparting knowledge, or at least true beliefs.

How, then, can Pyrrho's sceptical teaching benefit us? We shall return to this issue after discussing the first question.

Things are indeterminate

The fact that the first question addresses the nature of things might incline us towards the metaphysical interpretation. On this view, things are undifferentiated, unstable and indeterminate.

To say that things are undifferentiated appears to mean that there are no real, intrinsic differences between any two things. Similarly, they are indeterminate: no more one way than another. An atomist would accept a restricted version of this: there are no real differences between things with respect to secondary qualities such as colour since the atomic components of things are colourless. As Democritus famously asserts: "By convention, sweet; by convention, bitter; by convention, hot; by convention, cold; by convention, color; but in reality, atoms and void" (*M* 7.135; see DL 9.72). Since atoms really do have size and shape, however, things are differentiated and determinate with respect to these properties. But for Pyrrho, on the metaphysical interpretation not even size and shape differentiate one thing from another.

This may seem wildly implausible on the grounds that the regularity of our experience of the world strongly suggests some underlying structure. If things are really no more one way than another, it becomes difficult to understand why the sun always seems warming and an icy lake always seems cooling, or why heavy objects always seem to fall to earth and very light ones seem to rise and float. We do not know whether Pyrrho felt compelled to explain the apparent regularity of our experience. But given his rejection of scientific explanations (DL 9.65), it is likely that he would have dismissed such attempts as "empty theorizing". And indeed, if things were intrinsically indeterminate, it would be futile to think we could explain any perceived regularities by revealing some underlying structure. It would just be a brute, inexplicable fact that metaphysical indeterminacy is compatible with perceived regularities.

For sceptical purposes, it is more productive to focus on perceived irregularities, for example, that the same thing appears radically different in different circumstances: the wind feels warm to you and cool to me. The variability of phenomena along with seemingly endless disagreement is a staple of ancient Scepticism. Although there is no clear evidence that Pyrrho defends metaphysical indeterminacy on the basis of variability, this is at least a plausible route (DL 9.106; see Bett 2000). Even so, it requires a crucial premise linking variability to indeterminacy: if x is by nature F (= determinately F), then x is invariably F. This principle may be interpreted in a variety of ways, depending on how we understand the key qualifiers "invariably" and "by nature". Nevertheless, something like it is necessary to get us from the variability of the way things seem to the conclusion that they are not by nature any more one way than another (see Chapter 6 for Aenesidemus' later polemical use of invariability as a condition on truth).

Regardless of how he arrived at it, we can further clarify Pyrrho's view by interpreting his second adjective: what does he mean by saying that things are unstable? One attractive option is that Pyrrho defends the view Plato attributes to the Heracliteans in the *Theaetetus* (152d–e); namely, that everything is constantly changing in every respect (Bett 2000: 132–40; Powers 2001). The rate of change is irrelevant. The important point is that a thing never has precisely the same properties from one moment to the next. We should not think that we have stopped the process by taking a photograph, since this frozen moment does not correspond to the real nature of the thing. In fact, it is not really fitting to call it one thing in the first place. If *all* of its properties are in flux, it will not be the same thing over time; constant change will consume whatever momentary identity we may impose. In recognition of this insight, we should replace the verb "to be" with "becomes". It is never correct to say that *x* is *F*, but only that *x* becomes *F*. And even then, *x* does not remain *F*; nor does it even remain itself. So it is even misleading to talk about all of a thing's properties changing in so far as that presupposes some underlying substratum that might endure.

Because of this indeterminacy, Pyrrho concludes that neither our sensations nor opinions tell the truth or falsehoods. It is clear enough why he would think that they fail to report the truth. In order for our sensations or opinions to report anything it seems they must assert some definite, or determinate, proposition. And in order for an assertion to be true it must correctly report the relevant state of affairs. If things are inherently indeterminate, no assertion can correctly report how things are. So metaphysical indeterminacy eliminates the possibility that any sensation or opinion could be true.

But why does Pyrrho also say that indeterminacy eliminates the possibility that any sensation or opinion could be false? The more natural consequence to draw, it seems, would be that all propositions are false because they attempt to assert something determinate about things that are indeterminate. Perhaps Pyrrho thinks that in order for the proposition "*x* is *F*" to be false, some determinate state of affairs represented by "*x* is not-*F*" must be true. In other words, perhaps he thinks the possibility of error only makes sense in a world of determinate objects. In that case, indeterminacy would eliminate the possibility of anything being true or false.

Pyrrho might have adopted such a narrow conception of what is required for a statement to be false. But there is no evidence that he did.

Things are undecidable

The most convincing objection to the metaphysical interpretation is the decidedly epistemological focus of Aristocles' *On Philosophy*. One of his main tasks in this book is to defend Aristotle's view that both sensation and reason, properly employed, are reliable guides in seeking knowledge. To this end, he argues against competing accounts. Parmenides and his followers reject the evidence of the senses and trust only reason. Protagoras and Metrodorus reject reason and trust only sensation. Cyrenaics reject both sensation and reason and accept only their own affections or feelings. And, finally, Pyrrho and his followers reject all accounts of knowledge and maintain that it is our nature to know nothing (Brennan 1998; Chiesara 2001).

Aristocles clearly counts Pyrrho among those who proclaim that "we are so constituted that we know nothing" (*Praep. Ev.* 14.18.1–2). This is a statement not about things themselves, but rather our own cognitive and sensory capacities. Similarly, he identifies the subject to be investigated as our capacity for knowledge. If the metaphysical interpretation were correct, our inability to acquire knowledge would be due to the nature of things and not, as Aristocles says, due to any facts about us. Indeed, if things are indeterminate not even God can have any knowledge of them. So, if things are indeterminate, it does not matter how we are constituted, and Pyrrho's remark about our constitution would be idle.

But if the epistemological view is right, how can we explain the first question about the nature of *things*? When we refer to things it is sometimes unclear whether we mean to talk about the things themselves or their effect on us, or both. If I am asked about honey, I could respond either by talking about its chemical composition or about the way it tastes. Similarly, Pyrrho can reasonably be understood as saying:

[E] things are equally indifferentiable and unmeasurable and undecidable.

In that case, his answer tells us only about how we are affected by things, that is, it informs us only about our constitution and capacities. The epistemological interpretation allows us, and perhaps even requires us, to remain agnostic about the nature of things themselves.

On this view, what leads Pyrrho to conclude that we are so constituted as to know nothing is that "neither sensations nor opinions [consistently] tell us truths or falsehoods" (*Praep. Ev.* 14.18.4). The point is not that sensations and opinions have no truth-value, but that we are not able to determine what truth-value they have. They are not reliable guides; hence the qualification that they do not *consistently* tell the truth or lie.

Again, some sort of variability in the way things appear will motivate this position. And again we will need to supply a crucial premise, this time linking the variability of appearances to our inability to decide among them. Where the metaphysical view needs a requirement on truth, the epistemological view needs a requirement on justification. We start with the observation that the same thing appears in various, and incompatible, ways: both F and not-F. If we are unable to rationally prefer one of these appearances then we must suspend judgement about what x really is, by nature.

The later Sceptic Aenesidemus holds such a view of Pyrrho. He claims that Pyrrho determines nothing dogmatically because of contradiction (DL 9.106) and that he philosophized according to the principle of suspension of judgement (DL 9.62). But again, we must bear in mind the possibility that he is projecting his own view back in time (Bett 2000: 48–57). It is possible that even Timon projects his own epistemological scepticism on to Pyrrho. In that case, Timon, and not Pyrrho, would be the first Pyrrhonist (Brunschwig 1994). The later tradition, beginning with Timon, might have drawn only from the epistemological consequences of Pyrrho's metaphysical indeterminism.

I am not confident that the issue can be resolved on the basis of the evidence we have. But if Pyrrho is primarily concerned to show that recognizing our cognitive limitations is not a cause for despair but rather a route to tranquillity, either the metaphysical or epistemological view will do. Since I find the more modest, epistemological variety slightly more plausible, and since it wins the day historically, I shall develop this account in what follows; in effect, I shall proceed as if Timon got Pyrrho right.

Before moving on to the second and third questions, we shall need to consider what Pyrrho means to include in his claim about the nature of things.

The scope of "things" and Pyrrho's moral conventionalism

For Pyrrho, the most important matters that call for measurement or decision are evaluations of what is good and bad. So, we should focus on the claim that things are equally indifferentiable, unmeasurable and undecidable with respect to their value and choiceworthiness. This realization should make us appreciate that value judgements are contingent and groundless: we are unable to justify any conviction that something is not just apparently good, but really good. Accordingly, Pyrrho proclaims that "convention and habit are the basis of everything that men do" (DL 9.61), and "appearances prevail everywhere" (DL 9.105). Similarly, "there is nothing good or bad by nature, but 'these things are determined by men in accordance with convention' according to Timon" (M 11.140). Although this remark suggests the negatively dogmatic, metaphysical view that values do not exist in nature, we should note that only the latter half is attributed to Timon. So his point may still be that since we are unable to establish what is good or bad by nature, we must prescribe values conventionally.

Thus we may take Pyrrho's moral conventionalism as an immediate consequence of his view about our cognitive limits. We are not so constituted as to know what is by nature good and bad. These views may have been inspired by his compatriot Anaxarchus, who compares things to the painted scenes that we see at the theatre. We would think someone mad for taking such facades for reality.

Similarly, we behave like madmen or dreamers if we suppose our sensations are reliable indicators of the true natures of things (*M* 7.87–88).

Applying this to evaluative properties, we will behave like dreamers and madmen if we take apparently good things for genuinely good ones.[3] In one revealing anecdote we find this idea applied to justice and morality in general. Anaxarchus, along with Pyrrho, accompanied Alexander the Great on some expeditions and seems to have been by turns flattering and disdainful. After a drunken quarrel, Alexander kills his friend Cleitus, and then immediately feels great remorse. In his disdainful mood, Anaxarchus scoffs at him for behaving like a slave, fearing the law and disapproval of men, when he should realize that he, like Zeus, is the law (Plutarch, *Vit. Alex.* 50–52). Alexander's misery is the result of mistakenly thinking that his action was in reality unjust, shameful and worthy of punishment. But just as the writer of the play determines the plot, the king decides what justice is.

It is difficult to accept the notion that we cannot differentiate good from bad actions even in extreme cases; to think, for example, that Alexander's crime is really no better or worse than the good deeds he performed. But Pyrrho neither advocates a life of crime nor a life of virtue, as conceived by his contemporaries. His aim is to relieve us of poorly founded confidence and the disturbing desires that it produces.

The more common view among Greek philosophers is that the problem is desire for things that turn out to be bad. On this view, happiness requires choosing, if not acquiring, what is genuinely and not merely apparently good. We establish our goals in accordance with what we desire, and we desire what appears good. One might start out in pursuit of money, believing that it would be genuinely good to be rich, and then later decide that this is only an apparent good since some wealthy people seem to be miserable. Such experiences may convince us that there is an important distinction between merely apparent goods and genuine ones. Armed with this distinction, one would never desire something as only an apparent good. Thus we quickly arrive at the view that we must first determine what is genuinely good in order to establish the proper goals in the larger pursuit of happiness.

If we must justify our ends as genuinely good in order to be happy, scepticism about evaluative matters will eliminate the possibility of happiness. But Pyrrho does not take his scepticism to be such a wet blanket. So it seems he would have us replace the more familiar question of what one needs to know to live well, with the question of how one may live well in the absence of knowledge. In response to Aristocles' complaint about the possibility of any benefit coming to those who read Timon's books, we should say that imparting knowledge is not the only way to benefit one's students; in fact, it is not even a possible way.

The negative claim, then, is that we are incapable of acquiring evaluative knowledge, and the positive claim is that such knowledge is not necessary for tranquillity or happiness. Timon asserts both of these, apparently on behalf of Pyrrho, in the following couplet: "Having a correct yardstick of truth, I will relate a fiction, as it evidently is to me, / that the nature of the divine and good [exists] forever and from these life becomes most equable for man" (*M* 11.20; Svavarsson 2004; cf. Burnyeat 1980). There are actually two fictions here: first, that the nature of the divine and good exists forever; and secondly, that these are the source of a tranquil, equable life. To say that they exist forever may be taken to mean that they are stable measures of what is good, and not merely conventional or contingent. But according to Pyrrho, even if such standards were real, they are beyond our cognitive reach. So they cannot serve as standards or measures for us to actually use, and thus they cannot be relied on in attaining a tranquil life. He is able to confidently assert that these are fictions since this is an application of his more general claim that things are indifferentiable, unmeasurable and undecidable.

Cicero focuses on the practical consequences of this lack of evaluative distinctions in his remarks about Pyrrho (*Ac.* 2.130; *Fin.* 3.11–12, 4.43, 4.49, 4.60; *Off.* 1.6). He attributes to Pyrrho the view that all things are equal, that is, that they are all equally worthy of choice or of avoidance. But Cicero makes it clear that this is part of Pyrrho's conception of virtue as the only good; everything else is indifferent.

There are no rational grounds for preferring one thing to another for we are incapable of determining whether anything is more valuable or choiceworthy than anything else. We may feel a physiological compulsion one way or another, but this is no indication of having arrived at a correct assessment of a thing's worth. The fact that we are naturally inclined to seek food and shelter does not entail that we should, or that these things are by nature good.

In order to make sense of what we may call Pyrrho's conception of virtue we shall need to explore his answer to Timon's second question: what attitude should we adopt towards things?

Pyrrho's prescription: the sceptical attitude

In Aristocles' report (quoted above), Pyrrho advises that "we should not put our trust in [sensations and opinions] one bit, but we should be unopinionated, uncommitted and unwavering, saying concerning each individual thing that it no more is than is not, or it both is and is not, or it neither is nor is not". The suggestion that we should be unwavering *and* uncommitted raises the problem of consistency. Is Pyrrho advising us to firmly commit ourselves to the opinion that we should be unopinionated and uncommitted? We shall return to the problem of consistency in the next section. For now we shall concentrate on what Pyrrho advises us to say, and thus presumably to think.

What, for example, would Pyrrho have us say and think about death? An untimely death is generally thought to be unquestionably bad. But according to one anecdote, Pyrrho calmly faced his own imminent death onboard a ship in a storm. Unlike the others, he displayed no inclination to panic and flee. Instead, the story goes, he pointed to a contented pig happily eating in the midst of the storm and remarked that this is how we ought to be as well (DL 9.68). The pig had no beliefs about whether his situation was really bad, and indifferently carried on eating.

Pyrrho's attitude in this situation is captured by the expression that death is no more bad than good, or both bad and good, or neither bad nor good. This complicated utterance may be interpreted in two ways. First, it might be taken as one (or all) of three distinct claims: we may say either that (a) death is no more bad than good, or (b) death is both bad and good, or (c) death is neither bad nor good. Secondly, it might be taken as only one, four-part remark: death is no more (i) bad than it is (ii) good, or (iii) both bad and good, or (iv) neither bad nor good. This second alternative really does not allow us to say anything positive about death at all. What we are allowed to say, roughly, is that death is no more this way than that way, or neither way (see Aulus Gellius, *NA* 11.5.4; DeLacy 1958). And this is what we would expect if Pyrrho were committed to the notion that we cannot ever know anything about the nature of death.

Furthermore, the second and third claims of the first alternative – (b) and (c) – are problematic. It would make sense for Democritus to say, for example, that a patch of snow is no more white than not-white because in its real, atomic nature it has no colour. But Pyrrho would not accept such a definite account of the nature of things. He would not, in particular, accept the view that it is the nature of things to lack all colour. This is fundamentally different from his broader claim that it is the nature of things to be unknowable. So Pyrrho should not encourage us to say that (c) death is neither good nor bad in so far as that means he knows, or is even confident, that death lacks any particular value.

With regard to the second claim (b), it would make sense for Protagoras to say, for example, that a patch of snow is both white and not-white because a thing is what it appears to be, and if it appears white to you and not-white to me, then it is white for you and not-white for me. Again, Pyrrho should not be willing to endorse such a positive view about the nature of things. Far from claiming that appearances reveal the true (even if seemingly contradictory) nature of things, he absolutely denies that appearances can indicate the nature of reality.[4] Pyrrho would not encourage us to say, on the basis of conflicting appearances, that it is both good and bad.

In support of the second alternative, we should consider Timon's remark that "the expression ['no more'] means 'determining nothing, and suspending judgment'" (DL 9.76). If Pyrrho were to say that death is no more this than that, we may take him to mean that we can determine nothing about death and so must suspend judgement. We must remain unopinionated and uncommitted, and when faced with death we must be unwavering and firm in our refusal to take a position.

Whether or not Pyrrho would have called this disposition virtue, he did claim that those who develop it achieve tranquillity. Cicero reports that the followers of Pyrrho hold morality (or virtue) to be the only good (*Fin.* 3.12). But if nothing is known to be good or bad by nature, then it follows that Pyrrho does not know whether it is truly good to be firmly uncommitted and unopinionated; nor could he claim that tranquillity is good by nature. In that case, the sceptical disposition is only conventionally good, if it is good at all, and we could dismiss his advice as being out of step with our current conventions.

Pyrrho's firm lack of commitment and the problem of consistency

Pyrrho's position appears inconsistent. If we are so constituted as to know nothing, it seems we can never know that we are so constituted; nor can we know that tranquillity is good and worth striving for. And how are we to become firmly uncommitted and unopinionated if not by acquiring firm convictions and opinions? Generally, we think a firm, stable disposition to be a sign of deep commitment and, on the other hand, we suspect that the uncommitted are prone to vacillate.

Our evidence regarding Pyrrho does not reveal that he even considered these sorts of objections, much less what his response may have been. Nevertheless, there are several different responses available. These are worth considering as they foreshadow later developments in both Academic and Pyrrhonian Scepticism.

One way to avoid such inconsistencies is to allow for exceptions to Pyrrho's general claims. Perhaps all we can know is that we are so constituted as to know nothing, and that tranquillity is the only genuine good. These convictions will enable us to remain firmly uncommitted regarding everything else. That is, we should avoid all other opinions and convictions about knowledge and the good. If Pyrrho could provide some principled reason for making such exceptions we would have a convincing response to the problem. However, there is no evidence that he made such a move.

Another solution is to claim that Pyrrho had habituated himself to remain uncommitted and unopinionated. In that case, his tranquillity would not be the product of knowledge, or even belief, but rather the product of a deeply rooted habitual way of seeing things. In support of this solution we may appeal to the many reports focusing on his remarkable disposition. Timon is said to have clearly revealed this disposition in his book, *Pytho* (which is no longer extant; DL 9.67). Timon also consistently praises him in other works for his dispassionate tranquillity, highlighting his lack of disturbing beliefs or doctrines: Pyrrho is not weighed down with passion, opinion and futile legislation (*Praep. Ev.* 14.18.19); he has escaped from servitude to the opinions and empty theorizing of Sophists (DL 9.64). Another follower of Pyrrho, Nausiphanes asserts that we should become like Pyrrho in disposition, but that we should adopt his [Nausiphanes'] own doctrines (DL 9.64).

Some biographical details provide a sketch of how Pyrrho might have arrived at his remarkable disposition. While in India with Alexander, Pyrrho's teacher, Anaxarchus, was criticized for attending kings in their courts. Such behaviour, the Indian critic maintained, would make him unable to teach others what is good. While this probably did not trouble Anaxarchus, it did have an effect on Pyrrho, who had collected thousands of pieces of gold from Alexander for a poem he had written (*M* 1.282). Pyrrho withdrew into solitude (DL 9.62). He was perhaps concerned to avoid the appearance of believing that kings wield real power or that political involvement is beneficial.

In keeping with his disdain for worldly power, Pyrrho was fond of quoting a line from the *Iliad* in which Homer calls into question the premium the warrior culture placed on fame or glory: the generations of men come and go like leaves on a tree (*Iliad* 6.146). From this lofty perspective it seems silly to give oneself airs for having famous ancestors or for doing what may appear to be glorious deeds. Pyrrho frequently cited other passages in Homer displaying the inconsistency, futility and childishness of humanity (DL 9.67).

Pyrrho was even fonder of quoting from Democritus, who similarly railed against the destructive and disturbing effects of excessive ambition and desire. Democritus held that the proper goal in life is a persistently cheerful, fearless, calm and tranquil state of mind (DL 9.54). To achieve this he advised that we must attend to what is possible and be satisfied with what we have rather than allow ourselves to be consumed by envy and desire.

The practice and preaching of such detachment is not unusual in Greek philosophy prior to Pyrrho: in addition to Democritus, Diogenes the Cynic promoted a similar disposition. But on their views, detachment is supposed to arise from a correct evaluation of the goods of fortune, whereas in Pyrrho's view it arises from a refusal to evaluate such goods in the first place.

In any case, such detachment is a hard-won accomplishment. Pyrrho acknowledges this in the following report: "When he was terrified by a dog that had rushed at him, he answered his critic that it is difficult to entirely strip off one's humanity, but that one should struggle against things first by deeds and then, if that doesn't work, by reason" (DL 9.66; see *Praep. Ev.* 14.18.26). It probably seemed to Pyrrho that our most important struggle is to resist the very human tendency to evaluate things as genuinely good or bad. This tendency is most likely to surface when danger looms. We all tend to see imminent harm and an untimely death as genuinely bad. But Pyrrho advises that we learn to see them as neither good nor bad; that is, he promotes the development of a disposition *not* to evaluate things, and more generally not to suppose that anything is really, by nature, F.

It is unlikely that one could succeed in stripping away one's natural human tendency to consider pain and death genuinely bad without some very compelling reasons. In other words, one would probably not undertake a rigorous programme of conditioning unless one came to believe that the promised tranquillity would be worth it.

Plutarch attributes to Pyrrho the view that "freedom from suffering (*apatheia*) has to be gained through reason and philosophy" (*Prof. Virt.* 82F). And this leads us again to confront the problem of consistency. Why is the firmly uncommitted Pyrrho not still left with positive convictions about the value of tranquillity and our cognitive limitations?

In a passage probably from Timon's *Pytho*, we find a metaphor that plays a central role in later Pyrrhonism: the sceptic applies his characteristically sceptical utterances to themselves, which shows how the utterances are like purgatives in driving out the offensive substance before eliminating themselves (DL 9.76). Thus the expression "no more this than that" applies to itself and discharges the appearance that the sceptic has asserted something definite. When he says that he determines nothing, he should not be taken as having determined even that he determines nothing. Pyrrho's disposition is what is left after the sceptical purgatives perform their function. (We shall consider the purgative metaphor in greater detail in Chapter 9.)[5]

The outcome: Pyrrho's prudent tranquillity

We turn finally to the third question. Having become firmly uncommitted regarding the natures of things, one is initially speechless. It is not clear whether this should be taken literally, or rather as a withholding of any positive assertion about things. Even if the initial outcome is an amazed silence, we have to assume that the sceptic eventually adopts some form of speech to account for Pyrrho's willingness to hold forth.

Sextus describes a very plausible candidate for sceptically acceptable speech as a kind of non-assertion in which we refuse to assert (or deny) anything about the way the world is (*PH* 1.192–3, although he does not attribute this to Pyrrho). In this case we shall only report how things seem without any further commitment. If one succeeds in adopting the sceptical attitude and only says of things that they are no more this way than that or neither, then he would, obviously, no longer be asserting anything positive about the nature of things when he spoke.

Following speechlessness, or non-assertion, is tranquillity. The sceptic is no longer inclined one way or another; as Timon says, he will neither choose nor decline (*M* 11.164). As a result he is completely undisturbed by whatever course things take. The crucial assumption at work here is that it is the frustration of our beliefs and desires that is responsible for whatever disturbances we suffer. (We shall examine this diagnosis further in Chapter 7.)

But if Pyrrho came to see pain and death as not genuinely bad, he would not see them as "things to be avoided" either. According to Antigonus, Pyrrho was reckless, "avoiding nothing and taking no precautions, facing everything as it came, wagons, precipices, dogs, and entrusting nothing whatsoever to his sensations" (DL 9.62).

On this view Pyrrho was kept alive by his devoted students, who steered him away from speeding wagons and dangerous cliffs. But according to Aenesidemus, Pyrrho's suspension of judgement did not cause him to act carelessly in his daily life (DL 9.62). And Timon claims that Pyrrho did not depart from normal, habitual or customary practice (*sunētheia*; DL 9.105).

These latter remarks may seem to conflict with the anecdotes reporting Pyrrho's thoroughly unconventional behaviour. But prudence does not necessarily require social conformity. The tales of Pyrrho's recklessness appear to be sensational fabrications, probably devised to illustrate the supposedly terrible practical consequences of scepticism. Although there is no conclusive textual basis for choosing the prudent over the reckless Pyrrho, I defer once again to his student Timon, who announces in another lost work, *On the Senses*: "That honey is sweet I do not assert, but I agree that it seems to be" (DL 9.105). Aenesidemus takes such remarks to indicate that Pyrrho guides himself by the appearances (DL 9.106). Honey's apparent sweetness is sufficient to make me want to eat it; in this way appearances prevail over theories or arguments purporting to reveal something about the hidden nature of honey (see DL 9.105). If Aenesidemus is right, we may say that Pyrrho has no opinions about the nature of speeding chariots beyond what his senses report. But if one appears to be rushing towards him he will move out of the way, just as ordinary people do.

Conclusion

While I believe this account of Pyrrho makes the best sense of the fragmentary and sometimes conflicting evidence, it is vulnerable to the objection that it is the product of later Sceptics projecting their own views and practices back in time. Given the scarcity of evidence, however, we cannot be too confident about the extent to which the later tradition departs from or develops Pyrrho's sceptical position (but see Bett 2000). And given the fact that Pyrrho never wrote anything, we are largely dependent on Timon, whom Sextus describes as Pyrrho's prophet (*M* 1.53). But if Pyrrho is so oracular as to need a prophet, I believe we are right to accept the prophet's interpretation.

Furthermore, the account I have provided allows us to see the history of Pyrrhonism as the development of sceptical themes that emerge from the life of Pyrrho. First and foremost is his sceptical disposition, which inclines him away from arriving at any evaluative judgements. Later Pyrrhonists turn their attention especially to the development of argumentative strategies, the application of which leads them to suspend judgement and ultimately to acquire something like Pyrrho's celebrated disposition. In any case, Pyrrho's most important contribution to the history of Scepticism is to present our cognitive limitations in a positive light as the route to a good, tranquil life.

THREE

Arcesilaus: the origin of Academic Scepticism

Some time around 387 BCE, Plato began meeting with his students in a grove, or public park, just outside the city wall of Athens, where he had studied philosophy as a young man before becoming a pupil of Socrates (DL 3.5). This particular grove was named after a Greek hero, Hekademos. Thus was born Plato's Academy.[1]

Plato also bought (or was given) a private residence nearby where he and his students ate their meals and had the occasional drinking party (*symposium*). The main philosophical business was conducted both within the private house and in the open space of the park. With the exception of a few anecdotes recorded long after the fact, we have no explicit account of the methods and curricula of the original Academy.

However, given the prominent role played by the theory (or theories) of the Forms in Plato's dialogues, and Aristotle's extensive critique in *On Ideas* (and *Met.* 1.9), it is likely that they were much discussed in the Academy as well. Plato's first two successors, Speusippus, followed by Xenocrates, both developed elaborate and distinct metaphysical theories apparently designed, like the Forms, to explain the intelligible order in the world (among other things). Since Speusippus and Xenocrates were both members of the Academy prior to Plato's death, the origin of their metaphysical theories is probably to be found in their training with Plato.

The same may be said for Aristotle, who was a student in the Academy for twenty years before setting off to start his own school. His metaphysical view, which is apparently developed in reaction to the Forms, differs markedly from those of his Academic colleagues. Aristotle remarks that even though the Forms had been introduced by his friends, he is bound to honour the truth more highly (*NE* 1.6, 1096a12–17). Indeed, we may even say that one dishonours one's friend by not pointing out the flaws in his reasoning. And we might, somewhat optimistically, hope that Aristotle's friends in the Academy saw it that way as well. After all, Plato himself provides some devastating objections to the theory of the Forms in his own *Parmenides*.

The fact that disagreement was tolerated if not encouraged, and the fact that such a variety of positions emerged from the Academy, suggest that Plato was not interested in forcing an orthodox interpretation of the Forms on his students. In keeping with the dialectical spirit of his dialogues Plato probably sought to inspire his students to think for themselves.[2] A Socratic theme that emerges time and again in the dialogues is that we must arrive at the truth for ourselves if we are to arrive at all. Teaching is not a matter of pouring the answers in, but rather leading, enticing or aggravating the student to discover the truth for himself. In short, learning can never be forced (see for example *Rep.* 536e–f). And in so far as the development and promotion of an official account of Platonism involved such force, it would not have been part of Plato's plan for the Academy and his students.

Another theme from the dialogues that Plato's successors focused on is that virtue is sufficient (or nearly sufficient) for happiness. In making his case for the intrinsic value of virtue in the *Republic*, for example, Plato argues that it should be understood as a kind of health of the soul and fulfilment of our rational, human nature. Properly understood, virtue is worthwhile regardless of its consequences, although it is valuable for its consequences as well. The intellectual pleasures that are available only to the virtuous are far superior to any other. Without the knowledge of the Form of the Good that is necessary for virtue, even the fullest possible knowledge of other things is of no benefit to us, any more than if we acquire anything without the good of it (*Rep.* 505a–b). As long as we lack virtue, none of what we typically think of as good – for example, health, wealth, beauty – is necessarily good or beneficial for us. If I am in a vicious state, these apparent goods are in fact harmful in so far as they make me better able to achieve my vicious goals. As long as I do not know what is good for me, I am better off not being able to achieve my ends.

Speusippus and Xenocrates were probably thinking along these lines when they asserted that the best life for human beings is one in accordance with nature (Dillon 2003: 77, 142ff.). But it is also likely that they disagreed about the details of how the phrase "in accordance with nature" was to be interpreted.

The third successor, Polemo, led the Academy for nearly forty years from 314 BCE until his death in *c*.276 BCE. He does not seem to have diverged significantly from his predecessor, Xenocrates. Instead, he emphasized the importance of engaging in practical affairs. This is not to say that he ignored or avoided theoretical pursuits, but that he cautioned his students not to become so engrossed with them as to lose sight of their applications. We should not, he says, be admired for our skill with words, and yet be at war with ourselves in the ordering of our lives (DL 4.18). The conflict he refers to is probably a matter of having one's beliefs and dispositions at odds with one another: believing contradictory things and not living in accordance with the dictates of reason, and our common human nature, but instead learning how to talk a good game.

This is also a theme that Plato frequently develops in his dialogues; playing with words should never be mistaken for genuine philosophical discussion. The former aims only at victory while the latter aims at uncovering the truth. Many of Socrates' interlocutors suffer, at least in his eyes, from the misapprehension that the point of philosophical debate is to win and be thought superior to one's opponent. Not all of the Greek Sophists were unscrupulous; Plato presents both Gorgias and Protagoras as at least well-meaning, and there is good reason to believe that he is not especially fair in his general portrayal of the Sophists (see Woodruff 1999). Nevertheless, one of the Sophists' most highly prized skills was the ability to argue on both sides of any issue. This is especially valuable when political business is conducted by way of public speech. It is also crucially important when defending oneself from unjust accusations, although of course it would work equally well against just ones (see Aristophanes' *Clouds*).

In his dialogues, Plato expresses the worry that the mastery of such a skill too easily distracts us from the difficult work of examining our own lives. Those who seek to win by any means and who change their position solely to avoid being refuted are like patients who lie to their doctors.[3] This analogy assumes that one's interlocutor is qualified to diagnose intellectual conditions and that the pursuit of truth can in fact lead to a harmonious life. But Polemo is on solid Platonic ground in insisting that being a clever speaker is worthless if not harmful in the absence of a well-ordered, virtuous life.

No doubt this point was not lost on Polemo's student Arcesilaus, who was an exceptionally clever speaker. After studying astronomy and geometry in his hometown of Pitane, he came to Athens as a young man of about eighteen years old (*c.*298 BCE), roughly the time in which Pyrrho (*c.*365–275), Zeno (the founder of Stoicism, *c.*335–262) and Epicurus (*c.*341–271) were all flourishing. His older brother wanted him to become an orator, which is perhaps why he studied with Aristotle's successor, Theophrastus. Aristotle had included rhetoric as a legitimate science, worthy of philosophers' attention, and Theophrastus included it in his curriculum. But despite his rhetorical prowess, Arcesilaus was devoted to philosophy and, more importantly, to one of the leading Academics, Crantor.

Altogether, Arcesilaus spent about twenty years in Plato's school before becoming head himself, apparently with the approval of his colleagues (DL 4.32). The author of the *Academic Index* remarks, "At first he defended the position adopted by the School from Plato and Speusippus up to Polemo" (*Index. Ac.*, col. 18). If our evidence concerning Arcesilaus' predecessors is accurate, then no single, orthodox Platonism was shared among them all. So the position (*thesis*) that he initially adopted should be understood as more of a general stance or research agenda than a set of specific conclusions. In that sense (and with some simplification), the position, or agenda, of Plato's Academy prior to Arcesilaus' taking over prominently featured the proper interpretation of the Forms, including how or whether they make knowledge of the physical world possible, and the proper interpretation of the ethical ideal of living in accordance with nature.

Scepticism in the Academy: the Platonic and Socratic inspiration

Arcesilaus turned the Academy away from these projects and towards scepticism. In at least one important respect this move was not revolutionary. As we have seen, there had always been an intellectual freedom in the Academy that kept it from becoming a mere storehouse of dogma. But the move to scepticism did mark a new and distinct phase of the Academy.

By the time Arcesilaus became head of the school, there were probably no Academics alive who had personally known Plato. This made Plato's books all the more important. Despite having access to these books, Arcesilaus acquired his own copies (DL 4.32), from which he derived his sceptical interpretation.[4] As Cicero puts it:

> [Arcesilaus was] the first to adopt from the varied books of Plato and from Socrates' dialogues, especially the idea that there is no certainty that can be grasped either by the senses or the mind. In this complete rejection of the mind and senses as instruments of judgment, he is said to have employed an exceptionally charming manner of speaking, and also to have been the first to establish the practice – although this was very characteristic of Socrates – of not revealing his own view, but of always arguing against any view that any one else would assert.
>
> (*De Or.* 3.67 [May & Wisse 2001];
> see Plutarch, *Adv. Col.* 1121e–1122a)

That Arcesilaus derived his scepticism from Plato's dialogues will go some way in explaining why there is no record of any protest or upheaval following his innovation. Given his powerful rhetorical skill, he might have sold his colleagues on the idea that he was returning the institution to its real roots: Plato, and Socrates before him, had been sceptics.[5] Earlier Academics, including Arcesilaus himself, had misunderstood the spirit of Platonic philosophy by seeking to articulate, develop and defend positive doctrines. Thus he set out to reinvigorate the Academy with the sceptical spirit of its founder. In Plato's dialogues, Cicero claims, "nothing is affirmed, there are many arguments on either side, everything is under investigation, and nothing is claimed to be certain" (*Ac.* 1.46).

Arguing against all comers

The fact that Plato wrote dialogues provides some support for the claim that he never affirmed anything in his own voice. In Berkeley's and Hume's philosophical dialogues, by contrast, it is generally clear who speaks for the author, and what positions are being promoted. But in Plato's dialogues it is not clear who, if anyone, speaks for the author. It continues to be extremely difficult to discern what Plato thinks, and given the scholarly track record there is little hope of ever arriving at a consensus, let alone an enduring one, regarding an orthodox Platonism that is true to Plato's intentions.

That the dialogues contain arguments against whatever anyone asserts is also plausible enough. Socrates is constantly trolling for new answers to his questions and for new interlocutors who will finally reveal the truth to him. Cicero specifically tells us that Arcesilaus revived this Socratic practice of eliciting his interlocutors' views in order to argue against them (*Fin.* 2.2; *ND* 1.11; *Fat.* 4; *Ac.* 1.16), that is, to see whether their reasons really justify their beliefs.[6]

Socrates explains this practice in the *Apology* as part of his struggle to understand the puzzling pronouncement of the Delphic oracle; namely, that no one is wiser than Socrates (*Ap.* 20e–22e). He could not, at first, imagine how this statement could be true since he discerned no wisdom in himself, but he had no doubt that it was true, for the god would not lie. Seeking to resolve the oracle's riddle, he examined those who had a reputation for wisdom, perhaps to better understand what he was supposed to have himself. But after a lifetime spent searching for someone with expert, that is, irrefutable, knowledge of virtue, Socrates gradually came to the conclusion that what the oracle meant was that he is wisest because he does not believe he knows what in fact he does not. So he is slightly better off than all the rest who mistakenly think they know what they do not. (Note this is a far cry from the tranquil contentment that Pyrrho discovers from his ignorance.)

In pursuing this project, Socrates makes three important assumptions about knowledge and virtue. First, he implicitly identifies knowledge with virtue. In reaction to the oracle's assertion that no one is as wise as Socrates, he reflects on the fact that he is not aware of knowing anything worthwhile (*Ap.* 20c, 21b). In other words, he assumes that if he were wise he would have the relevant sort of knowledge. Accordingly, he investigates the oracle by looking for someone who has the sort of knowledge that he lacks. Secondly, if someone has this knowledge, then he cannot be refuted. To know *p* is to know why *p* is true in such a way that no argument can undermine your grasp of that truth (see *Gorg.* 473b; *Meno* 85c). This assumption is evident in the way Socrates goes about testing the oracle; namely, by seeing whether anyone can consistently defend his views on virtue. When Socrates shows his interlocutor is unwittingly committed to contradictory beliefs about *p*, we are supposed to conclude the interlocutor does not know *p*. The third assumption is the idea that knowledge of virtue is necessary (and possibly even sufficient) for performing good moral actions and ultimately for living a good life. This is rooted in another famous Socratic paradox: no one knowingly does wrong (e.g. *Prot.* 351b–358d).

The upshot is that as long as we lack this crucial knowledge, the only thing really worth doing is to earnestly pursue it. And, given the second assumption – if you have knowledge, you cannot be refuted – we must not rest content with even the most thoroughly defended position as long as it is possible that it might be refuted. As long as that possibility remains, we cannot justifiably claim to have the knowledge that is necessary for our flourishing.

Accordingly, Arcesilaus moves the Academy away from abstruse theoretical speculation regarding the Forms or other metaphysical first principles by emphasizing the negative character of Socrates' project. Under his leadership, the outcome of philosophical enquiry is the elimination of poorly founded beliefs. This is accomplished by arguing against anything that anyone is willing to defend.[7]

Nothing can be known with certainty

Given the nature of Socrates' project, it would not be surprising if he came to the conclusion that nothing can be known with certainty, at least regarding virtue. Such a conclusion would be hard to avoid after reflecting on his repeated failure to find someone with expert, (i.e. irrefutable, certain) knowledge. Whenever he discovers a promising candidate, Socrates eventually finds him lacking. Whether or not he articulated the implicit premises, the suggestion of an inductive argument is unmistakable. Interlocutors A to Y have failed to consistently defend their views and therefore their (implicit or explicit) claims to certain knowledge are false. On the basis of this experience one might reasonably expect that interlocutor Z will also fail. And on the basis of that enumerative induction one might reasonably infer that everyone will fail. Finally, in order to explain these failures, one might reasonably conclude that nothing (at least regarding virtue) can be known with certainty. For if knowledge of such an important matter were possible, surely someone would have acquired it.

This conclusion is necessarily tentative. The fact that no one passes Socrates' tests does not entail that nothing can be known. We may just as well conclude that Socrates has not chosen his interlocutors well enough or that there is something wrong with the tests. In particular, the second assumption mentioned above, namely that knowledge requires irrefutability, seems too demanding. In keeping with our ordinary ways of speaking, we might wish to say we know all sorts of things despite being unable to provide irrefutable justification. On the other hand, we might also insist that the degree of justification must be proportional to the importance of the matter

question. If, as Socrates maintains, beliefs about the proper way
live are the most important, then we might reasonably hold them
to such stringent requirements.

Be that as it may, if Arcesilaus pursued a similarly Socratic mission, and given his rhetorical power, he probably would have expe-
rienced the same string of disappointments. Thus he would have
arrived at the conclusion that nothing can be known with certainty
by means of the same sort of inductive reasoning.

Cicero also provides an alternative explanation. He tells us that
Arcesilaus, again following in Socrates' footsteps, arrived at his confession of ignorance from reflecting on the limitations of our minds
and senses and the shortness of life (*Ac.* 1.45).[8] If indeed he ever
formulated this as an argument, it need not exclude the inductive
reasoning. On the contrary, such limitations would in fact help to
explain the string of disappointments that figure in the inductive
argument. The crucial point is that Arcesilaus seems to have reasoned his way to the conclusion that nothing can be known.

The influence of Pyrrho

So Arcesilaus could have agreed with Pyrrho that we are not so constituted as to gain certain knowledge of the world. More importantly,
Arcesilaus seems to be following Pyrrho's lead when he insists that
wisdom requires the suspension of judgement. This is an idea that
we definitely do not find in Plato's dialogues.[9]

Both Sextus Empiricus (*PH* 1.232–4) and Numenius (*Praep. Ev.*
14.6.4–6) claim that Arcesilaus is like a Pyrrhonist in so far as he
refuses to assert anything about the way the world really is.[10] Like
Pyrrho, he refuses to accept the verdict of the senses or of reason as
being true or even likely to be true. Sextus further claims that Arcesilaus differs from the Pyrrhonist only in endorsing the suspension
of judgement as good.

It is likely that Arcesilaus, like so many others, admired Pyrrho's
legendary tranquillity. He may also have been impressed by Pyrrho's
insistence that we must suspend judgement in light of our ignorance.

But there is no evidence to suggest that Arcesilaus thought tranquillity is the proper goal in life. So while Pyrrho's influence is significant, it does not shape the contours of Arcesilaus' scepticism nearly as much as the influence of Plato and Socrates. It is only by pointing to the figure of Socrates that we can understand why Arcesilaus might have thought suspending judgement is good (*PH* 1.233). If he accepts the Socratic presupposition that virtue, as a form of knowledge, is necessary for a good life, then we are right to resist any temptation to settle for beliefs that are not known with certainty. To settle for such beliefs will put the search for truth to a premature end and so cannot be good. On the contrary, suspending judgement is good, but only with respect to our commitment to discover the truth.

Zeno and the Stoic inspiration

Around the time Arcesilaus arrived in Athens as a young man (*c*.298 BCE), Zeno, who also studied with Polemo in Plato's Academy, had established a new philosophical school. Since he typically met with his disciples at one of the covered colonnades (or Stoa), close to the Agora, they eventually came to be called Stoics. When Arcesilaus took over as head of the Academy in *c*.268, Stoicism was well established and flourishing.

One of the defining characteristics of the early Stoa is an empirically based epistemology that is supposed to show how the wisdom that Socrates sought was possible (Long 1988; Frede 1999). The essential ingredient is a type of impression that "arises from what is, and is stamped and impressed exactly in accordance with what is, of such a kind as could not arise from what is not" (*M* 7.248). The Stoics described such impressions as *kataleptikē*, graspable or grasping; I shall leave it transliterated as "kataleptic". Kataleptic impressions accurately convey all the relevant details of the object or state of affairs from which they arise. They somehow guarantee the truth of the propositions that articulate their content.

Kataleptic impressions provide a crucial path from foolishness to wisdom for the Stoics. By learning to distinguish kataleptic impressions from non-kataleptic ones, we may give our assent only to what is true. The kataleptic impression is a natural resource, so to speak, that is shared among sage and foolish alike. When one is in a normal and healthy condition, the impressions one receives are, for the most part, kataleptic. But when we assent to kataleptic impressions, we do not do so from the same firm and unwavering disposition that the sage does, nor do we grasp the complex, mutually reinforcing interrelations among these impressions. Unlike the sage's assent, ours is contingent on circumstances and is not rooted in a complete, systematic grasp of reality. So even if we assent to a kataleptic impression (or, more precisely, to the proposition implicit in the impression) we may still quite easily be convinced to abandon this truth by some argument or some other impression. The Stoic sage, by contrast, is irrefutable and unshakeable in his knowledge (e.g. DL 7.121, 162, 201; *M* 7.157). Here at last is someone, or at least a possible someone, who could stand up to Socrates' relentless questioning.

In the absence of a real sage to cross-examine, Arcesilaus turns his sights on those who would defend this ideally wise human being. There are two distinct accounts of his motivation for doing so. According to one, he wished to score points by taking down a widely respected philosophy and perhaps also to boost the fame of his own school in the process (*Praep. Ev.* 14.4.8; *Ac.* 2.15–16). According to the other, he simply wanted to discover the truth, and especially whether Zeno knew his optimistic epistemological view to be true (*Ac.* 2.76). These two accounts are compatible. There may well have been some petty professional rivalry at work in addition to the more noble aspirations.

Cicero reconstructs the debate this way:

> None of Zeno's predecessors had ever explicitly formulated, or even suggested, the view that a person could hold no opinions – and not just that they could, but that doing so was necessary for the wise person. Arcesilaus thought that this view was both true and honorable, as well as right for the wise person. So he asked Zeno, we may suppose, what would happen if the wise person couldn't apprehend anything, but

it was a mark of wisdom not to hold opinions. Zeno replied, no doubt, that the wise person wouldn't hold any opinions because there was something apprehensible [kataleptic]. So what was that? An impression, I suppose. Well, what kind of impression? Then Zeno defined it thus: an impression from what is, stamped, impressed, and molded just as it is. After that, Arcesilaus went on to ask what would happen if a true impression was just like a false one. At this point, Zeno was sharp enough to see that no impression would be apprehensible if one that came from what is was such that there could be one just like it from what is not. Arcesilaus agreed that this was a good addition to the definition, since neither a false impression, nor a true impression just like a false one, was apprehensible. So then he set to work with his arguments to show that there is no impression from something true such that there could not be one just like it from something false. (*Ac.* 2.77)

Both Arcesilaus and Zeno agree that the sage holds no mere opinions: that he is infallible (*Ac.* 2.66–67). The most plausible explanation for this agreement is their common Socratic inheritance. There is nothing short of infallibility that will satisfy the Socratic requirements on wisdom. As long as it remains possible that one might be refuted, he cannot rest content with mere beliefs or even with isolated bits of knowledge. In so far as our happiness and well-being rest firmly on such beliefs, one must continue to put them to the test until they are absolutely secured. This in turn requires grasping all of the systematic entailments that support the truth of each of the sage's beliefs. For example, in order to infallibly grasp the truth of Stoic ethical principles, one must see how they are logically related to the principles of physics and theology.[11]

But if there were nothing that we can be absolutely certain of, then it seems we can only attain the infallibility of the sage by refusing to believe anything at all. Believing nothing is the only way to assure that we will never be mistaken. Zeno agrees that the sage will withhold belief whenever he is uncertain. Although such caution is characteristic of the sage, his wisdom is constituted by irrefutable knowledge. To get to this comprehensive understanding, we have to rely on isolated bits of certainty. These are delivered to us by means of impressions that originate in what they represent, and that correctly report the details of what they represent.

Arcesilaus raised the obvious worry that an impression might appear to satisfy these conditions and yet fail to. Zeno then added the crucial claim that in order for an impression to be kataleptic, there cannot exist a false impression that is indistinguishable from it; or, in Sextus' account, a kataleptic impression is of such a kind as could not arise from what is not (*M* 7.252). We may take this requirement as merely a clarification or a substantive addition. As a clarification, we can see Zeno appealing to the principle of identity of indiscernibles in arguing that since no two things are ever exactly alike, their impressions will never be exactly alike, or indistinguishable, either. But that seems to miss the point of Arcesilaus' concern; namely, that two impressions might *appear* indistinguishable. For that reason, it seems preferable to read Zeno's addition as marking a first step towards an externalist view, according to which the subject does not need to be aware that the impression he assents to is kataleptic in order for him to grasp it as kataleptic.[12] On this view, Zeno begins to bring in considerations of how kataleptic impressions are formed – their causal histories – as a way of guaranteeing they arise from what is, and that they are stamped and moulded precisely in accordance with this.

Despite this move, Arcesilaus went to work constructing examples of false impressions that are indistinguishable from true ones. Cicero reports two kinds. One type illustrates cases of misidentification: for example, identical twins, eggs, statues or imprints in wax made by the same ring (*Ac.* 2.84–87). Another type involves cases of illusion, dreams and madness (*Ac.* 2.88–91). All of these examples illustrate Arcesilaus' general point that for every true impression there may exist a false one that is qualitatively identical to it, and thus indistinguishable from the true one. The issue, as Arcesilaus chose to understand it, is whether we are ever actually in a position to identify an impression as kataleptic, regardless of its causal history.

There is a good reason to agree with Arcesilaus' assessment here. In the Socratic spirit, the purpose of Zeno's account of knowledge is practical. He is not primarily interested in showing us that in some abstract, theoretical sense wisdom is a logical possibility, or that there is nothing conceptually incoherent about it. Rather, what he wants to establish is that with the proper training and use of our cognitive resources, wisdom is an attainable ideal. There is nothing about our human nature or about the world that prevents us from attaining wisdom; folly is due exclusively to the corruption of our nature. So Zeno needs to show that someone could actually develop his skills of discernment to such a level that he would never mistake a falsehood for a truth – and so the "arms race" begins. In response to each of the sceptical scenarios he will be forced to hypothesize an even greater level of expertise. Even if the sceptic grants that no two impressions are in fact qualitatively identical, he can always imagine that they are so infinitesimally close that no actual person's skill could differentiate them. The possibility of error appears to be inescapable.

If we accept this line of thinking, and if we accept the initial assumption that wisdom is incompatible with error, we have nothing left to do but suspend judgement. Arcesilaus is credited with doing just that:

> For these reasons [i.e. reasons that establish the impossibility of Stoic knowledge], he [Arcesilaus] thought that we shouldn't assert or affirm anything, or approve it with assent: we should always curb our rashness and restrain ourselves from any slip. But he considered it particularly rash to approve something false or unknown, because nothing was more shameful than for one's assent or approval to outrun knowledge or apprehension. His practice was consistent with this theory, so that by arguing against everyone's views he led most of them away from their own: when arguments of equal weight were found for the opposite sides of the same subject, it was easier to withhold assent from either side. (*Ac.* 1.45; see DL 4.28, 32)

we have a picture of a man who never believes he knows what ˌoes not. Nor does he even believe what may be false. It appears ᵤ.. ᵢ he believes nothing. But would he have considered mundane empirical beliefs regarding tables and chairs to be rash and shameful also? It is unlikely that anyone would pride himself on knowing that, for example, Crantor is walking in the Academy. If Arcesilaus had not needed to argue against such a claim, perhaps he would not object to believing it. Taken this way, suspension of judgement would be limited to those matters that have been tested and refuted, that is, shown to be unjustified.

Although this seems to be the more charitable reading, Arcesilaus in fact thought we must suspend judgement about everything (*PH* 1.232; DL 4.32; *Adv. Col.* 1120C). To attain wisdom we must develop the unwavering disposition to assent only to kataleptic impressions, regardless of what they are impressions of. More generally, and without presupposing Stoic epistemology, we may say that Arcesilaus aimed to develop the disposition to assent only to propositions sufficiently justified as to enable one to withstand Socratic examination. In either case, we must withhold assent not just to controversial and disputed impressions about justice and virtue, but also to impressions about tables, chairs and people as well (*M* 7.155–7).

The *apraxia* objection, I: suspending judgement renders us inactive

This interpretation makes the best sense of the *apraxia* objection: to suspend judgement about everything makes life unliveable. If Arcesilaus had allowed himself beliefs about the medium-sized objects we all encounter day to day, the objection would lose its punch. Plutarch records one version of this objection, aimed specifically at Arcesilaus: "how is it that someone who suspends judgment does not rush away to a mountain instead of to the bath, or stands up and walks to the door rather than the wall when he wants to go out to the market-place?" (*Adv. Col.* 1122E [LS 69A]; see also *Ac.* 2.37–38). The idea is that belief is a necessary part of any intentional action. In terms of Stoic psychology, one must first perceive the bath as something desirable and then assent to the related proposition "I should step towards the bath". Only then does the expected action occur.

If he were to withhold assent from his impression (or again, the proposition associated with the impression), then he would not move towards the bath; he might just as well move towards the mountain, or stand completely still. Imagine seeing a bowl of fruit on a table. You are hungry, so you perceive the fruit as something to be taken and eaten. According to Arcesilaus, we can never be certain about this impression – for example, the fruit may be wax – so we must not assent to it. But according to the Stoics, withholding our assent will keep us from acting. On their view, if we reach out for the fruit then we have assented to the proposition that the fruit should be taken.[13] To eliminate assent is to eliminate action.

Here is Arcesilaus' reply, as reported by Plutarch:

> The movement of impression we could not remove, even if we wanted to; rather, as soon as we encounter things, we get an impression and are affected by them. The movement of impulse, when aroused by that of impression, moves a person actively towards appropriate objects, since a kind of turn of the scale and inclination occur … So those who suspend judgment about everything do not remove this movement either, but make use of the impulse which leads them naturally towards what appears appropriate. What, then, is the only thing they avoid? That only in which falsehood and deception are engendered – opining and precipitately assenting … For action requires two things: an impression of something appropriate, and an impulse towards the appropriate object that has appeared; neither of these is in conflict with suspension of judgment.
>
> (*Adv. Col.* 1122B–D [LS 69A])

Reflecting on our actions will make this account seem plausible. Most of the time, when we choose to do something we do not lay out a list of all the pros and cons, carefully weigh the options and

then finally arrive at a conscious judgement or assent. In ordinary, everyday sorts of actions we simply respond to stimuli without being aware that we have assented. This does not mean that we have not in fact assented. But the way we usually use the term "assent" is to describe a conscious, deliberate approval of some impression or course of action. So in the everyday sense of the term, Arcesilaus is right to say that assent is not necessary for action.

But the Stoic account of assent is in fact more subtle and plausible than this. The idea that impressions might lead immediately to action could be challenged on the grounds that it does not explain the intentional nature of action. To merely respond is not to act in a sense that merits praise or blame, nor does it express anything about the agent's character. If we wish to explain these aspects of action, we will need more than a crude stimulus-response model.[14]

Nevertheless, Arcesilaus seems to have the better of this exchange. Some sort of action is clearly possible without assent. We shall next consider whether limiting ourselves to this type of action would be worthwhile.

The *apraxia* objection, II: suspending judgement makes virtue and happiness impossible

Another version of the *apraxia* objection claims that virtue and happiness will be impossible to achieve if we suspend judgement about everything (*M* 7.158; *Ac.* 2.23–25, 2.39). This objection presupposes something like the Stoic view that virtue requires firm convictions about what is morally right and good, and that it is both necessary and sufficient for happiness. Given this presupposition, Arcesilaus' proposal to suspend judgement about everything effectively eliminates any possibility of attaining virtue, and thus a happy life (in so far as we take virtue to be necessary for happiness).

According to Sextus, Arcesilaus felt compelled to respond to this objection. For the champion of the "true" Socratic tradition, such a charge would be devastating. Socrates' prime motivation was not simply to avoid error or rashness, but rather to learn how to lead the best possible life. If it turns out that Arcesilaus' method is incompatible with that end, he would be hard pressed to justify his claim to the Socratic mantle. Sextus asserts that since:

> it was necessary to investigate the conduct of life too, which is not of a nature to be explained without a criterion, on which happiness too, i.e. the end of life, has its trust dependent, Arcesilaus says that one who suspends judgment about everything will regulate choice and avoidance and actions in general by "the reasonable" [to eulogon]; and that by proceeding in accordance with this criterion he will act rightly; for happiness is acquired through prudence, and prudence resides in right actions, and right action is whatever, once it has been done, has a reasonable justification; therefore, one who attends to the reasonable will act rightly and be happy.   (M 7.158 [LS 69B])

Unfortunately this is the only piece of evidence for Arcesilaus' sceptical criterion of choice and avoidance. So we can only cautiously speculate about the details and how it is supposed to yield happiness. But first we must consider whether Arcesilaus endorses this criterion himself or not.

The dialectical interpretation

On the dialectical interpretation, Arcesilaus never asserts his own views; indeed, in so far as he heeds his own advice to suspend judgement, he has no views to assert in the first place. Instead, he elicits his opponents' views in order to show them that they are committed to inconsistent beliefs and therefore that they do not know what they think they know. His mission, like Socrates', is to deflate the confident dogmatists and encourage an open-ended pursuit of the truth.

We can easily see how this would work with Arcesilaus' arguments against the kataleptic impression. It is the Stoics who insist on unsatisfiable conditions; Arcesilaus merely draws out the implications without adding anything of his own. Given the further Stoic view that the sage never assents to what has not been grasped with certainty, it follows, again on Stoic grounds, that one must suspend judgement. Arcesilaus need not contribute anything of his own.

We may see his remarks about the *eulogon* in this dialectical light rather than as expressing his own views in the following way. The Stoic sage regulates his choice and avoidance in accordance with his unwavering, systematic knowledge. By proceeding in accordance with what he knows to be truly good, he acts rightly. This they understood to be prudence (*phronēsis*), which guarantees a happy life. Having undermined the Stoic account of knowledge, Arcesilaus then proceeds to show the Stoics that they have ample theoretical resources to answer their own objections about suspending judgement, even though the kind of prudence that remains possible is a much more modest sort. In effect, he vandalizes the Stoic system by replacing the sage's action based on certainty with the more down to earth and readily attainable action in accordance with the reasonable.

The greatest strength of the dialectical interpretation is that it saves Arcesilaus from a variety of potential inconsistencies. For example, if he personally believes we should suspend judgement, then it seems he should not also advise us to regulate our lives in accordance with the reasonable, in so far as that conflicts with suspending judgement. Nor should he endorse the three Socratic principles: (i) virtue is a kind of knowledge; (ii) the person with knowledge is irrefutable; and (iii) virtue is necessary if not also sufficient for a good life. But if he believes none of these things, he cannot be accused of inconsistency. Further support for the dialectical interpretation comes from the fact that all of the views associated with Arcesilaus can plausibly be seen as consequences of Stoic commitments that would be particularly unwelcome to the Stoics.

An objection to the dialectical interpretation

Although the dialectical interpretation is attractive, it is vulnerable to at least one powerful objection. It is odd for Arcesilaus to have bothered responding to the *apraxia* objections if he were only drawing consequences from the Stoic position. If it is only the Stoics who are unwittingly committed to the view that we should suspend judgement, then the charge that this makes life unliveable and virtue impossible is all the more damning for them. In that case it would make more sense for Arcesilaus to applaud the *apraxia* objections than to respond to them. He would have more effectively deflated his opponents if he left them with their own incoherent view. So his response suggests that he is defending his own view: Arcesilaus himself thinks that we should suspend judgement.

Similarly, if he were only concerned to show the Stoics the inadequacy of their view, it makes no sense for him to provide an alternative criterion of action. But let us suppose for the sake of argument that he generously offers the Stoics a viable alternative. If the dialectical interpretation is right, Arcesilaus must have employed the Stoic understanding of *to eulogon*, for if he provided his own understanding he would no longer be arguing dialectically. The Stoics defined the reasonable (*to eulogon*) as a proposition that has more chances of being true than false (DL 7.76). This is more or less the sense in which we typically use the term also. A reasonable proposition is credible; it is worth accepting as true even though we do not take the evidence or arguments to be conclusive.

If that is correct, then Arcesilaus has not in fact shown the Stoics that morally right action and happiness are possible for those who suspend judgement. The one who regulates his action in accordance with *to eulogon*, as the Stoics understand that term, will have all sorts of beliefs about what one should or should not do. Such a person will not have suspended judgement. In order for Arcesilaus to arrive at the desired conclusion, he will have to provide some interpretation of *to eulogon* such that acting in accordance with it is consistent with suspending judgement. This suggests, contrary to the dialectical interpretation, that his goal is to show the Stoics that the sceptic is able to live and flourish without the Stoic criterion; this seems to be Arcesilaus' own view of the matter (see Hankinson 1998a: 85–91).

Consistency and Arcesilaus' Socratic habits

As we have already seen, it appears inconsistent to believe that virtue is a kind of irrefutable knowledge *and* that one should suspend judgement about everything. If we suspend judgement we should not also hold beliefs about knowledge and virtue; on one account Arcesilaus made a point even of suspending judgement with regard to whether he was in fact ignorant (*Ac.* 1.45). On the other hand, Arcesilaus is frequently associated with views about what knowledge requires and with the advice that we should suspend judgement. How then are we to resolve this apparent inconsistency?

The rise of Stoicism, especially under the guise of a positive development of Socratic philosophy, would have incited Arcesilaus to bring the critical or sceptical elements of Socrates to light. In reviving this sceptical practice, he probably accepted Socrates' methodological assumptions as well. The point of arguing against everyone is to promote the Socratic search for truth. It would be unacceptably dogmatic, however, if he had never turned his sceptical sights on his own assumptions.[15] One should not uncritically believe anything. Once he had done so, he must have found powerful arguments opposing Socrates' assumptions.

In order for Arcesilaus to be a consistent sceptic he would need to suspend judgement regarding these motivating assumptions. It would follow that he did not believe virtue is an irrefutable kind of knowledge or that it is essential for a flourishing life. Why then did he carry on with his sceptical practice, behaving *as if* he believed these things?

I believe the most plausible speculation is to characterize the commitments that underlie Arcesilaus' behaviour as a-rational: they are neither in accordance with, nor violations of, any rational standards. Whatever attitude Arcesilaus continued to take towards his initially motivating assumptions, he cannot have thought that reason requires us to engage in this Socratic project. The dictates of reason, for Arcesilaus, are inconclusive. The irony is that this attitude arises from a deep commitment to follow reason wherever it leads. It appears that that commitment cannot itself be rational, even if Arcesilaus thought that initially he had good reasons for adopting it. As a habitual activity, Arcesilaus need not feel compelled to defend it. Even after acknowledging that there are no conclusive arguments in support of the notion that it is good or beneficial to behave this way, he merely finds himself inclined to continue.

Similarly, Arcesilaus' acceptance of the notion that knowledge is impossible may be habitual, and not rational. His argument against the Stoic criterion of knowledge is clearly dialectical, so he need not accept the conclusion that nothing can be known (in the Stoic sense). But considering his success in refuting all comers, it must have seemed that knowledge is out of our reach.

Here again we may appeal to Socrates for illustration. After a lifetime of refuting those who thought they had knowledge, Socrates continued to entertain the possibility that he might yet discover someone who could successfully defend himself. This must have seemed a very slim possibility. After years of successfully refuting his contemporaries, Arcesilaus would be inclined to expect that the next interlocutor would also fall. The idea that knowledge is impossible would take hold as more of a habitual expectation than a rational, philosophical judgement or belief that he would be willing to defend (Cooper 2004). At no point does Arcesilaus conclude, and hence believe, that knowledge is impossible, even though it must have seemed (in some sense) to be the case. (We shall return to this crucial contrast between appearances and judgements or beliefs later; see especially Chapter 9.)

Finally, what are we to make of living in accordance with the reasonable? Arcesilaus maintains that just as purposeful action is possible without assent or belief, so too is reasonable action. Some things will seem reasonable just as fire will seem hot; in both cases some action will ensue, regardless of whether I assent to the impression. All that Arcesilaus asks us to do is provide an explanation of why it appeared reasonable after the fact. Given the social importance of explaining our actions, it is likely that the "reasonable justification" is aimed at convincing others that one's action was appropriate. If my action or choice has some adverse effect and I fail to convince others that it was reasonable, I will probably suffer undesirable consequences. Even if my actions have a positive effect, my convincing explanation will help me to get the credit I deserve. By developing a disposition to provide convincing accounts of why I took my action to be reasonable, I will for the most part act rightly and prudently and will be happy. Assenting to these impressions and forming beliefs about what is right and wrong contributes in no way to my success; in fact, given Arcesilaus' mistrust of rationally supported conclusions, we are better off not assenting.

Conclusion

The kinds of prudence and happiness that one might expect from such a life are far more modest than the Stoic varieties. In fact, living in accordance with the reasonable seems extraordinarily easy. But we must recall that universal suspension of judgement is an essential part of this life, and we should not assume that this is a simple matter. From Arcesilaus' Socratic perspective, we all suffer from a pronounced disposition to prematurely put an end to enquiry and affirm our views with too much confidence. Without the irritating benefit of a Socrates who relentlessly puts us to the test, we are prone to settle comfortably into our convictions without even being aware of having done so.

FOUR

Carneades

None of Arcesilaus' first three successors (Lacydes, Evandrus and Hegesinus) are credited with any noteworthy achievements: they merely continue Arcesilaus' practice. Carneades, by contrast, surpasses even Arcesilaus in his rhetorical and philosophical brilliance. Accordingly, he invites an even greater measure of criticism:

> this man also would bring forward and take back, and gather to the battle contradictions and subtle twists in various ways, and be full both of denials and affirmations, and contradictions on both sides: and if ever there was need of marvelous statements, he would rise up as violent as a river in flood, overflowing with rapid stream everything on this side and on that, and would fall upon his hearers and drag them along with him in a tumult ... The evil results therefore were the more numerous [than Arcesilaus']. And nevertheless Carneades fascinated and enslaved men's souls ... In fact every opinion of Carneades was victorious, and never any other, since those with whom he was at war were less powerful as speakers. (*Praep. Ev.* 14.8.2, 9–10)

Carneades' persuasiveness only serves to accomplish greater evil if we assume that he leads people away from true, or at least beneficial,

59

beliefs. The pressing question is: what did he hope to achieve? It is uncharitable to assume that he was malicious. But it is easy to see how he might have appeared so.

Both Socrates (*Ap.* 23c) and Arcesilaus (DL 4.37) had attracted a large following by publicly deflating the intellectual pretensions of prominent people. And they earned scorn along with admiration: they were both accused of corrupting the youth (*Ap.* 23d; DL 4.40). By undermining conviction they appear to be leading people astray. They take away the moral compass and replace it with nothing.

In 156/5 BCE, Carneades, along with two other philosophers, was sent by Athens as an ambassador to Rome (*Tusc.* 4.5; *De Or.* 2.155; *Att.* 13.21; *Div. Inst.* 5.15.3–5). While there he publicly argued at length in defence of certain Platonic and Aristotelian conceptions of justice on one day and then refuted his own arguments the next. He did this, "not because he thought justice ought to be disparaged, but to show that its defenders had no certain or firm arguments about it" (Lactantius, *Epitome* 55.8 [LS 68M]). Cato was scandalized by this display and devised a clever plan to purge the city of Carneades and his fellow philosophers as quickly as possible. He criticized the Senate for detaining men who were able to get anything they might wish by means of their persuasive powers, and suggested they vote immediately on the embassy's proposal and send them home to Athens (Plutarch, *Vit. Cat. Mai.* 22–3). It probably appeared to Cato, and other Romans, that Carneades was indeed disparaging justice, even if that was not his intent. Undermining conviction, even poorly founded conviction, can be a dangerous business.

In order to determine more precisely what Carneades sought to achieve by means of his rhetorical brilliance and how he differs from Arcesilaus, we shall examine a selection of his arguments.

Theological arguments, I: against God's eternity

As with his arguments about justice, Carneades sought to undermine poorly founded convictions about the gods. Here again he did not wish to promote atheism, nor disparage the gods, but rather to show the Stoics that they had established nothing in their theology (*ND* 3.43–44; *M* 9.182–4). Although these arguments are aimed specifically at the Stoics, they apply just as well to any theological view that understands God as a living being, both eternal and benevolent.

If, as the Stoics maintain, God is alive (and is not a plant) then he is capable of sensation. But sensation, according to the Stoics, is a kind of alteration: "If God is altered, he is receptive of alteration and change; and being receptive of change, he will certainly be receptive of change for the worse. And if so, he is also perishable" (*M* 9.146–7). Sensation requires that the agent be the passive recipient of something that effects a change in him. Whether that alteration is for the better or worse is outside his control since he passively receives it. We do not choose to feel heat or cold when we do. Although we may try to avoid exposing ourselves to extreme conditions, freezing to death is ultimately out of our control (see *ND* 3.34). If one is stranded on a snowy mountain, whether or not one chooses to freeze is beside the point. So even though no one could strand God on a snowy mountain, he is, in principle, receptive of harmful or destructive alterations in so far as he is a sentient being. To be sentient is to be vulnerable to destruction, so God cannot be both sentient and eternal.

The easiest way out of this problem is to grant that God is not eternal. The problem with this is that an integral starting-point for Stoic theology is the commonly accepted notion that what is divine *is* eternal and imperishable. Thus Carneades may have pressed the following dilemma. Either God is imperishable or he is not. If he is, then it appears he cannot be sentient, since all sentient things are perishable. And if he is not, then we are no longer working with the common conception of God, contrary to the Stoics' claim.

Arguing both for and against the imperishability of God is supposed to leave us with no rational basis to prefer either view (see Long 1990).

Theological arguments, II: against God's benevolence

God's benevolence is part of his completely virtuous nature according to the Stoics. But if God has all the dispositions that we human beings consider virtuous, then he must be subject to at least some of the same conditions that make virtue possible and desirable for us. This led Carneades to argue as follows:

> if a being does not and cannot partake of evil, what need has he to make a choice between good things and evil things, and what need has he of reason and understanding? We apply these faculties to advance from what is revealed to what is hidden, but nothing can be hidden from God. As for justice, which apportions to each its own, it has no relevance to the gods, for as you Stoics put it, it was born when men banded together in community. Temperance consists in forgoing physical pleasures; if this virtue has a role in heaven, there must also be scope for physical pleasures there. As for the idea of God manifesting courage, how can we envisage that, seeing that pain or grief or danger does not impinge on God? Yet can we possibly visualize a God who does not use reason, and who is endowed with no virtue?
>
> (ND 3.38 [Walsh 1997]; cf. M 9.152–77)

This is evidently the inspiration for the sceptical dilemma that Hume advances (in Part V of his *Dialogues Concerning Natural Religion*; see Price 1964). On one hand, the more we make God like us the more he is vulnerable, imperfect and subject to human failings. On the other hand, the less we make God like us the less comprehensible he is. So we may either opt for a distant, incomprehensible God who satisfies our expectations of divine perfection or a closer, more comprehensible God who suffers from our human failings and is, to that extent, less worthy of the title.

Theological arguments, III: sorites

The Stoics believe both that the world itself is a divine being, and that it is possible to account for popular Greek, polytheistic religious views as well. They argue that elements or aspects of the divine being are themselves divine. But certainly not everything in the world is a god. So it is necessary to show how we may draw a clear line between what is divine and therefore worthy of worship and what is not. Carneades employs a sorites argument in order to show that no such principled line can be drawn (Burnyeat 1982b).

The term sorites comes from the Greek word for heap, *sōros*. If I place one grain of wheat on the table and ask you whether it is a heap, you will say no. If I add another grain to the first you will still say it is not a heap. But if I continue to add more and more, at some point it clearly becomes a heap. Yet, as a general rule, the addition of one grain does not transform a non-heap into a heap. So it seems that there can be no heaps or, more plausibly, it seems that our understanding of "heap" is too fuzzy to allow us to draw clear lines between heaps and non-heaps.

This form of reasoning exploits the fuzziness of concepts: by minute additions (or subtractions) of some property we find it impossible to determine whether the concept continues to apply. Imagine someone who is very poor. Adding a penny to his bank account will not make him wealthy, yet if we continue to add pennies, eventually he will become wealthy; it is just not clear when we reach that point, if indeed there is a point at which poverty is transformed into wealth. It does not follow that no one is wealthy. What follows is that we do not know the precise limits of this predicate.[1]

We can run this argument on countless other adjectives – for example, tall, bald, friendly – as well as many of the concepts that we use on a daily basis. Most would agree that football is a sport. But is golf a sport? How about Frisbee golf? How about video golf? Our inability to conclusively determine what counts as a sport or who counts as bald may not seem too threatening, but the dangers become more apparent when we consider the predicate "is a person". Deciding who or what is a person has important moral and legal implications, both for beginning-of-life and end-of-life issues. The microscopic cluster of cells of a newly fertilized egg is pretty clearly not a person. But adding a millisecond's worth of development does not seem to be significant enough to make the difference between a person and a non-person. And yet as development continues after birth we get to what obviously is a person. In these cases there is a greater urgency and necessity in confronting the sorites paradox because significant action may well be required.

Carneades applied the sorites to the predicate "is a god" in the following way:

> If Zeus is a god ... Poseidon too, being his brother, will be a god. But if Poseidon is a god, the [river] Achelous too will be a god. And if the Achelous is, so is the Nile. If the Nile is, so are all rivers. If all rivers are, streams too would be gods. If streams were, torrents would be. But streams are not. Therefore Zeus is not a god either. But if there are gods, Zeus too would be a god. Therefore there are no gods.
>
> (*M* 9.182–4 [LS 70E]; see also *ND* 3.43–4)

This is a creative use of the sorites since it does not proceed by the simple addition of some property. Instead, as in the sport example above, Carneades proceeds by drawing analogies. Both Poseidon and Achelous are large bodies of water; if it is true that one is a god, then the other must be a god also. But if the river Achelous is a god, then so too is every other river. We may continue this line of reasoning until we arrive at a puddle in the street: there is no principled place to draw the line.[2]

If one is inclined to worship the gods it seems one will have to determine who or what is worthy of such respect. What Carneades seeks to show with his arguments is not that nothing is a god, but that the Stoics have provided no convincing account of how we may maintain the common Greek conception of multiple gods without acknowledging the divinity of everything. And if reason can tell us nothing definitive about the nature or existence of God, or the gods, we must suspend judgement.

This is probably what Arcesilaus would have us do. However, it is not as clear in the case of Carneades, who is said to have departed from his great predecessor by claiming that we cannot, and need not, suspend judgement about everything (*Praep. Ev.* 14.7; see *Ac.* 2.59; *PH* 1.227–30). What attitude, then, would Carneades have us take towards our inconclusive enquiry into the nature of the gods? We shall return to this question later.

Ethical arguments: Carneades' divisions

Carneades' ethical arguments exhibit the same pattern. He is not interested in disparaging virtue or in convincing us to become vicious. Once again he is bent on undermining the poorly placed confidence of the dogmatists.

Unlike Arcesilaus, who argued against whatever his interlocutors actually believed (or were tempted to believe), Carneades broadened the sceptical attack in seeking to refute every possible ethical theory (*Fin.* 5.16). More precisely, he set out in a "division" every ethical theory that had been constructed or could be constructed in accordance with certain naturalistic assumptions. Since those assumptions were shared among his contemporaries, he employed his division to undermine the very project of Hellenistic ethical philosophy (Algra 1997; Annas 2001, 2007).

According to the naturalistic assumptions, an ethical theory must explain what sorts of goods we naturally desire, and why, or for what end, we desire them. Ethical development is, in one important respect, no different from the natural, physical development of an infant into an adult: the final stage of development is, in some sense, inherent in the person's initial condition. So our common human nature inclines us towards certain things and away from others, and it is only from those natural dispositions that we are able to construct a flourishing human life.

If our initial condition is nurtured appropriately, we fulfil our *telos*: our natural end or function. But there are many ways in which that development may go wrong. Just as a lack of good nutrition will prevent one from achieving the natural, physiological end, a lack of understanding about the proper goals in life will prevent one from achieving the natural, ethical end. Thus a crucial task for ethical theory is to teach us what the proper goals are.

By contrast, according to some non-naturalistic ethical views, our proper goal is to transcend the limitations of human nature. In some of Plato's dialogues, we are encouraged to escape this life as quickly as possible by becoming like God (Annas 1999). Later Christian thinkers developed this further, claiming that human nature cannot be perfected by merely natural means, but requires supernatural intervention.

Carneades offers three candidates for the objects our nature inclines us towards: pleasure, absence of pain and primary natural things (i.e. goods of the body and mind such as health, beauty or intelligence). These seem to be the only plausible candidates, as we can see by trying to find other naturalistic (non-theological) goods that do not fit into one of these categories. This immediately gives us three possible accounts of what we should organize our lives around. We may say the best life for human beings is: (1) to obtain pleasure; (2) to obtain the absence of pain; or (3) to obtain the primary natural goods. These are the simplest theories because they hold that nature implants in us a desire for the things we must obtain to live well.

But perhaps we should insist that it is not enough merely to get these things, but that we must do so in the right way, that is, virtuously. So they will only be components of a good life when accompanied with virtue. This will give us three more options. The best life for human beings is: (4) virtue plus pleasure; (5) virtue plus the absence of pain; or (6) virtue plus the primary natural goods. These theories will have to explain why it matters how we get the things we need to flourish.

Then again, perhaps we should only think of these as targets to be aimed at. In that case, we get three more possibilities. The best life for human beings is: (7) to strive for pleasure; (8) to strive for the absence of pain; or (9) to strive for the primary natural goods. The difficulty here is to explain why nature implants desires in us that we do not need to satisfy in order to flourish (see Figure 2).

Ethical ends: objects that human nature inclines us towards

Pleasure	Absence of pain	Primary nature things (mental and physical goods: health, wealth, intelligence)

Corresponding accounts of the good life in accordance with human nature

(1) Obtaining pleasure (EPICUREANS)	(2) Obtaining the absence of pain	(3) Obtaining (and enjoying) the primary natural things
(4) Obtaining pleasure in a morally good life	(5) Obtaining the absence of pain in a morally good life	(6) Obtaining and enjoying the primary natural things in a morally good life (ARISTOTELIANS)
(7) Striving for pleasure	(8) Striving for the absence of pain	(9) Striving for the primary natural things (STOICS)

Figure 2. Carneades' ethical divisions (*Fin.* 5.15–23, *Tusc.* 5.84–85; *Ac.* 2.128–31).

These theories are all supposed to give us actual, practical guidance in planning out our lives. Although they all place a significant emphasis on grasping what the proper targets are, they are not intellectualist: they do not maintain that becoming ethically good is simply a matter of acquiring the right sort of knowledge; or if it is, then acquiring knowledge will necessarily involve some change in our dispositions and desires. Nevertheless, they all maintain that knowledge is a necessary condition for virtue: if we do not know which targets are the right ones to aim at, we will only hit them haphazardly and by accident. To consistently and reliably hit the right targets we must know what we are to aim at (see *Tusc.* 5.15; *NE* 1.2, 1094a23–25 and 1.3, 1095a9–12).

The comparisons between ethical views implicit in Carneades' division shows that they cannot all be true. To defend one is to attack the others. But rather than taking the perspective of a participant in these ethical debates, Carneades places himself outside, surveying the whole field. This freedom from doctrinal commitment gives him a non-partisan appreciation of the strengths and weaknesses of the various positions, and it gives him a convenient frame for his sceptical attacks.

Such is Cicero's approach in *De Finibus* when he argues for and against the three most plausible and forcefully defended positions: the Epicurean (1), the Aristotelian (6) and the Stoic (9). The sceptical arguments that Cicero reports against these views are not always explicitly attributed to Carneades, but the context makes it reasonable to suppose that they are his, or at least were inspired by him.

Inconsistencies in Epicurean and Stoic ethics

One of Cicero's central complaints about the Epicurean view is that it is inconsistent. Epicurus, in fact, wavers between (1) and (2), since he sometimes conceives of pleasure as an active stimulation of the senses and other times as the tranquil absence of pain.[3] It is clear that maximizing one type of pleasure does not always maximize the other. Seeking the absence of pain will lead me away from many pleasures I might otherwise enjoy. And seeking those active pleasures will probably lead to some unwanted pains.

We are born with a natural desire for pleasure. But according to Epicurus it is the absence of pain that completes or fulfils our nature. If this is correct, nature seems guilty of misleading us. It would make much more sense to give us a desire for the absence of pain if that is what we need to flourish. Epicurus must explain why nature should implant in us a desire for pleasure when the satisfaction of that desire does not guarantee a good life.

There are powerful responses available to the Epicurean, some of which can be found in Cicero's defence (*Fin.* 1; see also DL 10.121–35). However, the sceptic does not need to provide irrefutable, conclusive evidence that the position in question is false. Sceptical refutation aims at showing that the dogmatists do not have an adequate defence, usually by pointing out inconsistencies within their theories. It is often possible to patch up the inconsistency by modifying the theory, but that in turn will provide a new target for sceptical refutation. The burden of proof always lies with those who are promoting a positive view.

Cicero's main objection to the Stoic account of the ethical end also points to an inconsistency. The Stoics claim that the primary natural goods are valuable, and thus choiceworthy, but also indifferent with respect to our happiness. It is supposedly a matter of striving in the right way that counts; whether or not we succeed is irrelevant. The Stoic sage will make every reasonable effort to maintain his health, for example, but this is consistent with his falling ill. His wisdom is not manifested in outcomes over which he has no ultimate control, but rather in a qualitative state of mind that directs him to act always in the right way. Once he has achieved wisdom, his happiness cannot be affected by the presence or absence of health or other such so called "preferred indifferents". The qualitative state of virtue allows for neither increase nor decrease: a chronically ill sage will be no less happy than one in great health. In effect, the Stoics appear to be saying that such things as health, strength and beauty are worth choosing because they are worth having, but also that it does not really matter whether you have them.

Cicero presents the Stoics with a dilemma: either they must say that the primary natural goods are really good, or that they are really neutral, neither good nor bad. If they go with the former option, their position collapses into the Peripatetic view that happiness comes only through a virtuous acquisition, use and enjoyment of good things. In other words, we will see that the Stoics do not really believe that striving is all we need for happiness. If they go with the latter option, their position can no longer offer any practical guidance; it will no longer matter whether I try to preserve my health since it can neither add to nor subtract from my happiness. So it will not matter whether I try to preserve my health or not. In general, such a theory will give us no basis on which to choose one thing and reject another.

Carneades used to get quite worked up by the Stoic claim that virtue is sufficient for happiness (*Tusc.* 5.83). One of the ways he sought to undermine this conviction was to argue in support of the first horn of the dilemma, that is, to show that their theory actually commits them to the Peripatetic position.

> Carneades used to judge the controversy [between Peripatetics and Stoics] as a respected arbitrator. Since the same things which the Peripatetics deemed goods, the Stoics regarded as advantages, and since the Peripatetics did not confer more value than the Stoics on wealth, good health, and other things of the same kind, he said that when the issue is weighed with respect to the facts, not words, there was no cause for dispute. (*Tusc.* 5.120; see also *Fin.* 3.41)

Carneades is clearly out to undermine a central component in Stoic ethics: the doctrine of the preferred indifferents. However, he is not trying to show that Stoic and Aristotelian ethics converge in order to defend it. Indeed, this is only one horn of the dilemma. Underlying the argument, at least in Cicero's presentation, is the notion that what really matters is the life one leads, the choices one makes, the way one responds to good fortune and adversity, not the words one uses to describe them, or the theory one appeals to in order to explain oneself. If the lives of morally upright Stoics are indistinguishable from the lives of Peripatetics, then the doctrinal differences are insignificant. This pragmatic attitude is not offered as an alternative to philosophical investigation. Carneades is not saying that rational enquiry is futile, but rather that dogmatic commitment to philosophical theories is futile.

So it would be surprising if the participants had *invited* him to sit as judge. If he thought they were all equally wrong, there is nothing for him to judge. But Cicero says that the controversy used to be decided by Carneades [*controversiam solebat iudicare*]. Since it is clearly a philosophical dispute, what needs to be decided is which side presents the most rationally compelling case. If Carneades judged that one position is more plausibly defended than the others, it is hard to see why he would not approve of that side himself. What attitude then would Carneades have us take towards these inconclusive ethical theories?

We shall postpone this question one last time until we have considered his arguments against Stoic epistemology.

Epistemological arguments

As with his sceptical attacks on theology and ethics, Carneades did not aim to show that no belief is true, but rather that none of the available epistemological theories had established anything about knowledge. Once again, Carneades was more ambitious than Arcesilaus:

> [He] positioned himself on the criterion not only against the Stoics but also against everyone before him. In fact his first argument, which is directed against all of them together, is one according to which he establishes that nothing is without qualification a criterion of truth – not reason, not sense-perception, not appearance, not anything else that there is; for all of these as a group deceive us.   (*M* 7.159)[4]

Despite disagreements regarding proposed criteria, it was agreed among Hellenistic philosophers that the successful candidate must play some role in differentiating the true from the false (Striker 1974). So Carneades attempts to show that nothing can fill this role, that is, that we have no reliable way to differentiate the true from the false.

As described by the Stoics, the criterion is more than just a theoretical account; it is supposed to be the tool that enables us to progress from folly to wisdom. We saw in Chapter 3 that becoming wise, for the Stoics, is a matter of learning to assent only to kataleptic impressions. The point of explaining the nature of such impressions is not simply to assure us that something is true, but rather to show how we can assent only to what is true.

Extending Arcesilaus' attack, Carneades makes a distinction between two aspects of an impression: one in relation to what it is an impression of, and the other in relation to the agent having the impression. The first relation determines whether it is true or false, and the second whether it is convincing or not. Separating these aspects makes Arcesilaus' objection more vivid, and it forces the Stoics to be more explicit about their position: an impression will be true or false depending on whether it agrees with its object(s), but this will not determine whether or not the agent finds the impression convincing (M 7.168). On the other hand, the fact that the agent finds the impression convincing need not tell us anything about whether it is true or false.

The Stoic criterion, the kataleptic impression, includes both aspects in such a way that its persuasiveness is supposed to indicate its truth. But, as Arcesilaus had argued, for any irresistibly persuasive and true impression we can imagine a false one that is indistinguishable. Carneades employs a sorites argument to further this objection. Advancing by minute degrees we can imagine transforming a kataleptic into a non-kataleptic impression, or vice versa. One reconstruction of the argument goes this way.[5]

[1] If God can present a sleeper with a persuasive impression [of what doesn't exist], then He can present the sleeper with an impression that is extremely truth-like, i.e. one which approximates the truth very closely.

[2] If ... one that is extremely truth-like, then ... one that's difficult to discriminate from a true impression.

[3] If ... one that is difficult to discriminate, then ... one that can't be discriminated.

[4] If ... one that can't be discriminated, then ... one that doesn't differ at all.   (*Ac.* 2.47–49)

The impression retains its persuasiveness throughout the steps; it does not become more persuasive as we proceed. What changes is the degree of difference between this vacuous impression and a true one. The impressions themselves gradually become more and more similar until we arrive at identical, that is, indistinguishable, perceptual contents. In the end, two equally persuasive impressions, one vacuous and one true, differ in nothing but number.

Chrysippus' customary way of dealing with the sorites is to stop answering before one comes to unclear cases: "in the case of appearances where the difference between them is so small, the wise person will hold fast and keep quiet, whereas in cases where a greater difference strikes him, he will assent to one of them as true" (*M* 7.416; see *Ac.* 2.91–2). So if the differences are minute, say between two imprints from the same ring, the sage will withhold assent. But in cases where there is a great difference between a kataleptic and non-kataleptic impression, the sage will not hesitate to assent to the former.

The problem with this response is that it assumes one can actually decide which situation one is in. Suppose that "fifty is few" is the content of a kataleptic impression, and that "ten thousand is few" is the content of a non-kataleptic and false impression. Clearly, fifty-one is about as far from ten thousand as fifty is. So the sage will assent to the proposition that "fifty-one is few" also (*M* 7.416–21). If there is a great difference between the evident truth of such claims and the falsity of "ten thousand is few", there should also be a great difference between "fifty-two is few" and "ten thousand is few". But once he starts down that road, there seems to be no principled place to stop answering.

Even if we suppose that somewhere along this road the sage would eventually receive the kataleptic impression that one hundred (or whatever the number may be) is not few, he must be able to recognize it as such. This impression must be quite distinct from the impression that ninety-nine is few. But this would be a remarkable feat of discrimination since in every other case the addition of one unit is not enough to transform few into many. So even if the sage receives the kataleptic impression regarding what is few and many, the sorites objection should undermine his confidence in being able to correctly identify it as such.

Similarly, one might be prevented from finding a kataleptic impression convincing due to external circumstances.

> For example, when Heracles stood by Admetus, having brought Alcestis up from below the earth, Admetus did

catch a kataleptic impression from Alcestis, yet did not trust it …. For Admetus figured that Alcestis was dead and that a dead person does not rise up. (*M* 7.254–56)

The impression of Alcestis seems to meet the requirements for being kataleptic: it is from a real thing, and in accordance with precisely that thing, and accurately depicts all the relevant details.

To deal with such eventualities, some later Stoics argue that the kataleptic impression can only serve as the criterion of truth if it has no obstacle (*M* 7.253–57, 7.424). As the Admetus example illustrates, the sorts of obstacles in question are beliefs or mental states. If I am in an anxious or fearful state of mind, I might very well receive a kataleptic impression and yet refuse to assent to it. Similarly, if I am firmly convinced of some false belief, I might also be reluctant to assent to some other truth. If there are no such obstacles, assenting to a kataleptic impression is like the sinking of a scale's balance when weight is put on it. The mind necessarily yields and cannot refrain from giving its approval to what is perspicuous (*Ac.* 2.38). When the kataleptic impression lacks any obstacles it practically lays hold of us by the hair and drags us to assent (*M* 7.257).

What these passages suggest is some sort of natural fit between kataleptic impressions and our rational faculty such that these impressions are, at least potentially, compelling in a way that false ones cannot be. According to this view, kataleptic impressions affect the properly trained mind in a way that is quite different from the way false impressions affect the same mind. The sage is the one who has habituated himself not to be tempted to assent to false beliefs. The fit between his rational nature and the truth explains how this habituation is possible. So perhaps it is possible to acquire the necessary level of discernment, if we can still call it that. Taken this way, the Stoic criterion is simply a guarantee that one might develop one's cognitive and perceptual equipment in such a way that one only finds kataleptic impressions persuasive.[6]

Such a guarantee is still cold comfort to the Sceptic. Carneades follows Arcesilaus in forcing the Stoics to live up to the more ambitious promise of their epistemology: show us *how* one might become a sage. This is especially urgent given their view that nothing but wisdom is really worthwhile. While we all languish in our vice and folly, it is of little use to be told that wisdom is possible. Carneades' sceptical attack emphasizes that the relation of an impression to the agent, its persuasiveness or credibility, is primary in our struggle for wisdom.

Epochē and apraxia

We come finally to the question of what cognitive attitude Carneades would have us take towards all this inconclusiveness. The simple answer is that we should withhold assent. But determining precisely what he means by this is complicated by the fact that he makes a distinction between two kinds of assent, only one of which we are supposed to withhold. The other is sceptically acceptable (*Ac.* 2.104).

Cicero reports Carneades' distinction as a key move in his response to the standard objection that suspending judgement makes life impossible (*apraxia*). The Stoics complained that if there are no kataleptic impressions, as Carneades argues, then everything would be unclear (*Ac.* 2.32). Carneades' sceptical attack calls into question the fit between human cognition and the world. In other words, it suggests that even if we use our cognitive equipment to the best of our ability we might not make any progress towards securing infallible justification for our beliefs.

We may develop this objection further in terms of the two aspects of an impression. By making this distinction Carneades draws our attention to the fact that the subjective plausibility of an impression is no *necessary* indicator of truth and vice versa. That is all he needs to assert for the sake of his objection to Stoic epistemology.

But this leaves open the question of whether the subjective plausibility of an impression is even a fallible indicator of truth, that is, whether there is *any* connection between plausibility and truth. If not, something seeming plausible has no greater likelihood of being true than something seeming wildly implausible. The convincing and familiar sight of a friend is just as likely to be true as the dream-like, hazy impression of a centaur. As far as we know, the way the world appears is not in any way an indicator of the way the world is. If that is what Carneades means, it is easy to see why the Stoics would assert that he is overturning life itself and depriving us of our minds (*Ac.* 2.31).

In countering the *apraxia* objection, Carneades maintains that there is an important difference between an impression being merely unclear and it's being inapprehensible (*Ac.* 2.32; *Praep. Ev.* 14.7). Everything is equally inapprehensible: no impression can be grasped or apprehended in such a way that we could not in principle be mistaken about it. But that does not mean that everything is equally unclear. Carneades only aims to do away with what never existed, the Stoic fiction of kataleptic impressions. But he leaves us what we have had all along, persuasive or convincing impressions, as our guide in practical matters.

Rather than give us advice about how we should act in the absence of certain knowledge, Carneades merely describes how we do act:

> … just as in ordinary life, when we are investigating a small matter we question one witness, when it is a greater matter, several witnesses, and when it is an even more essential matter we examine each of the witnesses on the basis of the mutual agreement among the others …   (*M* 7.184)

In the first level of scrutiny we apply the persuasive impression on its own as the criterion. If I receive an impression that is, at first sight, apparently true, I assent to it and act accordingly; we shall consider what is involved in such assent below. The fact that what is apparently true is sometimes false does not bother us, and nor should it. Carneades asserts that:

> one should not, because the rare occurrence of this [the apparently true impression being false], distrust the one that for the most part tells the truth. For both our judgments and our actions are, as a matter of fact, regulated by what applies for the most part.   (*M* 7.175)

The claim that such impressions "tell the truth" for the most part is simply a way of saying that they are reliable or trustworthy. If he had meant something more, he would be suggesting a dogmatic alternative to the Stoic account of truth. He does not (and should not) offer any speculation as to why such impressions are for the most part reliable.

But in presenting the persuasive impression as an alternative account of the criterion, he is making a significant departure from the standard use of the term "criterion". On the standard use, if something satisfies the criterion of truth then it is true. But a convincing impression may be true or false.

At the second level of scrutiny, where the stakes are a bit higher, we examine the impressions that appear along with the one in question. Carneades' makes the obvious, but important, observation that we typically do not receive isolated, individual impressions; rather, they come in groups. When I encounter my friend, I receive impressions of her clothes, her hair, her shoes and the sound of her voice, along with the objects she may be holding and other things in the immediate vicinity, and even the quality of the light. When the cluster of such impressions all appear true and mutually supportive, our trust is greater. But if one of these impressions appears false, if my friend's voice sounds completely unfamiliar, then I should reject the impression that this is my friend. Carneades describes this with the additional requirement that the convincing impression not be "turned away", that is, turned away by an apparently false impression accompanying it.

At the third level of scrutiny, in matters of the highest importance, we turn our attention to each of the associated impressions themselves and actively seek to discredit one on the basis of the others. Carneades claims that this is the sort of thing we do when scrutinizing candidates for public office. It is not sufficient that the candidate convincingly appears to be qualified. Commensurate with the importance of the position, we will examine his credentials and references. Each of these in turn will be put to similar tests. In the end, the most we can achieve is coherence among the examined impressions, but at this highest level of scrutiny, we will not settle for the coherence of the initial cluster of impressions. Thus we get the final requirement that the convincing impression that has not been turned away has also been gone over in detail.

Despite the fact that the highest level of scrutiny still fails to guarantee the truth of the impression, we continue to rely on it. If we do not, that is, if we find no impressions convincing, Carneades grants that life would be overturned (*Ac.* 2.99, 103, 105).

Carneades' practical criterion and the two types of assent

What exactly are we doing when we rely on such impressions? We may now understand the type of assent Carneades allows and the type he would have us withhold. For convenience we shall refer to these as sceptical and dogmatic assent, respectively. Sceptical assent is given to persuasive impressions that have received the appropriate level of scrutiny. (More strictly speaking, assent is given to a proposition associated with the impression. If we do not formulate such a proposition by interpreting the impression's significance, then it is not "saying" anything with which we might agree.)

The distinction between dogmatic and sceptical assent may be interpreted in two ways. One is that Carneades would have us withhold assent in the manner that would characterize assent to a kataleptic impression if we were able to identify it as such. In other words, since we cannot know whether any impression we assent to is kataleptic, we should never assent with absolute confidence.

On this *probabilist* view, all that Carneades would have us avoid is the rashness of taking ourselves to *know* what we do not; he does not object to cautiously believing that some impression is probably true. If this is correct, Carneades does not completely sever the connection between persuasive impressions and the truth. He merely points out that persuasive impressions are fallible and that as far as we know they are all we have. Accordingly, sceptical assent would yield fallible beliefs held with the appropriately modest awareness that they may be false.

The other alternative is that Carneades would have us withhold assent to the truth of any proposition. On this *sceptical* view, dogmatic assent is simply a matter of taking something to be true, whether in a modest or confident manner. Withholding this type of assent would rule out believing anything, as we commonly use the word belief. The corresponding type of sceptical assent would be a matter of going along with some impression without taking it to be true, or even probably true.

This issue continues to be controversial. Although a number of scholars in recent years have supported the second alternative, I believe the first is the correct interpretation of Carneades, at least with respect to ordinary, non-philosophical beliefs.[7]

As we saw in Chapter 3, Arcesilaus offers a version of the sceptical response. Action does not require assent, all we need is an impression and an impulse, neither of which need to be, or even can be, withheld. What makes compelling Arcesilaus' use of this response is the notion that we often act without consciously or deliberately reflecting on our situation.

Carneades incorporates such cases in his first level of scrutiny: "in cases where the situation does not give us an opportunity for exact consideration of the matter" (*M* 7.185). When being pursued by enemies, one does not have time to consciously deliberate about the evidence of one's senses; one must act on the basis of however things strike one at that moment.

But as we ramp up the level of scrutiny, this account no longer makes sense. Suppose I have carefully and thoroughly examined an apple. I have even fed a bit to my pet hamster, which appears fine afterwards. All of my impressions confirm that it is a good apple so I take a bite. The most plausible explanation is that I have come to believe the apple is probably okay to eat. The sceptical view would require me to say that although the apple appears good after my careful examination, I have no opinion as to whether it "really" is or not.

But Carneades offers his persuasive impressions as part of a description about how we in fact get along in the world. Most people take the evidence of their senses as good, although fallible, indicators of the way the world is. This is not to say that they accept some sophisticated metaphysical theory about reality, or even some explanation as to why the senses are generally reliable. When we raise the level of scrutiny, we expect to increase our chances of getting things right. We do not expect to merely feel more convinced.

The main problem with the sceptical interpretation is that it requires the Carneadean to find something convincing without thereby finding it likely to be true. Yet these notions are so closely linked that pulling them apart appears to make them both unintelligible. This is especially clear when we rely on impressions to determine the best course of action. It is quite implausible to think that an impression leads immediately to impulse when we are slowly and methodically considering possible courses of action along with the relevant evidence. Such deliberate judgement calls for some kind of assent.

This is where Carneades' persuasive impressions and his variety of sceptical assent come in. In differentiating two kinds of assent, and in describing the levels of scrutiny we typically employ, he shows how deliberation, and not just action, is possible for the sceptic. While this move strengthens the sceptic's response to the *apraxia* objection, it comes at the price of loosening up on *epochē*.

As a response to the *apraxia* objection, Carneades' practical criterion is only meant to show how we manage in ordinary life without kataleptic impressions. With one important exception, examples of Carneades' sceptical assent always occur in the context of making ordinary, everyday judgements: for example, whether this is Socrates (*M* 7.176–78), whether to flee (*M* 7.186), whether a coiled object is a rope or a snake (*M* 7.187), whether to go on a voyage, get married, sow crops and so on (*Ac.* 2.100, 109).

The possible exception occurs in response to the inconsistency objection. Carneades would not need to assert that he knows knowledge is impossible; instead he may say this is a persuasive intellectual impression to which he assents with the proper measure of caution (*Ac.* 2.110). Cicero does not explicitly assign this judgement to him, but it would have been an obvious move to make. Excluding this case, Carneades is never reported to have sincerely approved of any of the philosophical positions he debated. Sometimes he defended a view so vigorously he was thought to actually endorse it (*Ac.* 2.139;

see 2.131; *Fin.* 5.20). But Cicero makes it clear that he only argued for these positions dialectically. Even his close friend and companion Clitomachus could never figure out which philosophical views Carneades accepted (*Ac.* 2.139). The most plausible explanation for this is that he did not accept any of them, but continued, in good Socratic fashion, to seek the truth. In the meantime, he allows for the ordinary process of deliberation and a sceptically appropriate assent to persuasive impressions regarding the day-to-day maintenance of our lives.

The dialectical interpretation

As with Arcesilaus, it remains a distinct possibility that Carneades does not endorse any of his apparently positive claims, but instead develops them all on the basis of his opponents' views. On a purely dialectical interpretation, Carneades shows only that every positive, dogmatic view is rationally indefensible in terms of its proponent's own standards.

But if Carneades is showing the Stoics where their position leads, then once again the *apraxia* objection would be their problem, not his. Carneades should not respond to such objections but rather accept them as further confirmation of the untenable position occupied by dogmatists.

However, Carneades' dialectical strategy might be more indirect. He might have sought to show the Stoics that their position is not the best available. If he can show that Stoic epistemology is less rationally defensible than some other account, he will have established his goal. He will have shown that the Stoics' confidence in their epistemology is poorly founded. The elaborate account of persuasive impressions may be the centrepiece of this indirect strategy. This would also explain why the account of persuasive impressions is not derived strictly on the basis of Stoic commitments. Carneades would not be trying to show what the Stoics are unwittingly committed to, but rather that there is a better explanation available. Since such a modest, probabilist alternative would not be appealing to Stoics, who believed that wisdom requires irrefutable knowledge, in the end they would be left with no epistemological position; that is, they would be led to suspend judgement (Allen 1994).

But if this were Carneades' strategy it is unclear why he would not accept this alternative himself. He is not committed in advance to *epochē*, nor is he attributed any unequivocal view about what wisdom requires. Furthermore, if his description of sceptically appropriate assent is an account of how people do in fact deliberate, then he too will deliberate in this way. His admission that life would be overturned without convincing impressions to guide the way seems sincere. If so, Carneades will rely on convincing impressions just as everyone does.

The dialectical interpretation also requires that we explain away the evidence reporting Carneades' departure from Arcesilaus' position. Sextus marks this distinction, as we have seen, in terms of Arcesilaus' Middle Academy and Carneades' New Academy. Carneades deviates from Arcesilaus' more radically sceptical position by deliberately choosing to yield to some impressions rather than following along without any strong inclination or adherence (*PH* 1.230).[8] Apparently his point is that Carneades violates the sceptical spirit of *epochē* by being too actively involved or interested in getting things right, and in preferring one impression to another on the basis of how convincing they are. His yielding to convincing impressions accompanies a strong inclination towards things being as they seem. In other words, he accepts that convincing impressions have some evidential value, that they are fallible indicators of truth. And like everyone else, he relies on them in the countless ordinary judgements we make everyday.

Conclusion

Carneades was both more ambitious and more modest than Arcesilaus. He was more ambitious in extending his sceptical arguments regarding epistemology and ethics to cover every possible theory that might be propounded. And he was more modest in allowing for a kind of positive mental attitude that we take towards things we do not know, at least with regard to practical issues.

Carneades' view of sceptical assent makes for a more convincing response to the *apraxia* objection since it leaves in place all the ordinary measures of deliberation that people in fact employ. Arcesilaus, as I have interpreted him in Chapter 3, is only able to show how a very reactive form of action is possible. His criterion of action does not explain how the sceptic may adjudicate among his impressions after having reflected on them. Carneades' view also preserves the sceptic's consistency in allowing him to say that it appears convincing, but not certain, that knowledge is impossible (*Ac.* 2.110).

FIVE

Cicero: the end of the sceptical Academy

There are two narratives we can tell regarding the end of the sceptical Academy. According to the first, the fallibilist interpretation of Carneades is historically wrong, and philosophically ill advised. It was a mistake to positively endorse the claims that earlier Academics advanced dialectically. Compared to the originally radical and pure scepticism of Arcesilaus, the later product is an exhausted and degenerate compromise. Arcesilaus was right to insist on the universal suspension of judgement; to compromise on this point is to abandon what is best about Academic Scepticism. This is the line pursued by the renegade Academic Aenesidemus, whom we shall meet in Chapter 6.

According to the second narrative, one version of which we shall develop in this chapter, Arcesilaus' successors were right to modify and mitigate his originally radical scepticism. In particular they were right to limit the scope of what we must suspend judgement about, and to enlarge the scope of sceptically appropriate assent. Viewed in this way, their concessions constitute progress: the culmination of many years of philosophical debate with the Stoics.

At the heart of this dispute is the issue of whether it is ever wise to accept a proposition that is not known to be true.[1] In other words, what will the sage do in the absence of certainty? Arcesilaus and Carneades agree that he will suspend judgement. But by modifying what it means to suspend judgement, Carneades also allows for practical deliberation leading to fallible beliefs in accordance with convincing impressions. For example, it seems that the weather is fine and the crew reliable, so it seems likely that the voyage will be safe. But this convincing impression is not the product of arguing pro and con; it is simply a matter of examining the conditions and checking one impression against another. Carneades' fallibilism seems only to extend to practical matters and is not related to his dialectical method.[2]

The sceptical Academy's final concession is to accept that dialectical argument pro and con can provide fallible justification in support of one side of the dispute. The outcome is no longer the purely negative one of undermining conviction. This final step is the development of philosophical fallibilism as a kind of mitigated scepticism. On this view, the Academics continue to reject the Stoic account of knowledge, but they expand even further the range of sceptically appropriate assent.

The Academy after the death of Carneades

After Carneades' death in c.128 BCE, his long-time friend and associate Clitomachus became head of the Academy. Clitomachus wrote over 400 books, many (if not all) of which contained arguments he had heard from his much-admired friend (DL 4.67). Carneades praised him, sardonically, for saying the same things [as Carneades had], in contrast to another student, Charmadas, who said them in the same way (*Orat.* 51). This may simply be a matter of Clitomachus' lacking the oratorical skills of his teacher. But if so, it suggests that Clitomachus would not have been as effective at undermining his opponent's dogmatic confidence. It is worth remembering that both Arcesilaus and Carneades carried on their philosophical work primarily, if not exclusively, through conversation rather than writing.

After Clitomachus' death in c.110 BCE, Philo of Larissa became head of the Academy. He had been Clitomachus' student for about fourteen years, and was overjoyed at his promotion, returning the favour by preserving and augmenting the doctrines of his teacher. So at least initially he held to the Clitomachean orthodoxy. In Chapter 4 I have tried to articulate what that orthodoxy was; although this continues to be controversial, we shall take this position as the one Philo starts with. In addition to the continued opposition to the Stoic account of kataleptic impressions, the crucial element of this position, or practice, is that the outcome of dialectical argument is always negative: either the sceptic or his interlocutor suspends judgement, having come to see that reason provides no more support for one side of the dispute than the other.

Eventually Philo became disenchanted with Clitomachus' (i.e. Carneades') promotion of *epochē* because of the clarity and agreement of his sensations (*Praep. Ev.* 14.9.1–2). Precisely why Philo became disenchanted with *epochē* and changed his mind is as controversial as what he changed his mind to. Sextus explains what is distinctive about Philo's new position, which he labels the Fourth Academy, in this way (*PH* 1.220; see *Praep. Ev.* 14.4): "Philo and his followers say that as far as the Stoic standard (i.e. apprehensive [kataleptic] appearance) is concerned objects are inapprehensible, but as far as the nature of the objects themselves is concerned they are apprehensible" (*PH* 1.235; see *PH* 1.220; *Praep. Ev.* 14.4). In other words, things cannot be known in the manner the Stoics claim, but they can still be known in some less demanding way. This view was set out in detail in Philo's Roman books, so called because he wrote them shortly after coming to Rome in 89/8 BCE. Unfortunately, we have only a few references to these books in our sources, none of which elaborate the nature of Philo's novel position.

According to one plausible reconstruction, Philo's innovation is to drop the internalist requirement that caused so much trouble for earlier defenders of Stoic epistemology (Hankinson 1998a: 116–20). In other words, for Philo it is no longer necessary to know that one knows of any particular impression that it accurately conveys the relevant details. In effect, Philo allows that certain impressions reveal the nature of their object but not the fact that they are so revelatory. No impression is self-certifying in the way required by (some accounts of) Stoic epistemology, but on Philo's new account such self-certification is not necessary for knowledge.[3] Whatever his Roman view may have been, Philo's former student Antiochus was outraged by it. He had already abandoned the scepticism of the Third Academy for a form of Stoicism. Antiochus came to believe that the Stoic criterion is the only possible, or at least reasonable, account of knowledge (*Ac.* 2.18–31). This is probably why he was so put out by Philo's new, non-Stoic account of knowledge. He was even moved to publish his own extensive arguments in opposition (*Ac.* 2.11–12).

Despite his endorsement of Stoicism, Antiochus continued to consider himself an Academic because he believed his view was a return to the original position of Plato and his immediate successors (*Ac.* 1.17–18). Antiochus further argued that the Stoic view emerged as a development of this original Academic position (*Ac.* 2.43). So in defending Stoic epistemology, Antiochus took himself to be correcting the errors initiated by Arcesilaus' sceptical turn in the Academy.

Although Sextus associates Antiochus with the Fifth Academy, it is not clear whether he succeeded Philo in any officially recognized capacity. Shortly after Philo and other prominent Academics fled from Athens to Rome, Plato's Academy ceased to exist as an institution. But even if it had continued to exist, neither of the positions associated with the Fourth and Fifth Academies would qualify as sceptical in so far as both allow for some kind of knowledge. The sceptical Academy comes to an end in either case.

Cicero's mitigated scepticism

This end, however, is not a full stop. Between 46 and 44 BCE Cicero, who had studied with both Philo and Antiochus, as well as other prominent Stoic and Epicurean philosophers, wrote a series of dialogues defending and displaying the practice of Academic philosophy as he saw it.[4] In response to his critics, he insists that he has not come forward as champion of a lost cause: "When men die, their doctrines do not perish with them, though perhaps they suffer from the loss of an authoritative exponent" (*ND* 1.11).

Some forty years after the Academy closed its doors, Cicero presents himself as just such an authoritative voice. The problem is that Cicero's mitigated scepticism is a significant departure from his Academic predecessors. He accepts neither the Stoic epistemology of Antiochus' Fifth Academy nor the less demanding account of knowledge that characterizes Philo's Roman books. Nor does he accept the severe view of *epochē* championed by Arcesilaus and Carneades.[5]

As we have seen, for Arcesilaus and Carneades, suspending judgement on philosophical matters is completely unrelated to the issue of *apraxia*. Their sceptical criteria show only how we are able to act in practical matters. The application of these criteria has nothing to do with the dialectical skills of argument pro and con. For example, investigating some appearance in the manner proposed by Carneades is not a matter of articulating rational arguments for and against it. Whatever course of action one chooses in accordance with these practical criteria is not the product of a philosophical enquiry. As far as we know, Arcesilaus never describes the conclusion of an argument as *eulogon*, and Carneades never describes the conclusion of an argument as *pithanon* (with one possible exception to be discussed below).

Cicero, however, translates Carneades' *pithanon* with the Latin *probabile* (i.e. probable or plausible) and sometimes *veri simile* (i.e. truth-like), and maintains that the sole purpose of the Academic argument pro and con is to "draw out or formulate the truth or its closest possible approximation" (*Ac.* 2.7; see *Ac.* 2.60, 2.66; *ND* 1.11; *Fin.* 1.13; *Tusc.* 1.8, 2.9; Glucker 1995). Rather than merely revealing larger portions of our ignorance, Cicero thinks the Academic method allows for progress towards the truth.[6] And these judgements will clearly have a major impact on the choices one makes and the kind of life one lives. So Cicero uses the Academic dialectical method to accomplish both positive and negative ends: by revealing the strength of the opposed arguments it eliminates unwarranted confidence while establishing the degree to which one view is more probable than another.

Despite the apparent novelty of his view of the Academic method, Cicero claims that it had always been the practice of the sceptical Academy: the method of arguing against everything and *openly* judging nothing originated with Socrates, was revived by Arcesilaus, strengthened by Carneades and flourished right down to his own time. This approach requires the Academic to master all the schools of philosophy in order to make a well-informed judgement about where the truth probably lies (*ND* 1.11–12). Similarly, he claims that of all the competing philosophical sects that arose from Socrates, as immortalized in Plato's dialogues, he follows the one that he thinks Socrates himself used: "to conceal one's own opinion, to relieve others of error, and in every discussion to look for what was most probable" (*Tusc.* 5.11).

It is possible that Cicero sincerely thought he was presenting an accurate account of the history of the Academy. But even if he was aware of the extent to which his account was revisionist, it is not surprising that he did not present it as such. In the Hellenistic period, there was no premium on originality or novelty. And Cicero would probably have shied away from presenting himself as a philosophical innovator as he was already confronting the problem of convincing the ruling class of the value of Romanizing Greek philosophy. Given their suspicions of Greek philosophy, it would have been particularly unsuitable for a statesman of Cicero's standing to put himself forward as an innovator. Thus we find him uncharacteristically modest in this regard, describing himself as a mere transcriber, providing only the words with which to express the borrowed ideas (*Att.* 12.52).

Furthermore, Cicero may well have felt justified since other prominent Academics had provided their own revisionist accounts of the history of the Academy. Arcesilaus got the ball rolling by claiming to have returned to the original, sceptical views of Plato and Socrates; Philo and Antiochus later offered quite different accounts of the history of the Academy, each in support of his own innovation (Brittain 2001: 169–219).

In addition to the illustrious historical origins of this view, Cicero defends his Academic allegiance by arguing that it is the only prudent position to take for those starting out on philosophical investigations:

> [We Academics] are more free and unbiased since our power of judgment is impartial so we are not compelled by any necessity to defend all those things prescribed and, as it were, dictated by some authority. For ... [the dogmatists] pass judgment about matters which they have not comprehended either yielding to some friend or captivated by some single [philosopher] whom they first heard. And they are driven, as if by a storm, to that view which they cling to like a rock ... Although I don't know why, most people prefer to go wrong and to defend pugnaciously that view which they have learned to love rather than to seek without being stubborn for the view which can be maintained most consistently. (*Ac.* 2.8–9)

Becoming irrationally attached to a philosophical system is a tremendous irony since philosophers pride themselves on the rationality of their convictions. But philosophers are like everyone else when it comes to finding comfort in what is familiar. Adhering to a philosophical system can provide the comfort of making sense out of things: or at least the impression that one has made sense out of things. Cicero's point is that the satisfaction this provides may encourage us to discount or ignore objections to our position.

Such stubbornness is in no way necessitated by allegiance to a philosophical system. But to align ourselves, say to Epicureanism, would require us to judge that Epicurus had been a wise man. And yet, "deciding who is wise seems to be a particular function of people who are already wise" (*Ac.* 2.9). Since no one starts out with the knowledge and wisdom he desires, we should all begin with the Academic method, and carefully examine the rational merits of each competing account before making any judgements.[7]

Even so, why should we make *any* judgements as a result of our enquiry? This is an especially pressing question if we grant, as Cicero does, that finding one view to be more probable than another provides only a fallible justification; further enquiry may well show that a different position is more probable, so perhaps it would be more prudent to withhold judgement until we can conclusively settle the matter. Closely associated with this concern is a second question: why should we think that following this method will enable us to progress towards the truth rather than merely exchanging one view for another? We shall take these questions in turn.

Why should we accept any philosophical beliefs?

On some occasions, Cicero seems to endorse the view that it is never wise to believe what we do not know for certain (e.g. *Ac.* 2.66). In context, we should understand this as part of the earlier Academics' dialectical strategy. Carneades used to employ two related arguments against the Stoics (*Ac.* 2.59, 67, 78):

(A) If the sage assents (to something unknown) he will hold an opinion.
The sage will never hold an opinion (he is infallible).
Therefore, the sage will never assent to anything (since there is nothing worthy of his assent).

And he sometimes argued this way.

(B) If the sage assents (to something unknown) he will hold an opinion.
The sage assents (to something unknown). Therefore, the sage holds opinions (and is fallible).

Neither of these options is acceptable to the Stoics. Since they thought that assent is necessary for action, (A) would render the sage impassive. And since they thought assenting to what is unknown is a moral as well as an epistemic failing (*M* 7.157), (B) would render the sage foolish.

Within the context of this dialectical strategy, it makes sense for Cicero to affirm that the sage is infallible. But it would be very surprising if he believed this himself since the Academic method only yields fallible justification. If wisdom requires infallibility, Cicero would have to conclude that his favoured method is incapable of producing wisdom. Similarly, since he believes that human cognition is inescapably fallible, he would have to conclude that wisdom is unattainable. In fact, he maintains that *Stoic* wisdom is unattainable, or at least so far unattained. Despite his admiration for this lofty ideal, he often points out that there have never been any real life Stoic sages – it happens more often that a mule gives birth (*Div.* 2.61). Even the Stoics were reluctant to acknowledge any actual sages (see Brouwer 2002).

Unlike the Stoics, Cicero allows for a more modest conception of wisdom, one that is attainable by real, imperfect human beings:

> Those who act and live in such a way as to prove their loyalty, integrity, fairness and generosity, in who there is no excessive desire, licentiousness and insolence, and who have great strength of character ... let us consider good, as they were accounted good in life ...   (*Amic.* 19)

Although Cicero does not explain what cognitive state such real life virtue arises from, it is clear that the constancy of those described in this passage is not the product of Stoic wisdom. Similarly, when he refers to the courage or justice of real Roman heroes, he does not mean for us to understand these as perfect models of virtue. They achieved only a semblance and likeness to (Stoic) wisdom (*Off.* 3.16). But it is virtue nonetheless.

In general, what Cicero finds admirable about real people is their ability to balance principled, rational conviction with the gentleness and mercy that arises from an appreciation of human fallibility. The Academic method, as Cicero conceives it, is ideally suited to promote this balance. Since there is no conclusive end to enquiry, one must continue to put his fallible convictions to the test. The open-ended nature of enquiry is supposed to prevent us from becoming irrationally attached to our views; it keeps the virtue of perseverance from degenerating into the vice of obstinacy.[8]

But we have yet to see why we should persevere in the first place. Why should we believe anything as a result of philosophical enquiry? The answer is implicit in Cicero's philosophical dialogues: the most rationally defensible view is the most likely to be true and the most beneficial. Suspending judgement may guarantee that one avoids error, but it also guarantees that philosophical enquiry will yield no positive benefits. This is unacceptable for Cicero, who sees the aims of the philosophical art of thinking and the rhetorical art of speaking as intimately connected: wisdom and eloquence should not be sought in isolation from one another, for "wisdom without eloquence does too little for the good of states, but … eloquence without wisdom is generally highly disadvantageous" (*Inv.* 1.1; see also Long 1995). The separation of these arts yields either an inarticulate wisdom or a babbling stupidity (*De Or.* 3.142). If we remain unconvinced by what is true, or at least likely to be true, it does us no good. On the other hand, a foolish eloquence is like a weapon in the hands of a madman.

If the natural end of philosophy is to not merely aim at but to bring about the improvement of human life, the philosopher must master the art of persuasion. But he must also discover what is truly beneficial by means of rational enquiry. Otherwise, he will be guilty of a babbling stupidity. Since nature has not equipped us with the means of acquiring certainty, we can arrive only at probable beliefs regarding what is beneficial. Hence if philosophy is to accomplish its natural end, such beliefs must be sufficient to improve the human condition.

But why should we accept this pragmatic conception of philosophy in the first place? If, contrary to Cicero's view, philosophy arose simply as an expression of our natural curiosity, there would be nothing objectionable about treating it as a collection of intriguing puzzles. Indeed, it would be objectionable to pretend that philosophy can do more than satisfy, or at least stimulate, our curiosity and strengthen our reasoning skills. On this view, philosophy has no inherent social or political obligations.

Cicero's argument depends on the Stoic view that we all have a natural sympathy for members of our species, despite the fact that this sympathy is often thoroughly corrupted (*Fin.* 3.62–68; see *Rep.* 1.39; *Leg.* 1.16, 28, 32). It is in accordance with our nature to value and promote the public good. But this requires some understanding of what is genuinely beneficial. And this requires philosophy, broadly understood as the art of thinking. Once we acknowledge our natural sympathy and the corresponding obligation to discover what is genuinely beneficial, we will also be obliged to develop and practise the art of persuasion. Acquiring, defending and promoting fallible beliefs about the public good is thus a necessary part of discharging the social and political obligation of philosophy.

Another natural end of philosophy is to secure, as far as possible, a tranquil, happy and virtuous life. For Cicero, tranquillity does not come from suspending judgement as Pyrrho promises, but rather from embracing the view that virtue is sufficient for happiness. What is most characteristic of Cicero's real life sage is the conviction that all human possessions are inferior to wisdom. With this conviction, one is able to weather any storm and avoid disturbing emotions such as fear and distress:

> ... if there is someone who regards as endurable the power of Fortune and all the human lot, whatever can befall, so that neither fear nor anxiety affects him, if he lusts after nothing, is carried away by no meaningless mental pleasure, on what grounds is he not happy? And if this is brought about by virtue, on what grounds does virtue of itself alone not make people happy? (*Tusc.* 5.17)

This is the most audacious and important promise made by philosophy. Accordingly, Cicero repeatedly subjects it to careful scrutiny, arguing both for and against it in *Tusculanae Disputationes* 5 and *De Finibus Bonorum et Malorum* 3–5. But the sufficiency of virtue remains only a promise and a possibility in so far as we have failed to grasp the truth of this claim with certainty.

Although the most effective defence against the vicissitudes of life would be the firm conviction that virtue is sufficient for happiness, we cannot discount the opposed arguments. Again, the Stoic view appears to be too demanding, requiring not merely an unattainable epistemic ideal, but a degree of self-sufficiency that seems incompatible with our fragility. On the other hand, acknowledging our vulnerability may encourage us to set our sights too low and treat our weaknesses as inevitable. In the end, the extent to which a real person can preserve his tranquillity in the face of suffering is an empirical question. But the most effective defence, and the most rationally defensible view, is to believe either that virtue is sufficient for happiness, or at least nearly sufficient (*Off.* 3.31; see also *Tusc.* 5.3–4; *Ac.* 2.134).

Verisimilitude and philosophical expertise

However, it seems that unjustified, and even false, beliefs may be just as comforting and beneficial as justified, probable or true beliefs. So we should not think that the benefits of adopting some belief provide a good reason for thinking it is true. The fundamental claim of mitigated scepticism is that we should adopt the most rationally convincing, probable view because it is most likely to be true, and because it is worth risking error in order to believe what is true. Without this condition, it will still be reasonable to suspend judgement as long as conclusive justification is lacking. So assuming that we should believe the truth, and that we are better off with probable beliefs, it will follow that we should believe the most probable view.

But one might object that any attempt to establish that we should adopt the most rationally defensible view begs the question. More generally, attempting to rationally establish the reliability of reason seems to presuppose the reliability of reason. For example, Cicero's defence of the view that philosophy aims at the improvement of the human condition relies on the premise that we have a natural sympathy for members of our species. But why should we believe that, especially given the admission that justification always fails (or at least has failed so far) to be conclusive? No matter how extensively Cicero defends his premises, we will be left with this basic question: why should I adopt a belief on the basis of a fallible justification?

Fortunately, we may appeal to the existence of practical expertise as an indication that the proper use of reason leads us closer to the truth. In showing how expertise is possible, we may claim that it is a matter of learning to discern what is probable (*Ac.* 2.146). The best explanation for the fact that experts are more often successful than non-experts is that what they find probable is in fact true.

If expertise arises from learning to see what is probable, or like the truth, then truth must exist. Cicero acknowledges this assumption in his defence of the Academic method. Antiochus had objected that the Academics' worst mistake:

> is to take these two radically inconsistent premises to be consistent, first, [1] there are some false impressions (from which it follows that some are true); and then again, [2] there is no difference at all between true and false impressions. But they assumed the first premise as if there were a difference – hence the former is undermined by the latter, and the latter by the former. (*Ac.* 2.44)

In other words, the Academics inconsistently maintain both that there is and that there is not a difference between true and false impressions. Lucullus considers this to be the greatest possible refutation of the Academic method.

Cicero concedes that this objection would be right, "if we Academics did away with truth altogether. Yet we don't, since we discern as many true as false things. But our discerning is a kind of approval: we don't find any sign of apprehension" (*Ac.* 2.111). This is an odd response if we take it as merely reaffirming the first premise [1], that is, there is a difference between true and false impressions. If I am accused of inconsistently maintaining p and $\sim p$, it will not do for me to confidently reply that this would be right except for the fact that I hold p.

In order for this to be a response to Antiochus' objection, Cicero needs to disambiguate the kind of difference involved in each of the allegedly inconsistent claims. In the second premise [2], the difference between a true and false impression is a matter of what actual people are able to discern. So the point is simply that there is no difference that one can discern in practice. In the first premise [1], the difference between a true and false impression is a causal one. Cicero agrees with the Stoics that true impressions come from what is the case and accurately convey the relevant details of their object, whereas false impressions do not; he does not deny that truth exists. So despite the ever-present possibility of an impenetrable deception, Cicero can maintain that some impressions are true and some false.

So Cicero is not merely reaffirming the first premise [1]. He explains why Academics do not do away with truth by saying that he discerns as many true as false things. It is likely that some of the impressions he receives are true, even though he is not in a position to say with certainty which these are.

When limited to practical matters, this much is consistent with Carneades' scepticism. But Cicero believes we can discern what is probable even in philosophical, and especially ethical, matters. The Academic sage will guide his conduct, whether in ordinary, everyday matters or when deciding what is morally appropriate, by following what appears probable (*Ac.* 2.110). In order to extend the probable in this way, we must assume there is a kind of philosophical and ethical expertise, analogous to the more technical varieties.

The Stoics certainly conceived of philosophy this way. They maintain that dialectic was invented to enable us to distinguish truth from falsehood (*Ac.* 2.91; see DL 7.46). But, Cicero asks, in what subject is the skilled dialectician able to make such judgements? One must know more than the principles of dialectic to distinguish truth from falsehood. Cicero allows that the dialectician may judge which inferences are acceptable, which propositions are ambiguous and which conclusions genuinely follow from which premises. But this makes dialectic a far more modest enterprise than the Stoic variety, which promises, among other things, the discovery of substantive truths. On the more modest account, dialectic is a matter of reason judging about itself: the proper and improper use of logical inference.

On this view, it is clear that philosophical expertise will have to rely on something more than dialectic in leading us to truth. Even if the philosopher is able to reveal that some justification is inadequate, it will not follow that the view in question is false. It will always be possible to construct a more consistent and more convincing justification of that same view. But if we cannot conclusively rule any position out, we should have little confidence in those views that have not yet been refuted and continue to appear probable. Their survival may simply be a matter of not having subjected them to sufficient scrutiny. If so, the probable no longer seems to provide good grounds for even tentative approval.

The mitigated sceptic's prospects are particularly bleak when attempting to adjudicate among competing positions that are internally consistent. Determining who has the most rationally defensible view in such a debate may reveal more about the observers' preconceptions than the positions themselves. This seems to be the case with Cicero's own alleged refutation of Epicurean ethics in *De Finibus Bonorum et Malorum* 2. It is especially striking that Cicero himself provides the material, via his character Torquatus in Book 1 to meet many, if not all, of the objections he levels in Book 2. So one might object that Cicero's fallibilist pursuit of truth is really nothing more than the pursuit of persuasion (Inwood 1990).

In support of this objection, one might also claim that the analogy between the plausibility of sense-impressions and the plausibility of philosophical positions breaks down with regard to the crucial factor of prediction. Science and technical expertise rely heavily on predictive failure as a means of disconfirmation; the assumption is that the structure of the physical world provides an objective constraint. If the engineer's design is not consistent with the laws of nature, the bridge will collapse. But there is arguably no such constraint available for the philosophical version of this method. One can stubbornly maintain one's ethical or metaphysical views, whether they turn out to be true or false, without suffering any analogous collapse.

Socrates and epistemic optimism

What initially appears to be only a minimal commitment to a philosophical method turns out to require some optimistic views about human nature and reason. In order for Cicero to be confident that the proper application of the Academic method will lead us closer to the truth, he must suppose that there are such truths to be discovered in the first place. He must also suppose that human nature provides the kind of objective constraint on ethical theory that physical nature provides for scientific theory. Someone living in accordance with false ethical views will not in fact be happy, despite what he may say or think. It is simply not possible to live well if one has false beliefs about what is in accordance with our nature, and what is genuinely worth pursuing and what is worth avoiding.

In general, Cicero needs the epistemically optimistic view that through study and practice we can come to see what is intelligible in itself as persuasive (see *Rh.* 1.1, 1355a). This is necessary in order for us to trust that continued enquiry and argument pro and con in the absence of a criterion of truth is not a colossal waste of time. The most important expression of this optimism is the notion that the truth cannot be refuted, and hence that what has not yet been refuted, despite serious efforts to do so, is likely to be true.

Such optimism is also necessary to maintain the distinction between perseverance and obstinacy. If nature provides no constraints on philosophical enquiry, that is, if nature never gives us reliable indicators about how well we are doing, then all perseverance is equally foolish (or equally wise). The optimistic view that there are such constraints, however, indicates that if one is properly open-minded and dedicated to enquiry, if one has really acquired philosophical expertise, then what one finds persuasive will more likely be true than what others find persuasive.

Short of committing ourselves to some criterion of truth, this fallible, inductive confirmation is the best we can achieve. There can be no guarantee that the Academic method leads to truth; this is what we should expect from a sceptically cautious philosophy. But even without any such guarantees, it is nonetheless reasonable to pursue truth while lacking a criterion in the full sense. Even if the Academic never advances beyond verisimilitude, and even if he makes no measurable progress towards truth, we may still prefer his method on the grounds that it offers a reasonable compromise between radical scepticism and dogmatism. It is an attempt to balance the demand that we discover and believe the truth with the awareness of our cognitive limitations and imperfections.

Karl Popper identifies this as the most fundamental question of epistemology: "How can we admit that our knowledge is a human – an all too human – affair, without at the same time implying that it is all individual whim and arbitrariness?" (Popper 1963: 16). And he attributes the original discovery of his fallibilist solution to Plato's Socrates. Cicero seems to have drawn a similar lesson from Socrates. Despite sincerely believing that he failed to know the things he most wished to know, Socrates remains firm in his reasoned convictions. Even when on trial for his life, he refused to pander to the judges or compromise his principles. He continued to investigate the most pressing philosophical matters to the very end (*Tusc.* 1.71; see Plato *Phaedo* 107a).

Socrates' willingness to abide by the conclusions of his arguments is nowhere more apparent than when Crito tries to convince him that he is being unreasonable by staying in prison and forfeiting his life. Socrates replies:

> Not only now, but always am I the kind of man who is per-
> suaded by nothing except the argument that on reflection
> seems best to me. I am not able now to throw out those
> arguments I used before just because this misfortune has
> come upon me; for they seem pretty much the same to me.
> And I honor and value these arguments even as before. So
> unless we are able to produce better arguments right now,
> you can be sure that I will not agree with you ...
> (*Crito* 46b [Grube 1997])

Whether it is a question about the immortality of the soul or the justice of staying in prison, Socrates refuses to act on the basis of anything but the arguments that seem most rationally defensible. What makes Socrates a worthy ideal for Cicero is that he was neither fanatical in his convictions nor easily swayed from them.

Conclusion

Cicero's version of philosophical fallibilism provides a synthesis of Sceptical caution and Stoic confidence. As such it is subject to objections from both sides. Radical sceptics complain it is not sufficiently cautious, and committed Stoics complain it is not sufficiently confident. In reply to the radical sceptic we may say that although the fallibilist is not immune to error, he is still able to avoid the epistemic vice of rash or hasty assent. If we are inescapably fallible, it is unreasonable to insist we should believe nothing that falls short of certainty. Rational integrity for such imperfect agents should not demand infallibility. And in reply to the confident Stoic we may say that the fallibilist is able to avoid the vice of dogmatic or arrogant stubbornness. As we can see from the example of Socrates, absolute certainty is not necessary to maintain the courage of one's convictions.

Viewed in this way, Cicero's fallibilism is a positive development of the earlier, more radically sceptical practice of the Academics.

CERO

Aenesidemus: the Pyrrhonian revival

What I have described as progress in the last chapter was seen as decline by at least one member of the late Academy. Aenesidemus criticized his fellow Academics for being dogmatic.[1] The long dispute with the Stoics had effectively come to an end, and the Stoics had won. The Academics had completely abandoned their originally strict stance on *epochē* and now made firm determinations about a whole range of philosophical issues.

Aenesidemus committed his scepticism to writing, probably some time in the early-to-mid first century BCE.[2] Unfortunately, only some fragments and testimonia survive. The most extensive reports are about his *Pyrrhonist Discourses*. One of these comes from the ninth-century Byzantine patriarch Photius, who is remarkable in his own right. In his *Bibliothēkē*, Photius summarizes 280 books, including the *Pyrrhonist Discourses*.[3] It is clear from his summary that he thinks very little of Aenesidemus' work because it makes no contribution to Christian dogma and drives from our minds the instinctive tenets of faith (*Bib.* 170b39–40). Nevertheless, Photius is a generally reliable source (Wilson 1994). So despite his assessment of Aenesidemus' scepticism, he probably provides an accurate summary.

The proper interpretation of that summary, however, along with the general character of Aenesidemus' Pyrrhonism, is disputed. The

102

central issue is whether the revived Pyrrhonism is a type of relativism that affirms the impossibility of knowledge, or whether it is more consistent with Sextus Empiricus' later scepticism, according to which we cannot conclusively rule out the possibility of any kind of knowledge. The former, relativist view yields very definite conclusions about our cognitive limits while the latter, sceptical one shows only that we are not able to rationally resolve matters, positively or negatively.

In this chapter I shall defend the sceptical interpretation of Aenesidemus' Pyrrhonian revival and offer an explanation of how his apparently relativistic arguments are consistent with Scepticism. But first we need to briefly consider what he found objectionable about his contemporary Academics.

The late Academy's dogmatism

As far as Aenesidemus is concerned, the only live disagreement that remained between the Stoics and Academics of his day was regarding the kataleptic impression. And since the Academics had taken so much Stoic dogma on board, even this was no more than a fraternal quibble. The Academics now agreed that the proper use of reason brings us closer to the truth; they only disagreed about whether we could achieve certainty. Within the Academy, Antiochus defended the Stoic view against Philo's weaker conception of knowledge, leading Aenesidemus to dismiss them as "Stoics fighting against Stoics" (*Bib.* 170a14–17; Striker 1997).

In fact, matters were far worse: the followers of Philo were not only dogmatic, but they unwittingly contradicted themselves (*Bib.* 170a28–38).[4] The contradiction is to maintain that one both can and cannot distinguish the true from the false. The fallibilist seems to want it both ways: we cannot reliably, or conclusively, determine the truth, but we can fallibly or provisionally do so. One difficulty is to explain why fallible justification falls short while remaining a reliable indication of truth. We confronted a similar problem for Cicero's fallibilism in Chapter 5: how is it that we cannot identify the truth, but we can identify what resembles the truth? If we can detect verisimilitude, why can we not detect truth itself?

Aenesidemus appears to be exploiting this problem. He probably argued, much as Antiochus did (*Ac.* 2.34), that if we are aware of the truth of some sense perception or thought, there is no longer any ground for perplexity or doubt. On the other hand, if what we are aware of is unclear, we should not make firm assertions regarding it. The intuition is that only conclusive justification is genuine justification. If the Sceptics are able to produce some convincing evidence or argument against every claim, then there will always be some reason for thinking the belief in question is false. And in so far as I have good reason to think the belief is false, I have good reason to think I do not know it, and that I am not (at least currently) able to justify it. There is thus a tension between cautious doubt and the confidence that derives from justification; Philo and his followers cannot have it both ways.[5]

The defining mark of the dogmatism that Aenesidemus rejects is confident and unambiguous assertion and denial (*Bib.* 169b38–40). This is not simply a matter of uttering words with a certain inflection, but must include some degree of commitment to, or belief in, the propositions asserted. By arguing that there is no firm basis for grasping the truth, he sought to reinstate *epochē* as the proper goal (or at least outcome) of investigation.[6]

Pyrrhonian relativism

While all of our sources associate Aenesidemus with *epochē*, many also attribute to him what appear to be negatively dogmatic conclusions: for example, things are inapprehensible, and cannot be known in themselves (*De Ebr.* 175, 187; DL 9.88).[7] Similarly, he is said to have argued that signs (in a precise, epistemological sense) do not exist, ends (in the precise sense of objectively correct ethical goals) do not exist, and all sorts of issues are necessarily beyond our comprehension, including the nature of truth, causes, affections, motion, generation and destruction (*Bib.* 170b3–35; see also *M* 11.68–95; Bett 1997, 2000).

How then are we to reconcile Aenesidemus' *epochē* with these negatively dogmatic views? According to the relativist interpretation, Aenesidemus would only have us suspend judgement about a restricted class of statements, which does not include the conclusions to his sceptical arguments. These arguments are supposed to show that we should not believe any proposition of the form "*x* is by nature *F*". In place of such assertions, and with a backward glance to Pyrrho, he encourages us to say only that: "things are no more of this kind than of that, or are sometimes of this kind, sometimes not, or for one person they are of this kind, for another person not of this kind, and for another person not even existent at all" (*Bib.* 170a1–3). So it is only correct to say a thing has certain properties *relative* to some perceiver, or some specific conditions.[8] Nothing is just what it is *simplicter*. Honey, we may say, is no more sweet than not-sweet; but this is consistent with saying that it really is sweet relative to a perceiving agent in the right circumstances.

Since acceptable assertions take the form "*x* is contingently, or variably *F*", we may suppose the objectionable assertion "*x* is by nature *F*" means "*x* is invariably, without qualification, *F*". So to withhold judgement about the natures of things means to withhold judgement from any proposition of the form "*x* is invariably *F*".

On the other hand, there are two sorts of acceptable beliefs. First, we may believe that it is *not the case* that *x* is by nature *F*; for example, it is not the case that honey is by nature sweet. Denying that any property holds invariably of some object does not count, on this view, as being about the nature of that thing. Aenesidemus only wishes to exclude positive characterizations of a thing's nature (Woodruff 1988). Secondly, we may believe that honey is sweet in certain circumstances. Properly relativized beliefs are not about the nature of things either, and hence are not included in the scope of the relativist's *epochē*. In general, when *x* appears *F*, we may believe that *x* is contingently, or variably *F*: it is *F* for me, at this moment, in these circumstances.

A problem arises at this point. Typically we think that a belief is either true or false, whether or not we know which it is. So it should be at least possible that some properly relativized beliefs are true.

105

One way to explain how this is possible is to say that something need not be invariably *F* to be really *F*. The fact that it is only *F* in certain circumstances does not mean that it is not really *F*. The properties a thing has are determined by the context in which we encounter it. Honey really is sweet for me as I taste it right now even though it is not invariably sweet. So my belief that honey is sweet for me right now as I taste it is true.

What is attractive about this interpretation is that it enables us to explain why so many negatively dogmatic conclusions are attributed to Aenesidemus. He really did try to establish that we cannot know anything about the invariable nature of things, including truth, causes, motion, signs and ends. It is impossible to know what these things invariably are because they are not invariably anything.

However, such a position seems too dogmatic to attribute to Aenesidemus. It is hardly the sort of view we should expect to find as a reaction to the excessive dogmatism of his contemporary Academics. This is especially the case given that a similar view had been embraced much earlier by the Epicurean Polystratus in the third century (see LS 7D). So it seems unlikely that this view would have been perceived as a sceptical threat in Aenesidemus' time (first century BCE). Also, in so far as it suggests a causal or dispositional account of properties – something is the way it is at some moment *because* of certain contextual facts – it would be at odds with Aenesidemus' own arguments aimed at undermining causal explanations (*PH* 1.180–6).

Alternatively, we might say that properly relativized beliefs are not about things themselves, but only about the way things appear. Thus my belief that this honey tastes sweet to me right now will be true in virtue of the appearance that it is sweet. Such a belief is not about honey itself, but only the way it appears.

This account avoids the charge of dogmatism in so far as it commits the sceptic to no beliefs about the way the world really is. But, with the notable exception of the Cyrenaics, Greek philosophers do not conceive of truth in terms of the way things subjectively appear rather than the way they objectively are (Burnyeat 1982a). So if Aenesidemus meant to promote the idea that properly relativized beliefs are only about the way things appear, he would also have to endorse a very unorthodox view about truth in order to explain how such beliefs could be true. So it is unlikely that this was his view. But even if it were, it would provide no help in explaining his apparently negative dogmatic commitments. For on this view, his bold claim that signs do not exist would reduce to the much weaker observation that they do not seem to exist, to him, at this moment, in these circumstances. And even if that were true, it would constitute a pretty toothless scepticism. A dogmatic opponent could merely counter that it appears to him that signs do exist.

So on either attempt to explain how properly relativized beliefs could be true it seems we are left without a sceptical position that would have suited Aenesidemus' ambition to revive Pyrrhonism in response to Academic dogmatism.

A more promising approach, I believe, is to reject the assumption that gives rise to the problem in the first place. If rather than assenting to properly relativized assertions Aenesidemus suspends judgement about them, we do not need to explain how such assertions can be true. This remains an interesting philosophical question, but it poses no particular problem for one who has no beliefs. Furthermore, his negative dogmatism can be dissolved by placing the suspicious claims within the context of his oppositional strategy; his arguments for the non-existence of signs, for example, are not expressions of his own view but part of his attempt to balance things out. And finally his relativism is best explained as a modest, semantic form, according to which, whenever I say "x appears F", it must be understood that I mean "x appears F *in certain circumstances*". Semantic relativism involves no metaphysical or epistemological commitments and is thus consistent with a general *epochē* (Annas & Barnes 1985).

In what follows we shall develop this sceptical interpretation and examine how well it accords with the fragmentary evidence for Aenesidemus' Pyrrhonism.

Pyrrhonian Scepticism

The sceptical interpretation provides a different account of what it means for *x* to be by nature *F*, and consequently what it is we must suspend judgement about. On this view, the distinction between how things appear and how they are by nature makes no reference to invariability; it amounts more simply to a contrast between appearance and reality. Some such distinction is fundamental to the entire history of Western philosophy and, unsurprisingly, it gets worked out in a large number of ways. We do not need to specify a precise sense for the distinction in this context. The crucial point is that any proposition of the form "*x* is (really as opposed to only apparently) *F*" should be read as "*x* is by nature *F*". This is a wider construal of the expression "by nature *F*" than its relativist counterpart since it does not limit the nature of things to what they invariably are.

Accordingly, the scope of sceptical *epochē* is also much wider. On this view, Aenesidemus would not allow us to believe that honey is (really, or even apparently) sweet in the appropriate circumstances. But neither would he allow us to believe that nothing is by nature good or bad, that epistemological signs do not exist, or that nothing can be known as it really is. All such beliefs are about the nature of things and involve illicit inferences from how things appear to how they really are, whether contingently or invariably. On the sceptical interpretation, the purpose of Aenesidemus' arguments is to block any such inference.

Undecidability and the ten modes

As part of his Pyrrhonian revival, Aenesidemus assembled various kinds of sceptical arguments, or modes, designed to induce *epochē*. In Sextus' presentation of these modes, the central strategy is to show that we are not rationally able to adjudicate between conflicting appearances in order to decide which one is true.[9]

The first mode calls our attention to the various ways the same thing appears to members of different animal species. Although we do not, and perhaps cannot, know what it is like to be a bat, it is overwhelmingly likely that things appear differently to bats than they do to us. The same point could be made regarding any other animal species. We can only guess at what it is like to navigate at night by radar, what a grain of rice looks like to an ant, how it feels for a fish to extract oxygen from water, or how it feels to have ones feathers ruffled by the wind. It is reasonable to suppose that all animals are attracted by pleasure and repulsed by pain, and perhaps even that there is some fundamental similarity in the experience of pleasure and pain across all species. But the point remains that the same things are objects of choice and avoidance to members of different species.

Given this variety of competing experiences of the same things, we are inclined to wonder which, if any, are correct and how we might determine this. It is unacceptable to merely assume that our sensory equipment provides exclusive access to the nature of reality. And according to Aenesidemus, any attempt to provide rational justification for such a stance is necessarily biased: "we ourselves will not be able to adjudicate between our own impression and those of other animals: we are ourselves parties to the disagreement, and hence in need of an adjudicator, rather than capable of judging for ourselves" (PH 1.59). This is a clear statement of the undecidability strategy: being party to a dispute compromises one's judgement. This is not a matter of being swayed by some pragmatic interest (as often happens in legal cases); it is a matter of calling into question one's very ability to correctly adjudicate among the appearances.

In the fourth mode, Sextus observes that whatever condition one happens to be in affects the way things appear: for example, whether one is waking or sleeping, young or old, in need or satisfied, drunk or sober, confident or fearful and so on (PH 1.100). But if one is always in some set of such conditions, then he will be party to the dispute. The very issue is whether, for example, the world is as it appears to a person who is insane. Since my sanity affects how things appear to me, I am not in a position to adjudicate. Any attempt to provide a rational justification of my preference will presuppose the very matter at issue, namely, whether I am right to prefer sanity.

Sextus supplements this point by considering the possibility that one might offer a proof in support of one of the conflicting appearances. In that case:

> The so-called proof must be either apparent to us or non-apparent. If it is non-apparent, we will not propound it with confidence. But if it is apparent to us, since our inquiry is about what is apparent to animals and proof is apparent to us, who are animals, it will itself in so far as it is apparent be subject to inquiry as to its truth ... (*PH* 1.60)

In other words, if the premises and inferences contained in the proof are not apparent to us, we have no proof. And if they are apparent to us, they will not be apparent to someone else, or to some non-human animals. And this brings us back to the question of how we may decide without being guilty of irrational bias. In effect, any attempt to provide a proof will lead us to an infinite regress or beg the question.

Infinite regress is an integral part of the strategy of a later set of five modes, developed by Agrippa (*PH* 1.164; DL 9.88; see Chapter 8). It seems unlikely that Aenesidemus ever propounded this argument himself. Sextus probably appends it to the original Aenesideman modes in order to strengthen the case. But we do not need to set off an infinite regress in order to argue that being party to a dispute puts us in the position of begging the question. The only presupposition necessary is one that also plays a central role in Sextus' Pyrrhonism; namely, that an arbitrary preference cannot serve as rational justification.

In any case, this undecidability strategy is clearly antithetical to metaphysical relativism. In one sense, the relativist has no need to decide between the appearances; properly relativized they may all be true, and hence there really are no conflicts in the first place. So it would be misleading to describe the relativist's assembly of variable appearances as an oppositional method (as both Sextus and Diogenes do: *PH* 1.31–33; DL 9.78). At best we could say the relativist argument aims to dissolve the misleading impression that such appearances conflict. But again, it would be odd to describe this as pitting one appearance *against* another. Undecidability is just as clearly antithetical to negative dogmatism. The negative dogmatist refuses to decide between conflicting appearances not because he is unable to determine which is true, but rather because he has decided that none of them are true. Unlike the sceptic he is not even in principle open to the possibility that he may eventually discover the truth about things because he believes there is no such truth to discover.

Invariability

However, Philo reports that Aenesidemus' first mode provides a clear warrant that things are inapprehensible (*De Ebr.* 175). And similarly, Diogenes formulates the conclusions to some of the modes in terms that suggest not merely our inability to decide among competing appearances but the impossibility of doing so (DL 9.81, 85, 86, 88). Even if Aenesidemus is not a relativist, he would need a strategy other than undecidability to arrive at such conclusions.

The most plausible candidate for such a strategy requires the use of an invariability condition. According to Sextus:

> Aenesidemus says that there is a difference among apparent things, and that some of these appear in common to everyone, while others appear privately to someone, and that the ones that appear in common to everyone are true, while the ones not like this are false. (*M* 8.8)

The contrast suggests that what appears in common appears the same to everyone. Thus we may articulate an invariability condition this way:

[C] Appearances that appear in *common* to everyone [invariably] are true, while those not like this are false.

Similarly, Philo states, in his introduction to the modes:

> if it were the case that the same unvarying appearances were
> produced from the same things, then no doubt we should
> of necessity admire as unerring and incorruptible those two
> standards, perception and thought ... and we should not be
> in two minds and suspend judgment ...   (*De Ebr.* 169)

Sextus also makes use of something very much like this invariability
condition in his attack on ethics, which is apparently derived from
Aenesidemus:

> If there is anything by nature good, and there is anything by
> nature bad, this thing ought to be common to all and to be
> good or bad for everyone. For just as fire, being by nature
> warming, warms everyone and does not warm some but
> chill others, and in the same way as snow, which chills, does
> not chill some people but warm others, but chills everyone
> equally, so that which is by nature good ought to be good
> for everyone, and not good for some but bad for others.
>   (*M* 11.69; see *PH* 3.179; DL 9.101)[10]

If we understand the "appearing in common" in [C] and at the beginning of this passage as "affecting everyone the same way", we get:

[A]   If *x* is by nature *F*, then *x* *affects* everyone as *F*.

We may observe by means of the observations assembled in one of
the modes that:

x does not affect everyone as *F*.

And we may then conclude by *modus tollens* that *x* is not by nature
F. Since this argument can be applied to anything for which we can
assemble variable appearances, we may conclude quite generally that
knowledge of the natures of things is impossible. But in order to

get the negatively dogmatic conclusion that *x is* not by nature *F*, we have to read [A] as a statement not merely about how things appear, but rather how they really are. To clarify [A]: if *x* is [*and not merely appears*] by nature *F*, then *x affects* [*and not merely appears to affect*] everyone as *F*.

Although neither [A] nor [C] are explicitly mentioned in reports of the modes, all of them can easily be understood as following this pattern. The variability of the collected appearances of *x* will not present us with an undecidable conflict, but rather direct evidence that we cannot reveal the nature of *x* on the basis of those appearances, for that would require that *x* affect everyone in the same way.

But interpreting the modes in this way yields strikingly feeble arguments. The seventh mode, for example, draws our attention to the difficulty of determining what quantity of stuff reveals its true nature. A moderate amount of wine benefits, but a large amount stupefies; bars of silver appear white, shavings appear black; and in the correct proportions, drugs are beneficial, but mixed improperly they can be lethal. The motivating assumption is that the true nature of something will be expressed invariably in any quantity of it, and in any compound. If a drug is by nature beneficial, then it will affect everyone beneficially regardless of the quantity and the proportions in which it is mixed with other substances.

Such a simplistic view of causal properties would not be likely to convince anyone; it does not require a sophisticated causal theory to observe how easily the potency of drugs may be varied. This line of thinking would be effective at promoting the view that drugs really have certain powers only relative to their compounds and quantities. But by the same token it would also promote the idea that this is all there is to be known about the potency of drugs. In other words, it simply serves to reveal the implausibility of the invariability condition in this context.

Applying the invariability strategy to the modes generally produces feeble results. Rather than conclude that the truth is beyond our grasp, we will probably think, for example, that snake venom really is harmful to one person, but not to another, and playing with hoops really is serious business for children, but not for old people, and metals really are valuable when scarce, but not when abundant. In other words, the fact that nothing seems to meet the invariability condition might be taken as grounds to reject that condition and embrace some sort of relativism.

The tenth mode, however, is a more plausible candidate for the invariability strategy. This mode could be read as revealing the contingent and variable nature of value by pointing out the differences among lifestyles, customs, laws, beliefs in myths and dogmatic suppositions. In general, the contingency of what we find valuable is indicated by the correlation of belief and the time and place of one's birth. In some cultures it is appropriate to tattoo babies: in others it is not. If you grew up in ancient Ethiopia you would probably believe it is good to tattoo your child. But if you grew up in Victorian England you would probably believe it is bad. Homosexuality is customary in some places, illegal in others. Egyptians embalm the dead and Romans cremate the bodies (DL 9.83).

But if any of these practices were good by nature, they would affect all of us as good, that is, they would seem good to everyone just as fire seems warming to everyone. Hence we may conclude that nothing is good or bad by nature.

All ancient ethical theories offer some account of what is good by nature, and they all contend that whatever it is, it is beneficial. These are supposed to be objectively true accounts of what is good, and beneficial, for all human beings. So, the following conditional would be commonly held by ancient ethical theorists: if x is good by nature then it is beneficial for everyone. If we suppose that in order for x to be beneficial for someone, it must actually benefit him, we may restate the requirement this way:

[B]   If x is good by nature then everyone affected by it will be *benefited*.

Admittedly, this is quite distinct from the further claim:

[R]   If x is good by nature, then everyone affected by it will *recognize* it as beneficial.

It certainly seems possible that one might be benefited without recognizing it. Indeed, it often happens that what seemed initially like a problem turns out to be a blessing. And more generally, it seems one does not have to have any particular beliefs about what is good or bad to be benefited.

However, this is not the case for Stoic ethics, according to which, one must know what is good by nature to be virtuous. You might receive all sorts of apparently good things and develop the dispositions valued by your culture, but until and unless you grasp the distinction in theory and practice between what is by nature good and what is not, you will not be virtuous and none of these apparently good things can truly benefit you. Consequently, the virtuous Stoic cannot fail to be aware, at least on reflection, of the fact that he is virtuous and that his virtue is beneficial for him. So, given the Stoic view of what it means for x to be good by nature, Stoics would accept both [B] and [R].

In that case, if the argument were directed at a Stoic or anyone else who accepted these propositions [A, B, R], there would be no need for Aenesidemus himself to believe them. He may argue that as a result of his interlocutors' convictions, nothing is by nature good or bad. The confident assertion of any of these requirements takes us well beyond scepticism and even a merely negative dogmatism. The dialectical strategy, on the other hand, also anticipates and probably informs Sextus' dialectical use of [A].

It is clear that Sextus does not himself believe that fire heats by nature (*PH* 1.82; see *M* 9.242–43). But in the context of arguing against dogmatic ethical theories, he finds it useful to claim that it does: "Fire, which heats by nature, appears heating to everyone; and snow, which chills by nature, appears chilling to everyone" (*PH* 3.179; see *M* 8.189, 197–99). This makes it seem quite reasonable to expect that the natural property of goodness should also affect everyone the same way.

But in another passage, Sextus offers an important modification to [A], apparently in order to block the objection that fire does not warm everyone:

[A'] If x is by nature F, then x affects everyone *who is in what they call a natural state* as F (*PH* 3.179).

[A'] makes the natural warming power of fire more plausible. But by the same token it opens the door for the dogmatist to argue that his account of the good is the right one. Those who disagree, he might say, are simply not in a natural state; so the fact that the good does not seem good to them, or affect them beneficially, is exactly what we should expect.

As Sextus concludes the argument he drops the modification in [A'] without comment, reverting to [A]: "if things which affect us by nature affect everyone in the same way, while we are not all affected in the same way in the case of so-called goods, then nothing is by nature good" (*PH* 3.182). The only convincing explanation of his flexibility in this regard is that he uses [A] and [A'] dialectically to undermine his interlocutor's confidence, and not to establish any negatively dogmatic conclusions of his own.

The same is probably true for Aenesidemus as well. Indeed, the dialectical use of [C] is the key to understanding his puzzling connection with Heraclitus. Before turning to this issue, we shall consider why relativism and invariability came to be so closely associated with Aenesidemus, and how they can be understood to be consistent with scepticism.

Incorporating relativity and invariability within scepticism

It is possible that undecidability is a later strategy inspired by dissatisfaction with the invariability condition, or whatever principle is required to derive negatively dogmatic conclusions. Later Sceptics may have found Aenesidemus' collections of variable appearances a useful resource. But rather than appeal to [C] or [A], they may have argued that we are not in a position to decide among the variable, and crucially incompatible, appearances. Such a development is suggested by comments we find in two of our sources for Pyrrhonism that predate its sceptical expression in Sextus. According to the anonymous commentator on Plato's *Theaetetus* (probably from the first century BCE):

> The Pyrrhonists say that everything is relative, inasmuch as nothing exists in its own right but everything relative to other things. Neither shapes nor sounds nor objects of taste or smell or touch nor any other object of perception has a character of its own. For otherwise things that are the same would not affect us differently depending on their intervals and the things observed together with them ...
>
> (*In Tht.* Col. 63 [Annas & Barnes 1985: 97])

Similarly, the Roman author Aulus Gellius remarks that:

> Absolutely everything that affects the human senses is relative. That means that there is nothing at all which exists in its own right or which has its own power and nature: everything is referred to something else and appears such as its appearance is while it is appearing, i.e. such as it is made in our senses to which it has arrived and not such as it is in itself from which it has set out.
>
> (*NA* 11.5.7–8, probably mid-second century CE
> [Annas & Barnes 1985: 96–7])

These remarks may be interpreted in support of a metaphysical relativism. However, we may also reasonably suppose that their authors mistakenly attribute some principle to Aenesidemus that warrants the inference from the relativity of appearances to the relativity of things themselves. This would be an easy mistake to make if Aenesidemus in fact argued dialectically for such negatively dogmatic conclusions.

Furthermore, we can account for the prominent role of relativity by considering Sextus' discussion of the relativity mode, which he takes to be the generic form for all of the modes (*PH* 1.135–40, 1.39).[11] Sextus apparently saw relativity as the common feature binding this set of arguments together. All of the modes can be seen as relying on two types of relativity – variable and incompatible appearances of *x* are produced either relative to the subject judging (e.g. *x* appears *F* to human beings, not-*F* to dogs) or relative to the things observed along with *x* (e.g. *x* appears *F* when mixed with *y*, not-*F* when mixed with *z*). The general, and mundane, observation is that things appear as they do only *relative* to certain circumstances. And the sort of relativism at stake is the modest, semantic variety referred to above: whenever I say *x* appears *F*, it must be understood that I mean *x* appears *F in certain circumstances*. I cannot meaningfully talk about an appearance of *x* absent all circumstances. Having systematically generated a wealth of incompatible appearances, the sceptical work is done by the argument that we are unable to decide among them, that is, that we have no rational grounds on which to hold one set of circumstances as epistemically privileged. If this were Aenesidemus' view it would explain why he is closely connected with relativism, and why it is a mistake to see this as a metaphysical position.

If Aenesidemus promotes the suspension of judgement in the broad sense, regarding any claim about the way the world really is, as opposed to how it appears, then it is consistent for him to use both the undecidability and invariability strategies, provided he employs such principles as [A] dialectically.

Aenesidemus and Heraclitus

One of the virtues of this account is that it lends itself to a very plausible explanation of Aenesidemus' puzzling relation to Heracliteanism.[12] Aenesidemus took an active interest in Heraclitus, developing his own distinctive interpretations of the notoriously obscure sayings of the Presocratic. The most important of these, for our purposes, are his statements regarding Heraclitus' view of truth and the doctrine of the unity of opposites.

We have already encountered Aenesidemus' statement ([C]) that appearances that appear in common to everyone [*invariably*] are true, while those not like this are false (*M* 8.8; cf. *M* 7.126–34). Judging from the context and other related passages, [C] appears to be one of Aenesidemus' interpretations of Heraclitus.[13] In another passage, we find an important application of [C]:

> Aenesidemus and his followers used to say that the Sceptical persuasion is a path to the philosophy of Heraclitus, because the idea that contraries appear to hold of the same thing leads to the idea that contraries actually do hold of the same thing; and while the Sceptics say that contraries appear to hold of the same thing, the Heracliteans go on from there to the idea that they actually do hold. *(PH 1.210)*

This is a reference to Heraclitus' famous, and controversial, unity of opposites doctrine, illustrated by such claims as "sea water is both pure and polluted, bringing life to fish and death to human beings". And it is easy to see how, given [C], one can reason from the common appearance that contraries hold of the same thing to the claim that they actually do.

However, Sextus does not attribute this inference to Aenesidemus. It would be unacceptably dogmatic for a sceptic to endorse the unity of opposites doctrine as long as we understand it to be an assertion about the way things really are. For the sceptic, even if it is a common appearance that contraries hold of the same thing, this remains an appearance. He is not willing to apply [C] in order to arrive at the bold metaphysical conclusion that contraries actually do hold of the same thing because he does not subscribe to [C] in the first place.

This much Sextus and Aenesidemus agree on. But Sextus disagrees with Aenesidemus' claim that Pyrrhonian Scepticism is a path to the philosophy of Heraclitus. First, Sextus points out that the appearance that contraries hold of the same thing (e.g. honey tastes sweet to healthy people, bitter to sick ones) is not in the least peculiar to Sceptics or distinctive of Scepticism. Given the truly common nature of this appearance, it makes no sense to single Pyrrhonism out, rather than some other philosophy or even ordinary life, as a path to Heracliteanism.

Furthermore, the two views conflict. Clearly one cannot belong to both camps since that would require believing in the unity of opposites *as well as* suspending judgement about it. Sextus then claims "it is absurd to call a conflicting persuasion a path to the school it conflicts with" (*PH* 1.212). And this is the case if we take the path metaphor in either of the following ways. In logical terms:

If *A* is a path to *B*, then *A* entails *B*.

Or more broadly, in rhetorical terms:

If *A* is a path to *B*, then one who finds *A* convincing will find *B* convincing also.

In neither of these interpretations of the metaphor is it reasonable to say that Pyrrhonian Scepticism is a path to Heracliteanism. Scepticism certainly does not entail Heracliteanism. And if a Sceptic were to find Heraclitus' view convincing, it would not be because of his sceptical persuasion; just as if an agnostic became a theist it would not be because of his agnosticism.

A more plausible reading of Aenesidemus' metaphor is evident from *PH* 1.210, even if Sextus did not see it. One can arrive at a positive view of the nature of things, the Heraclitean unity of opposites, by applying the principle [C], which Pyrrhonists characteristically use only for the sake of undermining claims about the nature of things. Sextus mistakenly takes Aenesidemus' metaphor in an approving sense, as if to say one would do well to travel this sceptical road to Heracliteanism, whereas Aenesidemus meant it without any such approval; one *can* get to Heraclitus' view by way of a principle the Sceptics characteristically use.

Conclusion

In conclusion we shall briefly consider Aenesidemus' position in the history of Scepticism. Pyrrhonism, in whatever form it might have taken after Timon's death in 230 BCE, was utterly neglected until Aenesidemus brought it back to public attention (*Praep. Ev.* 14.18.29). What he brought back was not precisely Pyrrho's view, but a Scepticism clearly inspired by it. The most important element of inspiration seems to have been Pyrrho's novel association of *epochē* with tranquillity. Aenesidemus also appropriates Timon's view (echoed in the sceptical Academy) that appearances are adequate guides to life.

> We [Pyrrhonists] affirm the appearance, without also affirming that it *is* of such a kind. We too [i.e. like dogmatic philosophers] perceive that fire burns; but we suspend judgment about whether it is its nature to burn. We see that a man moves and that he dies; how it happens we don't know. We only object to the non-evident substance underlying appearances. (DL 9.104–5 [LS 1H]; see 9.106)

We do not need any special insight into the nature of things in order to live, and even to live well.

However, drawing on the dialectical tradition of the early sceptical Academy,[14] Aenesidemus develops an oppositional method designed to undermine anyone's confidence that he has rationally determined how things are. So his Pyrrhonist revival is actually a synthesis of two earlier traditions, combining the arguments and methods of the sceptical Academy in the service of attaining the kind of life exemplified by Pyrrho.

This interpretation also allows us to see the later Pyrrhonism, as outlined by Sextus, as a more potent version of Aenesidemus' version. By contrast, if we read Aenesidemus as a relativist, we are forced to conclude that Sextus either wilfully misrepresents or badly misunderstands him.

But, as we shall see, Sextus' version of Scepticism has much in common with Aenesidemus'. This is especially important with regard to the issue of the consistency of Scepticism. Since Aenesidemus accuses his contemporary Academics of rashly contradicting themselves, it is no surprise that he is concerned to preserve his own consistency: "The Pyrrhonist determines absolutely nothing, not even this very claim that nothing is determined ... by entertaining doubts about every thesis, they maintain consistency" (*Bib.* 169b27–28, 39–40). In other words, Aenesidemus' refusal to believe any proposition of the form "x is by nature F" should not itself be congealed into a doctrine. He believes that it is neither possible nor impossible to determine that x is by nature F. Determining nothing is not therefore a statement of an epistemological position that one might defend or attack, but rather a report of the Sceptic's general attitude towards investigation.

The nature of this attitude is captured in a metaphor: sceptical arguments are like purgatives that eliminate themselves along with the offending substance (DL 9.76). The self-defeating, or purgative, nature of sceptical arguments, as well as the nature of "the offending substance" are topics to be explored in Chapter 7 as we examine the later development of Pyrrhonian Scepticism.

SEVEN

Sextus Empiricus: the consistency of Pyrrhonian Scepticism

Whatever became of Pyrrhonian Scepticism in the wake of Aenesidemus, it did not make much of an impression on Seneca, who remarks in the early 60s CE that there is no one to hand on the teachings of Pyrrho (*Natural Questions* 7.32). On the other hand, looking back from the third century CE, Diogenes draws a lineage of Pyrrhonian teachers and students from Pyrrho all the way up to Sextus Empiricus and his student Saturninus (DL 9.115–16). The list probably exhibits Diogenes' passion for genealogy more than historical truth. But it is likely that there was some continuity of sceptical practice from the time of Aenesidemus since, more than 200 years later, Sextus draws on a rich tradition of sceptical argument that clearly was not the work of just one Sceptic.[1]

Indeed, Sextus himself sometimes seems not to be just one Sceptic either. There are a number of strands in his works, not all of which fit comfortably together. The most likely explanation is that there were earlier, incompatible versions of Pyrrhonism recorded in his sources, and that Sextus drew from them with little concern for consistency. Whether he should have been concerned with consistency is a topic to be explored later. Despite these apparently inconsistent sceptical strands in Sextus' texts, we can discern a distinctive voice at work, and we can extract a coherent philosophical position, or rather practice. This will be our task in this and the following two chapters.

The works of Sextus Empiricus

Sextus was a practising physician, probably at work in the late second century CE, possibly in Alexandria or Rome, or both.² His books reveal much philosophical and psychological detail about the practice of Scepticism, but they tell us virtually nothing about its historical development, the influence and size of the Sceptical movement or the relationship between Sceptical teachers and students. Also, since his sources are now lost we cannot determine the extent to which Sextus is an original thinker and the extent to which he merely compiles and arranges the arguments of his predecessors.

Whatever the case may be, his books represent the culmination of Pyrrhonian Scepticism and, along with Cicero's work, are the most important sources of transmission for the entire tradition of ancient Scepticism. And given his interest in setting out the arguments of past philosophers on various topics, he is one of our most important sources for Greek philosophy in general. Sextus' surviving works consist of the *Outlines of Pyrrhonism*, five books of the *Sceptical Commentaries* and *Against the Professors* (see Figure 3).

In the *Outlines of Pyrrhonism* (abbreviated as *PH* in accordance with its Greek title, *Pyrrhōneioi Hypotypōseis*), Sextus sets out a general account and a specific account of his sceptical practice. The general account explains the distinctive character of Scepticism, its principles, methods and aims, and how it differs from other philosophies with sceptical elements. The specific account, by contrast, sets out an array of arguments targeting claims made within each of the three traditional subdivisions of Hellenistic philosophy: logic, physics and ethics. Here the focus is on specific applications of the general argument forms and sceptical strategies outlined in the general part.

Outlines of Pyrrhonism is divided into three books. The first contains the general account, and the second and third contain the specific account. Sextus covers the same ground, with the same plan, in his *Sceptical Commentaries*. The general account was probably presented in much greater detail in the first five books, which have not survived. He then followed through with the specific arguments against logic, physics and ethics in the remaining books, which have

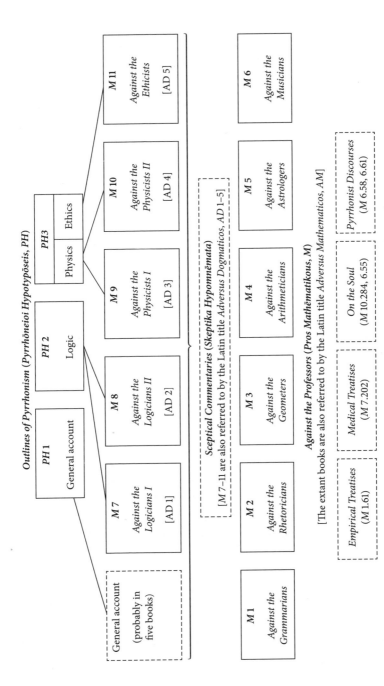

Figure 3. The works of Sextus Empiricus. Dotted lines indicate that the work or complete work is no longer extant.

125

survived. These were mistakenly thought to continue the six books titled *Against the Professors* (*Pros Mathēmatikous*; *M* 1–6), in which he records Sceptical and Epicurean arguments aimed at showing certain kinds of technical expertise to be a sham. So the surviving books of the *Sceptical Commentaries* are misleadingly named *M* 7–11. *M* 7 and 8 are also known as *Against the Logicians*, *M* 9 and 10 *Against the Physicists* and *M* 11 *Against the Ethicists*. Many of the same topics and arguments from *PH* 2–3 appear, often in greater length and detail, in the surviving books of the *Sceptical Commentaries*, *M* 7–11.[3]

The means and ends of Scepticism: normative versus causal accounts

Sextus characterizes Scepticism as a way of life (*agōgē*), and defines it as an ability (*dynamis*) to balance the persuasive force of arguments as well as appearances for and against any disputed claim. This balance, or equipollence, leads to suspension of judgement (*epochē*), which in turn leads to tranquillity (*ataraxia*; *PH* 1.8). We shall start by considering the relation between these three elements in the Sceptic's practice: equipollence, suspension of judgement and tranquillity. What does it mean to say that the first leads to the second, and the second to the third?

In ordinary circumstances, one does not start out as a sceptic in a state of *epochē* but rather ends up there. Sextus says the causal principle, or origin, of scepticism is the hope of becoming tranquil:

> Men of talent, troubled by the anomaly in things and puzzled as to which of them they should rather assent to, came to investigate what in things is true and what false, thinking that by deciding these issues they would become tranquil.
> (*PH* 1.12)

One might, for example, worry about whether or not a benevolent God exists. It is easy to imagine how conflicting accounts on this matter might be disturbing (although we shall look more closely at the nature of the proto-sceptic's disturbance later in this chapter). It is also easy to suppose that the way to relieve such a disturbance is by determining the truth. Once I come to know that God exists (or does not exist) I can stop worrying about it.

So the proto-sceptic sets about examining all the relevant arguments and evidence they can find. Instead of discovering the truth, however, "they came upon equipollent dispute, and being unable to decide this they suspended judgment. And when they suspended judgment, tranquility in matters of opinion followed fortuitously" (PH 1.26). The fortuitous appearance of tranquillity is also related in the following story:

> They say that [Apelles] was painting a horse and wanted to represent in his picture the lather on the horse's mouth; but he was so unsuccessful that he gave up, took the sponge on which he had been wiping off the colors from his brush, and flung it at the picture. And when it hit the picture, it produced a representation of the horse's lather. Now the Sceptics were hoping to acquire tranquility by deciding the anomalies in what appears and is thought of, and being unable to do this they suspended judgment. But when they suspended judgment, tranquility followed as it were fortuitously, as a shadow follows a body. (PH 1.28–29)

Sextus is clearly not advocating sponge-throwing as a painting technique. Imagine how frustrating that would be. The chances of hitting the canvas at precisely the right spot with a properly saturated sponge travelling at just the right speed are very slim. It just is not a reliable way of getting the desired outcome.

By analogy, Sextus is not suggesting that we jump straight to *epochē* and give up on the enquiry before even starting. Apelles' frustration, just like the proto-sceptic's disappointment at not finding the truth, is a necessary prelude to their unforeseen successes. The point of the story is to illustrate the surprising nature of the sceptic's initial discovery: tranquillity arises not in the way she originally supposed it would, but rather as the unforeseen outcome of bringing her intellect to a standstill.

How then does the sceptic bring her intellect to a standstill? We cannot force the scales of judgement to balance, in so far as we cannot make ourselves feel that both sides have equal rational force if they do not seem to. Of course one can pretend to find something convincing just as one can force the scales to balance by pushing down on one side; but this does not mean the objects weigh the same, and the person with her finger on the scale must know this.

So *epochē* is brought about in the sceptic as the effect of her argumentative practice. Sextus indicates this causal relation by means of a variety of passive constructions: because of equipollence, the sceptic is brought to, ends up in, or is forced to arrive at *epochē*.[4] Similarly: because of equipollence, *epochē* is brought about, is introduced, or follows for the sceptic.[5]

On the other hand, Sextus sometimes indicates the necessity of suspending judgement with an active construction: because of the sceptic's inability to decide among competing appearances, or philosophical accounts, it is necessary to suspend judgement.[6] Some of these assertions are clearly normative: one must, or should suspend judgement.[7]

So which is it? After becoming aware of the equipollence of opposed arguments, does the sceptic then decide that the reasonable thing to do is suspend judgement? Or does becoming aware of equipollence simply eliminate all inclination to believe one way or the other, and hence bring about *epochē* without the sceptic doing anything (else) to help it along?

We cannot opt for both since they are incompatible, at least in the following sense. Either the sceptic first makes the normative judgement that she should suspend judgement before arriving at *epochē*, or not. Similarly, either suspension of judgement arises immediately from her production of equally compelling, opposed arguments or it requires also a normative judgement about what one should do in such a case.

If the normative account is correct, the sceptic suspends judgement in accordance with a general principle:

[I]   It is *irrational* or irresponsible to believe either of two contradictory propositions that one finds equally convincing.

When confronting equipollence, it is still possible to opt for one or the other side. Perhaps as William James ([1897] 1979) suggests in "The Will to Believe", we may assent in accordance with some non-rational inclination when reason cannot settle the matter. And more prosaically, many people believe in things such as an afterlife owing to non-rational factors such as wishful thinking, even when the arguments on either side of the matter are inconclusive.

But because she endorses [I], and because she thinks one should not do what is irrational or irresponsible, the sceptic will think that she should not opt for either side.[8] Whether or not she consciously decides to suspend judgement in accordance with [I], each time she does so is governed by her acceptance of this general policy. She may still, on occasion, violate the policy, just as we all seem able to act contrary to our considered opinions. But on reflection she will think that she should not believe either of two contradictory positions that she finds equally convincing.

On the other hand, if the casual account is correct, *epochē* is simply what happens to the sceptic when she encounters equipollent arguments. In that case, the sceptic has no need of [I], just as I have no need of normative principles to digest my lunch; getting food into my stomach is sufficient (assuming everything is working properly). In place of [I] the causal account offers a description of the sceptical disposition:

[D]   The sceptic's *disposition* inclines her away from believing either of two contradictory propositions that she finds equally convincing.

Where [I] contains a generally applicable normative principle, [D] is a non-normative description of a very specific sort of person; [D] says nothing about what you or I should do, or even about what the sceptic should do. Lacking any inclination to believe, she suspends judgement; there is nothing to tip the scales one way or the other.

Choosing between these interpretations is crucially important for the overall interpretation of Sextus' Pyrrhonism, for they involve dramatically different attitudes towards reason. On the normative account, the sceptic shares with the dogmatist a commitment to [I]. They are involved in the same project of seeking the truth by examining and assessing arguments and evidence. They will also agree on the closely related principle:

> [R] It is *rational* and responsible to believe a proposition that one finds convincing (if it is sufficiently supported by reason and evidence).

They only disagree about whether any candidates are sufficiently supported by reason and evidence.

On the causal account, the sceptic starts out committed to both [I] and [R], but in her conversion to scepticism she leaves these behind along with all the other dogmatic beliefs she may have held. After developing the sceptical disposition, she no longer has any belief about what reason demands, or what she should do in virtue of being a rational agent. This sceptic is no longer engaged in the same project that she started out with; she is agnostic not only with respect to the positive claims made by dogmatists but also with respect to whether there are any normative requirements implicit in the use of reason.

Sceptical enquiry

The main point in favour of the normative account is that it supports the view of the sceptic as an open-minded enquirer. In order for anyone to sincerely hope to find the truth, she must be willing, at least in principle, to believe what reason establishes. If she is not willing to act in accordance with [R], then it seems she is not willing to follow where reason leads, and has foreclosed on the possibility of a successful end to the pursuit of truth. In that case, her scepticism appears to collapse into negative dogmatism.

If so, the causal account is mistaken, since Sextus insists on the distinction between scepticism and dogmatism, whether positive or negative. He opens the *Outlines of Pyrrhonism* by remarking that an investigation will end in one of two ways: a discovery of the truth or a denial that the truth can be found. Otherwise, the investigation will continue (*PH* 1.1–4). Aristotle, Epicurus and the Stoics are dogmatists since they think they have discovered the truth. For example, having determined that there is nothing but atoms and the void, Epicurus no longer needs to investigate that particular point: he would not go looking for what he has already found. He may go on to investigate other matters, but this will not make him part-sceptic since he will rely on the truths already discovered in seeking to expand his knowledge.

On the other hand, all enquiry must appear futile to those who have determined that the truth cannot be discovered; you would not go looking for what you have decided cannot be found. The negatively dogmatic Academics, for example, have determined that knowledge is impossible. Although this is not a fair description of Carneades (as we have seen in Chapter 4), it does clarify Sextus' view. In contrast to both types of dogmatism, the sceptic has neither discovered the truth nor found that it cannot be discovered, so she continues to investigate (*PH* 1.2). And in fact, Sextus leans on the etymology of the Greek term *skeptikē*, pointing out that scepticism is so named from its activity in investigating and enquiring (*skeptesthai*; *PH* 1.7).

If we understand this investigation as a continuation of her original, pre-sceptical project of trying to become tranquil by means of discovering the truth, then she will continue to accept [I] and [R]. But there is no compelling reason to suppose that her project remains the same after her sceptical conversion. On the contrary, there are both philosophical and textual reasons to suppose that it undergoes a radical transformation, like the sceptic herself. In that case, we will need to see how Sextus can preserve the distinction between scepticism and negative dogmatism, and we will need to clarify the kind of investigation the mature sceptic is engaged in.

The first time she stumbles on tranquillity by bringing her intellect to a standstill must be quite a surprise. But as she repeats the experience it will come to seem quite ordinary. She will come to expect that tranquillity follows *epochē*, and to expect that *epochē* follows equipollence. Each repetition of the cycle of equipollence–*epochē*–tranquillity will reinforce her sceptical disposition [D]. At some point in this process she will realize that she has no good reason to maintain her original expectation that tranquillity arises from rationally resolving the disputed issue, so she will no longer have the same motivation to accept [I] or [R]. For all she knows, discovering the truth might produce tranquillity, or it might produce greater disturbance. Never having discovered the truth, she is unable to predict or expect any particular outcome.

The more expert she becomes at balancing competing accounts the more unlikely it is that she will ever discover the truth. In fact, Sextus even envisages the possibility of a dogmatist presenting an argument that the sceptic cannot refute. His advice is to respond in the following way:

> Before the founder of the school to which you adhere was born, the argument of the school, which is no doubt sound, was not yet apparent, although it was really there in nature. In the same way, it is possible that the argument opposing the one you have just propounded is really there in nature but is not yet apparent to us; so we should not yet assent to what is now thought to be a powerful argument. (*PH* 1.34)

Suppose, for example, someone presents you with a compelling version of the problem of evil.[9] As a result, you are strongly inclined to think that a God meeting the Judeo-Christian description does not, and in fact cannot, exist. A fallible Academic who is committed to following the normative rules [I] and [R] will tentatively endorse atheism while maintaining that some theistic arguments may eventually prevail. Even if it is disturbing to think that he *could* be wrong, there is no incentive for the fallibilist to suspend judgement. In fact, it would be downright dishonest to do so.

This situation is quite different for the sceptic. Her inability to articulate an effective counter-argument right now does not override her sceptical disposition. In accordance with Sextus' advice, she will say that for all we know there is some powerful theodicy that could neutralize the force of the problem of evil, or that such an argument is awaiting "discovery". The mature sceptic has always, or nearly always, found the arguments necessary to achieve equipollence on the issues she has examined so far. So it would be rash and precipitous to endorse some view just because it has not yet been refuted.

In this situation, the sceptic is not in possession of the counterbalancing argument, and yet she somehow prevents the scales of judgement from tipping. What, then, is doing the work of the missing argument? If the sceptic actually finds the view in question convincing and still does not assent, the normative account could explain the situation this way: the sceptic must decide whether or not to suspend judgement; and when there is no counterbalancing argument, she will still believe that she should not assent. This amounts to an important expansion of the normative principle:

[I*] It is irrational and irresponsible to believe any proposition as long as it is possible to construct an equally convincing argument against it.

Since it has, so far, always been possible for the sceptic to construct an equally convincing counter-argument for any view, [I*] should lead her to think that it will always be irrational and irresponsible to believe any proposition. If so, her commitment to [I*], along with a well-honed sceptical talent for producing equipollence, make it exceedingly unlikely that any view will ever be sufficiently supported by reason and evidence. In that case, the normative account of Sextus' promissory note (*PH* 1.34) leaves the sceptic unable to sincerely expect that she will ever discover the truth.

Alternatively, the causal account can explain Sextus' promissory note by making a parallel modification:

[D*] The sceptic's disposition inclines her away from believing any proposition as long as it is possible to construct an equally convincing argument against it.

On this view, not only has she become habituated to suspend judgement when the arguments are equally balanced, she is not even inclined to accept views that are currently unopposed. Because of her experience, the mere possibility of a convincing counter-argument is enough to balance the scales of judgement. And (again) since she has so far always been able to construct an equally convincing counter-argument for any view, the sceptical disposition has the effect of leaving her unmoved by any rational considerations. She has developed an attitude towards reason that is radically different from the one she started out with.

A major advantage of the causal, or dispositional, account is that it provides a much better defence against the charge of negative dogmatism. The normative principle [I*] commits the sceptic to an extraordinarily high standard of justification. But given the sceptic's passion for arguing against any and every epistemological theory, such a commitment is suspicious at best, self-refuting at worst. If, in applying her sceptical skill, she constructs equally convincing arguments for and against [I*], adhering to this principle would require her to reject it. By contrast, attributing the disposition [D*] to the sceptic involves attributing no beliefs, and hence preserves the distinction between scepticism and negative dogmatism.

The causal account also fits nicely with the distinction Sextus draws between the Pyrrhonian Sceptic and Arcesilaus. In other regards their sceptical views are virtually the same but Arcesilaus says that particular suspensions of judgement are good and particular assents bad (*PH* 1.232). In other words, Arcesilaus thinks we should suspend judgement and we should not assent. The Pyrrhonist, by contrast, makes no such evaluative or normative judgement about suspending judgement (see *PH* 1.196 and Chapter 3).

Furthermore, in some passages Sextus indicates that the sceptic does in fact aim at acquiring and preserving tranquillity. For example, he says that the sceptic will study natural science, not for the sake of making firm assertions about scientific matters, but "in order to be able to oppose to every account an equal account, and for the sake of tranquility" (*PH* 1.18). So the investigation of scientific issues is a matter of collecting material and developing the sceptical ability to produce equipollence. Similarly, when explaining the aim (*telos*) of scepticism, he remarks: "Up to now we say the aim of the Sceptic is tranquility in matters of opinion and moderation of feeling in matters forced upon us" (*PH* 1.25; see also 1.30). We should not take this sceptical *telos* to be the sort of normative goal established by a dogmatic ethical theory. It is rather a description of the outcome of the sceptic's practice; at least so far, such practice, in Sextus' experience, has ended in *epochē* and tranquillity (Hankinson 1997b).

And finally, the sceptic's inability to ever discover the truth is only a problem if we suppose that the mature sceptic's enquiry is aimed at truth. Sextus never explicitly says that it is despite the fact that a number of passages can be read that way (see especially *PH* 1.3, 2.11; Palmer 2000). When we find, for example, that the sceptic has not *up to now* discovered a criterion of truth (*PH* 3.70; see 2.53), we do not need to suppose that she sincerely expects to someday find it. With regard to the discovery of truth, she no longer has any expectation one way or the other.

Granted, enquiry in the ordinary sense, is naturally aimed at revealing the truth. But the sceptic is not engaged in an ordinary enquiry after her conversion. What the sceptic investigates:

> is not what is apparent, but what is said about what is apparent – and this is different from investigating what is apparent itself. For example, it appears to us that honey sweetens (we concede this inasmuch as we are sweetened in a perceptual way); but whether (as far as the argument goes)[10] it is actually sweet is something we investigate – and this is not what is apparent but something said about what is apparent.
>
> (*PH* 1.19–20)

Before her surprising discovery about how to achieve tranquillity, the sceptic is engaged in the pursuit of truth (*PH* 1.12, 1.26). She wants to find out about the things themselves, not what is said about those things. She wants to determine whether or not a benevolent God exists, not merely what can be said *about* the existence of God.

These may seem to be inseparable. Why, after all, would one investigate what is said about the existence of God if not for the sake of determining the truth about whether God exists? Cicero, for example, seeks out arguments pro and con for the sake of making the most informed judgement about where the truth lies. Similarly, when Socrates examines the beliefs of his interlocutors, he wants to discover the truth *by means of* determining whether they know the truth. In Socrates' case, his second-order enquiry into what people say and believe about virtue is still aimed at revealing the first-order truth about virtue.

What the mature sceptic wants to discover, however, is not the truth about *x*, but rather what theories and arguments have been proposed regarding *x*, and how they are supposed to establish their conclusions. Before her conversion, her enquiry was aimed at discovering the truth and was guided by such normative principles as [I] and [R]. After her conversion, her enquiry takes on this second-order nature and is no longer governed by any normative considerations; as a matter of habit and disposition, she continues to seek out what is said on all sides of disputed issues. And as a matter of habit and disposition, her enquiry leaves her in a tranquil state of *epochē*.

The mature sceptic's investigation of arguments pro and con various issues will appear indistinguishable from the investigation of someone who accepts normative rules governing enquiry. The single, crucial difference is in their attitudes towards these rules. (In Chapter 9 we will find a similar difference between the sceptical and dogmatic attitudes towards cultural, ethical and religious practices.)

Therapeutic scepticism and Sextus' diagnosis

The sceptic's distinctive attitude towards reason is illustrated by the self-refuting nature of the attempt to rationally establish that there are no demonstrations (see Burnyeat 1976). Dogmatists seize on this peculiar feature in the following anti-sceptical argument (*PH* 2.185):

(1) If an argument establishes its conclusion, then (at least one) demonstration exists.

(2) The sceptical argument either establishes that there are no demonstrations or it does not.

(3) If it does not, then the argument has not shown there are no demonstrations.

(4) If it does establish its conclusion, then by (1), demonstration exists.

So it is self-refuting to rationally establish that there are no demonstrations. If we further suppose that one cannot in fact accomplish such a task, the sceptic will necessarily fail in her attempt. Similarly, one cannot *coherently* say in a loud and clear voice, "I'm not speaking right now". The fact that we can utter these words does not establish that we can communicate anything meaningful, or at least coherent, by making these noises.

Sextus responds by claiming that the sceptic finds no arguments probative, not even the one that is supposed to establish that there are no demonstrations. So the impossibility of coherently establishing that there are no demonstrations is not a problem. By achieving equipollence on the issue, the sceptic will not be inclined to accept either side. But this is consistent with, and indeed requires, that each side appear equally convincing or plausible.

The sceptical project will only be self-refuting if the sceptic seeks to prove that there are no demonstrations. But she does not; she does not seek to rationally establish anything, and nor is she bound by any normative principles associated with the rational pursuit of truth. Her use of reason has, so far, only led to equipollence, *epochē* and tranquility. The sceptic seeks to purge by means of reason the dogmatic assumption that the proper use of reason reveals the truth (see *PH* 1.20). This is suggested by Sextus' evocative metaphors:

> … there are many things that put themselves in the same condition as they put other things. For example, just as fire after consuming the wood destroys itself as well, and just as purgatives after driving the fluids out of bodies eliminate

themselves as well, so too the argument against demonstration, after doing away with all demonstration, can cancel itself as well. And again, just as it is not impossible for the person who has climbed to a high place by a ladder to knock over the ladder with his foot after his climb, so too it is not unlikely that the sceptic, having got to the accomplishment of his task by a sort of step-ladder – the argument showing that there is no demonstration – should do away with this argument.

(M 8.480–81; see also PH 2.188, 1.206; DL 9.76;
Praep. Ev. 14.18.21)

Sextus is happy to apply his negative conclusions to themselves, just as he is willing to say that the phrase "nothing is true" applies to itself as well (PH 2.188). But in that case, what is Sextus saying? Are we left with a sceptical idiot absurdly proclaiming that he is not speaking right now?

This depressing assessment is easily avoided. On many occasions, Sextus argues dialectically, relying not only on his dogmatic opponents' beliefs as premises, but also on their commitment to normative, rational principles. Like Arcesilaus and Carneades, the Pyrrhonist simply holds his opponents to their own rational standards in order to show how far short their beliefs fall. Such dialectical arguments, in their pure form, require no substantive or logical commitments on the part of the sceptic.

On other occasions, Sextus seems to insert his own premises and to speak in his own voice. But all of these propositions must be understood with the crucial qualifying disclaimer set out at the beginning of the Outlines: "By way of preface let us say that on none of the matters to be discussed do we affirm that things certainly are just as we say they are: rather, we report descriptively on each item according to how it appears to us at the time" (PH 1.4). Similarly, Sextus explains that we must understand the sceptic's use of such characteristic phrases as "some object or state of affairs is no more this than that" as a report on the way he is affected, that is, as an expression of how things appear to him at that moment (PH 1.187–191; see also PH 1.15, 1.135, 1.193, 1.197–198, 1.200). This applies to the sceptic's awareness of the equipollence of opposed arguments. "Whether they *are* equal, we do not affirm: we say what appears to us about them, when they make an impression on us" (*PH* 1.196). The sceptic will only report descriptively on how the arguments affect her. She will say nothing about how they should affect her, or how they should affect others. In this way, reason is stripped of the impersonal, normative force that we typically attribute to it (see Chapter 9 for more on the sceptic's reliance on appearances).

For example, if it seems to a dogmatist that the problem of evil is a good reason to be an atheist, he will hold that it is a good reason for anyone to be an atheist. Regardless of whether or not anyone finds the argument rationally compelling, he will hold that everyone *should*.

By contrast, when introducing the sceptical modes, Sextus insists that he is affirming nothing about their number or about their force: they may be unsound, and there may be more than the ones he describes (*PH* 1.35). The context makes it clear that he does not intend a specifically logical sense of soundness. He is not suggesting that the modes may be invalid, or that their premises may be false, but rather that they may be impotent, they may appear to some to be unsound. As to whether they are unsound in some objective sense he will have no opinion. He is simply acknowledging that different arguments affect people differently.

Sextus' concern for such variability is best explained in terms of his therapeutic and philanthropic agenda. In the conclusion to the *Outlines*, he writes:

> Sceptics are philanthropic and wish to cure by argument, as far as they can, the conceit and rashness of the Dogmatists. Just as doctors for bodily afflictions have remedies which differ in potency, and apply severe remedies to patients who are severely afflicted and milder remedies to those mildly afflicted, so Sceptics propound arguments which differ in strength – they employ weighty arguments, capable of vigorously rebutting the dogmatic affliction of conceit, against those who are distressed by a severe rashness, and they

> employ milder arguments against those who are afflicted
> by a conceit which is superficial and easily cured and which
> can be rebutted by a milder degree of plausibility. This is why
> those with a Sceptical impulse do not hesitate sometimes to
> propound arguments which are sometimes weighty in their
> plausibility, and sometimes apparently rather weak. They do
> this deliberately, since often a weaker argument is sufficient
> for them to achieve their purpose.   (PH 3.280–81)

Here the sceptic's purpose is clearly not the discovery of truth, but rather the alleviation of disturbance brought about by dogmatic inclinations.[11] But if a balanced diet of opposed arguments is the prescription that leads us to tranquillity, what is the diagnosis? What is the cause of psychological disturbance?

Sextus thinks that some disturbances are avoidable and others are unavoidable. As animals we are subject to the unavoidable kind: hunger, thirst, sexual urges and so on (PH 3.183). Sensations are not all pleasant. But as animals we have a natural inclination to remove disturbances whenever and wherever they arise. In combating a lofty Stoic conception of reason, Sextus appeals to the abilities of the humble dog. He points out that dogs not only remove thorns from their paws but also clean their wounds, favour injured legs in keeping with good Hippocratic practice and, by eating grass and vomiting, relieve an upset stomach. Thus the dog attains what the Stoic Chrysippus would (allegedly) have to admit as the perfection of reason in choosing what is appropriate and avoiding what is disturbing (PH 1.70–71, 1.238).

In this regard, we are no different from the other animals: we too naturally seek to eliminate disturbances. Unlike the other animals, however, we are subject to a host of unnecessary disturbances. These arise from believing that something is *by nature* good or bad, appropriate or inappropriate (PH 1.29–30, 3.236–8; M 11.118, 145–6, 158). For something to be by nature good means, as we saw in Chapter 6, that it is invariably and really so, despite the way it may appear. If something is good by nature, dogmatists believe, then it is good for everyone, at any time and in any circumstance.

Having judged that money is by nature good, I will feel a strong impulse towards acquiring it. I will feel just as strongly about avoiding poverty in so far as I judge it to be by nature bad. If I am poor, I will be disturbed by my poverty. Seeking to eliminate this disturbance I will intensely pursue money. If I fail to get it, I will be even more disturbed by my poverty. On the other hand, if I do get it, I will then live in fear of losing it. So becoming rich does not put an end to the disturbance: it merely shifts the focus.

By suspending judgement about what is really good and bad, the sceptic neither pursues nor avoids anything intensely. Nevertheless, he is not completely free from disturbance. The sceptic's method is only effective against the "distortions of reason" and "worthless opinion", that is, against voluntary motions of the mind (*M* 11.148). The aim of the sceptic is to be tranquil in matters of opinion and to be only moderately affected by matters that are forced upon him (*PH* 1.30). So he will still suffer from hunger, thirst and cold, but he will not believe these are bad. To do so merely makes the disturbance more severe. We naturally strive to rid ourselves of involuntary disturbances, just as a dog removes a thorn from its paw. The belief that such disturbance is bad adds nothing to the effort to be rid of it but only makes matters worse (*M* 11.158).

Stoic disturbances

So far the diagnosis only seems to implicate a small category of beliefs: those that lead to intense pursuit or avoidance. The Stoics would agree, pointing out that the reason such beliefs are disturbing is that the good and bad things pursued and avoided are not within our control, and are not in fact genuinely good or bad. Despite our best efforts, we may suffer from hunger, thirst, cold, poverty and so on. The tranquillity of the Stoic sage, however, is as firm and inviolable as possible. He is immune from the whims of fortune.

But this tranquillity is not the result of suspending judgement. Quite the contrary, it is (in part) the result of an irrefutable conviction that virtue is the only genuine good, and that unlike the apparent goods of fortune, it is entirely within our control. The Stoic sage calmly and confidently pursues apparently good things such as wealth and health and avoids the apparently bad ones such as pain and poverty, but always with the full realization that they are not genuinely good or bad; the sage's pursuit and avoidance is never intense. His knowledge that virtue lies entirely with himself and is the only genuine good produces a state of permanent tranquillity.[12]

Yet Sextus thinks that the Stoic, like anyone else who believes something is good or bad by nature, will suffer unnecessary disturbances. To substitute virtue for the goods of fortune does not remove disturbance, but rather rearranges it:

> ... the philosopher's reasoning produces one disease in place of another, since in turning away the person who is striving for wealth or glory or health as something good towards pursuing ... virtue, he does not free him from pursuit, but transfers him to another pursuit.   (*M* 11.135 [Bett 1997])

This is aimed not at the ideal Stoic sage, but rather at the flesh and blood Stoic who has not yet attained virtue. Lacking virtue, he will feel compelled to intensely pursue it. And he should consider himself miserable as long as he lacks it. The claim that virtue is entirely within our control will not, or at least should not, alleviate his disturbance as long as he lacks this good.

The Stoics argue that the proper response to the recognition of vice is not to become disturbed and despondent, but rather to redouble one's efforts to attain virtue. Besides, the Stoics maintain that mental disturbance can only arise with our permission. So we may admit that we lack the only thing worth having and set about trying to get it while remaining tranquil (White 1995).

But the Stoics also maintain that their philosophical convictions are rationally justified and not merely arbitrary preferences. And this provides an opening for the sceptic. Sextus remarks, "As for those who say that good things cannot be lost, we shall bring them to suspension of judgment as a result of the impasse arising from dispute" (*PH* 3.238). The sceptic accomplishes this by producing opposing arguments that appear equally convincing. The Stoic will then be at a loss as to what to believe. His former preference for Stoicism will appear arbitrary, and his inability to rationally resolve the puzzle as to whether good things can be lost will result in disturbance. He must either try to overcome the disturbance by finding a non-question-begging, non-arbitrary justification for his Stoicism, or join the sceptic in suspending judgement.

The only route to continuous tranquillity is to suspend judgement not merely about all evaluative matters, but also about whether reason is capable of producing a good life by stocking our minds with true beliefs. If, however, the real life Stoic never discovers that his preference is merely arbitrary (assuming it is), he will never feel distressed at violating his own commitment to reason. This undetected delusion, it seems, will serve just as well as the sceptical suspension of judgement in producing tranquillity. Nevertheless, delusional tranquillity is a fragile and contingent affair. And in any case, there is nothing admirable about refusing to put one's beliefs to the test, while supposing nonetheless that they are rationally justified.

The disturbance of non-evaluative beliefs

Not all of our beliefs seem to inspire pursuit or avoidance: for example, that seventeen is a prime number, or that material substance exists independently of my perception. Imagine a modestly fallible Academic who examines the arguments for and against the existence of material substance. Let us suppose he decides to tentatively accept the more convincing conclusion while continuing his investigations. Believing in the existence (or non-existence) of material substance will probably not affect the way the world appears. Presumably my desk will appear as solid to one convinced by Berkeley's idealist view of substance as to one convinced by Locke's realist view. Both of them will use the desk in the same way. Taken in isolation from other beliefs and attitudes, beliefs about material substance will probably have no practical effect at all. So if such beliefs have no impact on what we pursue and avoid, why should we think accepting them will produce any disturbance?[13]

We must note first that such beliefs are the product of the pursuit of truth. And even if we do not think there is any practical value in determining the truth of some matters, we must also suppose that the truth-seeker sees *some* value in it. He will probably see truth as intrinsically valuable, and thus worth acquiring regardless of the consequences. In that case, the dogmatic truth-seeker is subject to disturbance whenever he acknowledges that his justification falls short. For this will amount to an admission that while he might be in possession of an intrinsic good, he might not be.

What, then, about the dogmatist who acknowledges the imperfections in his justification of some belief but remains tranquil? We may even imagine that his greatest joy lies in debate with other dogmatists, and that he occasionally changes his views on things, approving first one view as more truth-like, then another. Lacking what he sees as intrinsically good is supposed to be disturbing, and yet it is quite easy to imagine cases in which it is not.

To take this as an objection presupposes that Sextus' diagnosis is meant to reveal some psychological truths about human nature. This is clearly not the spirit in which he offers his therapy. Instead, we should take his diagnosis as a descriptive report of his past experience. It seems to him that some have suffered from the intense pursuits and avoidances inspired by dogmatic commitments and even by the very pursuit of truth. Whether this pursuit manifests itself in evaluative or non-evaluative beliefs, the good that is sought, knowledge, is elusive. Since the satisfaction of this desire does not seem to be within our control, it seems to lead to frustration and disturbance.

A prime example of this is Sextus' remark that "Geometers are burdened with no small disturbance with regard to the existence or conceivability of a line having length without breadth" (*M* 3.57; see *M* 8.130). If this is the object they wish to instruct us about, and if they have no clear conception of it, then they will not be able to teach us anything about it.

Sextus' objection is simply that we cannot conceive of length without breadth. His point is that the very existence of a line, whether on a chalkboard or in someone's thoughts, presupposes breadth. Sextus believes neither this nor the geometer's contradictory claim; nor does he believe it is intrinsically good to resolve the issue. So he will not be troubled. The geometer, by contrast, will feel compelled to pursue a resolution; in addition to the intrinsic good at stake, he may also suffer from the more mundane worry that he is a fraud, or that his livelihood is at stake. Lacking such beliefs, the sceptic has no worries.

To sum up Sextus' diagnosis: the source of psychological disturbance is (seems to be) the epistemically optimistic belief that the proper use of reason will lead to the truth, and that the resulting improvement in our beliefs is somehow instrumental to our well-being. Thus when confronted with controversial issues that we feel we must resolve, we are driven to a troubling and intense pursuit. Even those who are motivated exclusively by disinterested curiosity are vulnerable to disturbance in so far as they deem the object of their enquiry to be genuinely good. For as they enquire they must acknowledge that they lack what they believe to be good, and after they convince themselves that they have obtained it, they must admit that their argument and evidence may eventually be overturned.

Conclusion: the consistency of Pyrrhonian Scepticism

Sextus describes the Pyrrhonist not as one who adheres to certain distinctive beliefs, as a Stoic or Epicurean would, but rather one who lives in accordance with the general account of Scepticism (*PH* 1.16–17). I have argued that this account is purely descriptive, and requires us to understand the conversion to Scepticism as involving the adoption of a very different project along with a radically different attitude towards reason. The mature sceptic sheds her original belief that the way to tranquillity is to rationally resolve the troubling issues. After developing the sceptical disposition, she no longer has any expectations or beliefs about the potential benefits of truth or the possibility of attaining it by means of reason. And with the radical revision of her investigation, she no longer feels that her use of reason is governed by the normative principles she originally adhered to, although her behaviour may still appear to be in conformity to them.

If we understand scepticism as an activity or set of practices aimed at relieving dogmatic disturbance, then we can see how misplaced the charge of inconsistency is. It is simply a category mistake to accuse a practice of inconsistency. Just as it is neither consistent nor inconsistent to ride a bicycle, the practice of scepticism, in so far as it is something the sceptic *does*, can be neither consistent nor inconsistent, although it can be either effective or ineffective, skilful or clumsy.

The charge of self-refutation is more difficult. I have briefly indicated how Sextus deals with this in arguing that there are no demonstrations. We shall return to the issue of whether he can sustain his peculiar attitude towards reason. But first, in Chapter 8, we shall consider the sceptic's arguments in order to better understand the tools with which Sextus would philanthropically relieve us of our beliefs. If we suppose that these arguments are effective, we may then consider two final questions about Pyrrhonian Scepticism. In Chapter 9, we shall examine how the sceptic is able to practise scepticism without beliefs, and how she is able to engage in the ordinary business of life without beliefs.

EIGHT

Pyrrhonian arguments

In this chapter I hope to show that even if we are uninterested in the prospects of tranquillity, Pyrrhonian Scepticism continues to provide an important, and perhaps insurmountable, challenge.[1] For this challenge to take effect, one must simply accept that an arbitrary preference is not a rational basis for belief, and that we have some sort of obligation as rational agents to justify our beliefs. If the sceptic can systematically block all of our attempts at justification, we will be left in the troubling position of believing that we ought to do what we cannot.[2]

The five modes

As we saw in Chapter 6, the modes are the Sceptic's tools; they are argument forms that may be employed against a wide variety of claims. After presenting Aenesidemus' ten modes, Sextus turns to another set of five that he describes as the property of "more recent Sceptics" (*PH* 1.164; see 1.36).[3]

What all routes to *epochē* have in common is that they oppose one thing to another (*PH* 1.31): for example, the appearance that the tower appears round with the appearance that the tower appears square, or the argument that providence exists with the argument that providence does not exist. The only logical requirement is that the opposed propositions must be contraries: they cannot both be true, but they may both be false. As long as they are contraries, there will be a problem for the proponent of either side: he cannot accept that both are true, so he must explain or justify his preference. The sceptic will then apply a mode or combination of modes to show this preference is ultimately arbitrary and thus not rationally justified.

Dispute, relativity and the sceptic's dialectical strategy

The first of the five modes proceeds by citing a dispute or disagreement that has not been decided (*PH* 1.165). The adjective Sextus typically uses, *anepikritos*, is ambiguous: it could mean either undecided or undecidable. To decide a dispute means to determine which side is right, or at least more justified and hence more likely to be right. But Sextus does not mean that certain disputes are impossible to resolve. If that were the case, it would be impossible to settle the matter, and Sextus would be a negative dogmatist. What he means is that the issue has not in fact been resolved to the satisfaction of all interested parties; otherwise there would be no disagreement to speak of. So the sceptic will say that such disputes have proved undecidable until now – they are currently undecided – but he will not say that they are in principle undecidable. His sceptical ability to achieve equipollence will prevent him from ever judging an issue, even the issue about whether some dispute might be resolved in the future.

The third of the five modes is relativity (*PH* 1.167). Although it plays a central role among Aenesidemus' ten modes, providing the general form for the rest, here it appears to be more of an adjunct to the mode deriving from dispute. The notion that everything is relative (i.e. appears relative) provides an easy formula for opposing one thing to another thereby generating a disagreement. In analogy with the first mode, we should understand this as an undecided relativity.

But why should I worry if I have not been able to persuade those who disagree with me? If I had granted that the dispute has not yet been resolved, I would have to suspend judgement. But I do not need to grant this. I might insist that I have resolved the dispute to my own satisfaction, and that adequate resolution does not require universal agreement. My view may still be the right one even if it is disputed. Not everyone is equally wiling or able to follow complicated arguments. So it is no surprise that not everyone shares my correct view of things.

This response will seem considerably less arrogant once I present my defence. For then it will no longer seem to be a matter of preferring my beliefs just because they are mine. But the sceptic is prepared to rebut any possible defence. Suppose I believe that providence exists, that is, that the world is governed by the wisdom of the gods (see *ND* 2.76). Suppose also that I am aware that some people disagree with me. Whatever I advance in support of my belief will be the subject of an undecided dispute. If I say that the universe exhibits a high degree of orderliness, I will also have to admit that some believe the orderliness we see is the exception and not the rule, or that this orderliness need not be the product of divine providence. And if I cite the authority of scripture as evidence I will have to admit that some believe scripture is not authoritative. Whatever reason I give for my belief will itself be subject to dispute. And I will have to provide yet another justification.

In this way the sceptic will drive me to an infinite regress, claiming that I have failed to justify my view. We shall consider this second mode in greater detail in the next section. For now, note that the regress is generated by my desire to show that my belief is neither arrogant nor arbitrary. The sceptic is not responsible for the regress. Unlike the persistent child who keeps asking why, the sceptic's challenge arises from the dogmatist's own conception of justification and rational agency: the sceptic only reflects the dogmatist's epistemic ambitions.

As long as I continue to see myself as this sort of rational agent, I will have to try to put an end to the regress. But there appear to be only two options. First, I may assert that some belief is self-evidently true and needs no other justification. The sceptic will then apply the fourth mode from hypothesis and argue that this is no better than an arbitrary assertion. Alternatively, I may claim that the reasons I have cited mutually support one another. So every reason I have advanced is justified by some other reason I have advanced. The sceptic will counter this with the fifth, reciprocal mode, and argue that circular reasoning provides no justification.

So we have a brief sketch of the general sceptical strategy. The dogmatist asserts his belief *P*. The sceptic points out that others endorse some logically incompatible claim *P**; or they assert that it only appears *P* in situation *S*, but *P** in some other situation *S**. For example, I might assert my belief that wealth is the greatest good. Someone else might assert that the greatest good is health or that it only appears to be wealth when one is healthy, while it appears to be health when one is ill. As a rational agent, the dogmatist is compelled to explain why he has decided in favour of *P*, that is, he must justify his belief. This leads to a trilemma: his belief is held on the basis of an infinite series of reasons, an arbitrary hypothesis or circular reasoning (*PH* 1.166–9). According to Sextus, each of these three lead to suspension of judgement (see Figure 4). We shall consider them in turn.

Infinite regress

There is nothing necessarily problematic about the notion of a potential infinity. We can always imagine making a further division of something or a further addition to it.

The problem arises when, as in the case of justification, we need to complete the task. Sextus presents a non-epistemic version of this problem in reporting an argument against the reality of motion:

> If anything is moved, it is moved either by itself or by something else. If by something else, then since what produces motion acts and what acts is moved, that item too will need something else to move it, and the second a third, and so *ad*

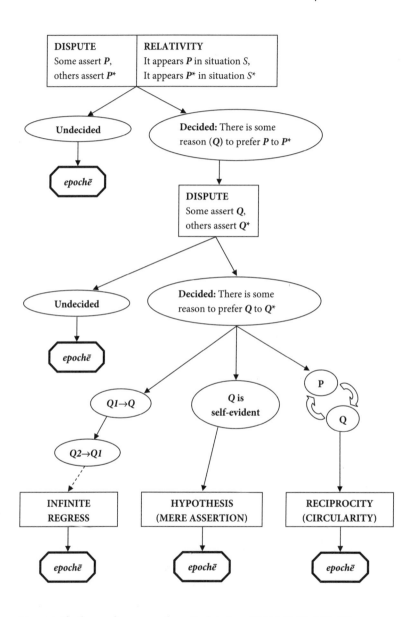

Figure 4. The five modes: a general sceptical strategy (*PH* 1.164–77, 2.19–20).

infinitum, so that the motion comes to have no beginning
– which is absurd. Not everything which is moved, therefore, is moved by something else. Nor by itself ...

(*PH* 3.67; see *M* 10.76)

The absurdity is the notion that the effects of some process occur
without the relevant cause having occurred to get things going. If
there is not a first step in the process, it has not started. And if it has
not started it cannot be completed.

But perhaps there does not really have to be a first cause. If the universe is eternal, motion will just be a brute fact, a feature of the way
things are. There will be no first cause of motion because objects in
the universe have always been in motion. So any instance of motion
that you care to name will have a preceding cause. No instance of
motion lacks an immediately preceding cause, and yet there is no first
cause. It will be futile to seek a first cause of motion because it does
not exist. But clearly things are, and always have been, in motion.

Whatever Sextus might say about this cosmological possibility, he
would not accept it in the epistemological context. He typically sums
up his application of this mode by remarking that it is *impossible* to
prove infinitely many propositions, to grasp an infinite number of
demonstrations, to make infinitely many decisions or judgements
and so on. We simply do not have the time.

The cosmological promissory note is unacceptable when seeking a justification. Even if I am able to provide a justification for
any randomly selected belief in the infinite regress, I am not able to
provide *every* justification. So, while we can admit that the infinite
series is potentially justified, it does not follow that it is actually
justified. For example, in order to actually decide between contrary
appearances, one:

> will need another appearance in turn to judge this second
> appearance, and another to judge that, and so *ad infini-
> tum*. But it is impossible to make infinitely many decisions.
> Therefore it is impossible to discover which appearances one
> must use as standards and which not. (*PH* 2.78)

The crucial point is that before my belief P can be justified, *all* of the preceding beliefs on which it depends must themselves be justified. The defender of the promissory notes mistakenly assumes that the justification of some randomly selected belief depends only on its predecessor. As long as there is even one actually unjustified belief in the series, we cannot count the final belief justified. So in order for a series of beliefs to produce a justification, it must be finite, that is, there must be a first, assuming the series is not circular.

How, then, does the mode deriving from infinite regression lead to the suspension of judgement? Since few would rest their justification on an infinite regress in the first place, this mode is most commonly used in conjunction with the hypothetical and reciprocal modes.[4] So for the most part, revealing the unacceptability of an infinite regress blocks a logically possible route to justification. Like every other sceptical argument, it aims to undermine the dogmatist's confidence by balancing opposing reasons in order to achieve equipollence.

Hypothesis

One tempting way to put an end to the regress is to set something down as true, claiming it needs no further justification. Contemporary epistemologists call such beliefs foundational or basic, and some describe them as self-evident. A hypothesis is, and should be, accepted as true without any demonstration of its truth.

Sextus' objection is obvious: "if they can be trusted on the basis of a bare assertion, the people who say the opposite can also be trustworthy when they bring forward their equally strong assertion" (*M* 8.436). The equal strength is a matter of psychological conviction. In other words, the proponents of hypothesis H are just as convinced as proponents of a logically incompatible hypothesis H^*. The sceptically inclined will acknowledge the intuitive force of both H and H^*; he will see why someone might find either hypothesis compelling. This will lead him to equipollence and the suspension of judgement.

The proponent of H, however, will not concede that H^* is equally compelling. He may insist that in order for something to be self-evidently true it does not have to be self-evidently true for everyone. Again, the dogmatist will not be impressed by disagreement. He might invoke Aristotle's distinction between what is better known to us and what is better known by nature, or without qualification (*Met.* 1.1, 184a16–21).[5] The idea is that the world is intelligible to us because of the kinds of animals we are. However, it is not immediately intelligible. It does not immediately reveal its order, pattern or structure, or generally why it is the way it is. But it does reveal itself to those who are properly trained and in the right physical and intellectual condition (compare [A'] from Chapter 6).

Aristotle thinks the things better known by nature are primary features of the world. They explain why things are the way they are, but they are not themselves explained in turn. So even though we can only arrive at knowledge of these first principles by starting with what is more familiar or better known to us, they are not justified or explained by appealing to anything else. Crucially, they are not frivolous or arbitrary assertions. In this sense the dogmatist does have a reason to prefer his first principles to what others might set down hypothetically. But he is still unable to provide any external justification for the truth of his hypotheses. Such principles will only appear compelling to those who have been properly trained.

A Platonist could tell a similar story, explaining why only some people are able to grasp certain basic truths that need no further justification. He will claim that statements about Forms only seem arbitrary to those who have not acquired the Platonic discipline. Again, the point is that disagreement about self-evidently true propositions need not cause one to abandon what appears self-evidently true.

Sextus does not explicitly address this type of reply, but it is easy enough to see what he could say. First, the notion of what is better known by nature, like the notion of Platonic Forms, is deeply embedded in philosophical theory. If we balance equally powerful arguments for and against Aristotle's teleology we will have no inclination to believe that there is a natural fit between human cognitive equipment and the metaphysical structure of the world. This in turn will lead us to suspend judgement about the intelligibility of the world and the very existence of things that are better known by nature.

Furthermore, there is disagreement regarding the proper training and the proper condition necessary to grasp self-evident truths. And there remain disagreements regarding the content of those supposedly self-evident truths. So we find ourselves back once again at the mode of dispute.

But perhaps we can differentiate among competing hypotheses on the basis of their predictive or explanatory success. The dogmatist might claim that:

> ... an assurance of the hypothesis being strong is the fact that the consequence that is drawn from the things assumed by hypothesis is found to be true; for if what follows from these is sound, the things from which it follows are also true and unquestionable. (*M* 8.375)

So some hypotheses are rationally preferable to others because they improve our predictive success: the consequences of the hypothesis are true.

Now the problem is to explain how we are able to determine that the consequences are true. They will not confirm themselves; if that were the case it would not be necessary to derive them from the premise or hypothesis. But they will not be confirmed by the premise either, because this has not been established as true and is itself the point under examination. For example, one might hypothesize that scripture is the literal word of God, and then infer that some specific scriptural claim is true. Since there is a dispute about the hypothesis, it is as unconvincing as the contrary hypothesis that scripture is not the literal word of God. So it cannot warrant the consequence.

Since for every hypothesis *H* there is at least one contrary hypothesis *H**, the sceptic finds the very act of hypothesizing suspicious. No one feels the need to hypothesize what is so evident as to be undisputed. Sextus returns to this theme in his discussion of the hypothetical mode:

... since apparent things display just that – that they appear – and have no further power to teach us that they also exist, let it be supposed both that the premises of the demonstration appear and similarly that the consequence does. But in this way the conclusion being sought will not be drawn and the truth will not be brought forward, since we are limited to bare assertion and our own affection. And wanting to show that they not only appear, but also exist, is the mark of men who are not content with what is necessary for normal use, but are eager also to help themselves to whatever possible.

(*M* 8.368)

If we acknowledge that reports about how things appear or how I am affected are mere assertions, there is no problem. But a hypothesis goes further. To hypothesize is to pretend that one's mere assertion is in fact true and to request that others treat it that way as well, whether it appears true to them or not.

In so far as we are committed to avoiding beliefs that are merely arbitrary preferences, we must not accept any argument that proceeds from hypotheses. Whenever the issue in question is supported by hypotheses on both (or all) sides, we must suspend judgement.

Reciprocity (circularity)

The final route to justification is to try to claim that one's beliefs are mutually supportive of each other. So none of my beliefs provide the foundation for the rest, but each is supported by the others. When the sceptic points out that there is a dispute about my claim *P*, I may respond that *P* is true because of *Q*. And when the sceptic points out that there is a dispute about *Q*, I respond that *Q* is true because of *P*. Sextus will then invoke the reciprocal mode.

"The reciprocal mode occurs when what ought to be confirmatory of the object under investigation needs to be made convincing by the object under investigation" (*PH* 1.169). If I wish to establish that (*P*) scripture is the literal word of God, I cannot rely on (*Q*) scriptural passages. Before I can rely on the authority of the passages I have to establish the original point under investigation: that scripture is the literal word of God. If the only way I can do that is by appealing to scriptural passages, I cannot succeed. I can never be justified in believing *P* as long as this presupposes that *Q* has been justified, because *Q* cannot be justified until *P* is.

This applies also to definitions. Consider the maddening experience of looking up the word "profligacy" in the dictionary and discovering that it means "dissoluteness". Naturally you turn to the definition of "dissoluteness" and find that it means "profligacy". If these are the only entries, you will be frustrated, because you need to understand one in order to understand the other, and vice versa. Sextus provides an example of this with "cause" and "effect":

> If in order to conceive of a cause, we must already have recognized its effect, and in order to know its effect … we must already know the cause, the reciprocal mode of puzzlement shows that both are inconceivable: the cause cannot be conceived of as a cause nor the effect as an effect; for each of them needs to be made convincing by the other, and we shall not know from which to begin to form the concept. Hence we shall not be able to assert that anything is a cause of anything. (*PH* 3.21–2)

We may nonetheless find ourselves in possession of the concepts of cause and effect, or at least, as Hume would put it, we will continue to expect that a certain type of event will be followed by another type of event. Sextus allows that the sceptic will expect to find fire when he sees smoke (*PH* 2.100; see the discussion of recollective signs below). What the reciprocal mode blocks in this case is the attempt to argue that anything is a cause in the metaphysical sense, that is, something that produces its effect necessarily. The sceptic's expectations are not the sort of thing he will argue for; he merely finds himself expecting that smoke will follow fire. The dogmatist's assertion that *P* is the cause of *Q*, however, will be disputed and thus in need of justification. But in order to justify his account of cause and effect he first needs to provide informative definitions of the key terms. The reciprocal mode shows this to be impossible, assuming the only way to define the terms is reciprocally, and this blocks the dogmatist's attempt at justification.

Reciprocal definitions are not arguments. But they suffer from the same shortcoming as reciprocal arguments (for more on definition, see *PH* 2.205–12). Just as the definitions are not informative, the arguments are not probative. They do not provide independent reasons for accepting the conclusion as true. If I were to collect a number of examples of courageous action in order to see what they all have in common, it seems that I first need some criterion or definition so that I do not mistakenly include a cowardly act among my examples. So I cannot collect my examples in order to reason inductively to the nature of courage since I must first know what courage is in order to correctly choose my examples (cf. *PH* 2.197). Of course, there may always be other, non-reciprocal grounds on which to justify one's claims or define one's terms. The charge of circularity does not necessarily lead by itself to *epochē*. Sextus uses it effectively in conjunction with the hypothetical mode in the following example.

If anyone claims to have apprehended something that is disputed, he will claim either that it is self-evidently true or that he has established its truth after having investigated it. If he opts for the former, the sceptic will apply the hypothetical mode. If he opts for the latter, the sceptic will apply the reciprocal mode, arguing that one can only apprehend what has been investigated, but that one can only investigate what has already been apprehended (*PH* 2.6–9). Sextus' argument is strongly reminiscent of Plato's paradox of enquiry (*Meno* 80d–e; cf. *PH* 3.174). One cannot search for what one already knows or for what one does not know. In the first case, there's no need to search for what you already know. In the second case, you cannot search for what you do not know because you do not know what to look for, so will not know if you happen by accident to find it.

For example, to investigate the soul I must already know enough to differentiate a soul from other things. Either I will claim that this knowledge is self-evident or that I have acquired it on the basis of enquiry. The former claim invites the hypothetical mode, and the latter invites the reciprocal: I cannot apprehend the soul, or anything about it, until I have investigated what a soul is, but I cannot investigate what a soul is until I have apprehended enough to be able to isolate my object of study.

Responses to this puzzle typically attempt to break out of the circularity, implicitly acknowledging the effectiveness of the reciprocal mode. For example, according to the solution that Plato experiments with in the *Meno*, we already know (in some sense) what we wish to discover by investigation. Learning turns out to be a kind of recollection and, contrary to appearances, we do in fact search for what we already "know".[6] Of course, any such solution will commit the dogmatist to other controversial, and disputed, claims. So the sceptic will still have ample opportunity to challenge his opponent.

But, we should note that Sextus presents this argument initially as a problem for the sceptic. If enquiry is impossible, it is impossible for everyone, and the sceptic cannot investigate the dogmatist's claims. For either he apprehends the things the dogmatists talk about or not. If the sceptic apprehends what the dogmatists mean by "soul", then he cannot be genuinely puzzled by it. On the other hand, if he does not apprehend "soul", then he cannot refute dogmatic claims about it.

Sextus disputes both horns of this dilemma by making a distinction between two senses of "apprehension". In one sense it means simply to think of something without affirming its reality, and in a stronger sense it means to grasp as true. So the sceptic apprehends "soul" in the weaker sense, but is still puzzled by whether such a thing actually exists. He understands the way his opponents use their terms, he understands what they think these words mean. But he does not thereby take himself to have grasped them as true (*PH* 2.4–6, *M* 8.334a–336a).[7]

Sextus claims that this dilemma is in fact even more problematic for the dogmatist. When, for example, the Stoic disputes the Epicurean claim that pleasure is the only good, he either apprehends the truth of this claim or not. If he apprehends it, then he must reject his Stoicism. And if he does not apprehend it, he cannot dispute it, for he does not even know what they are talking about. Of course, the Stoic can appeal to the same distinction the sceptic does, claiming that he grasps what the Epicurean means, and not that what the Epicurean means is true. So this distinction allows both dogmatists and sceptics to carry on their investigations. But it also emphasizes the point that we only investigate what we do not comprehend. In so far as dogmatists believe they have arrived at the truth, they have put an end to enquiry (*PH* 2.11).

The specific account of Scepticism

In his specific account, Sextus investigates an array of particular dogmatic doctrines. Rather than take these arguments piecemeal, he approaches them in a systematic fashion, first grouping the topics in accordance with standard dogmatic divisions, and secondly targeting the most basic, foundational principles or conclusions within each division.

In the opening passages of *M* 7 (the first book of *Against the Logicians*), Sextus sets out the three standard divisions of philosophy in the Hellenistic period: logic, physics and ethics.[8] This provides a useful, although crude, framework for organizing the history of Greek philosophy and, more importantly, for arranging his sceptical targets in a systematic way. As the story goes, most of the Presocratics cared only for the physical part, whereas Socrates cared only for the ethical, and Plato, Aristotle, Epicurus and the Stoics turned their attention to all three.

The Stoics were particularly fond of explaining the interrelations between these three parts metaphorically: for example, ethics is the yolk, physics the white and logic the shell of an egg (*M* 7.17–19). Others compared philosophy to a living being, comparing logic to the bones and sinews, ethics to the flesh and physics to the soul, although some preferred to see ethics as the soul and physics as the flesh. Nevertheless, logic plays either a structural or defensive role in all the metaphors. It shows us how we may win truth for ourselves and then how we may defend the ground.

Sextus decides to start with logic since every part of philosophy, whether Stoic or not, is dedicated to the discovery of truth, and this in turn requires reliable methods of differentiating the true from the false (*PH* 2.17; *M* 7.24). Logic provides the basic tools for all three parts of philosophy (*PH* 2.13). So, if the sceptic's arguments are successful, the dogmatists would be unable to differentiate the true from the false, and *a fortiori* unable to defend their claims in physics and ethics.

Sextus follows this standard division not because he endorses it, but rather "for the sake of an orderly and methodical search" (*M* 7.2). His focus on the more fundamental claims within each sub-discipline is similarly motivated. Appealing to a hunting metaphor, he notes that just as it is more skilful to be able to catch many prey all at once with a net than to pursue them one at a time with a line, so too it is more accomplished to bring down many claims in common with a single refutation (*M* 9.3). Appealing to a different metaphor, he suggests the way to do this is by undermining the foundation of the structure we wish to bring down (*M* 9.2; *PH* 3.1, 2.84). So, for example, he begins his examination of physics with arguments against the intelligibility of the active principle, God. In so far as dogmatic explanations of physical phenomena rely on the intelligibility of the active principle, Sextus will have effectively brought them all down by means of his arguments against the dogmatic conception of God.

We should be cautious about the import of all these metaphors, however. When Sextus "undermines" or "brings down" some dogmatic assertions, he does not take himself to have proven them false. The goal is once again to balance the rational force of arguments on each side of an issue, thereby leading the reader to suspend judgement. Sextus himself has no view on whether the dogmatist's foundational claims entail other propositions. It is enough that the dogmatist thinks so.

If the view I have defended in Chapter 7 is correct, Sextus is not searching for the truth about these disputed philosophical issues, but rather for what can be said about them in order to articulate equally compelling arguments on both sides. Given the therapeutic and philanthropic nature of the Sceptical project and the variability in what people find persuasive, Sextus wishes to find a variety of ways of bringing about equipollence. This explains the concessive nature of many of his arguments; in particular, it explains why, after presenting the generally applicable strategy of the five modes, and then undermining dogmatic logic, he nonetheless presses on to attack their specific arguments in physics and ethics. Even if his "patients" are not sufficiently impressed by the Sceptical assault on the roots of their dogmatic positions, he will attempt to cut off the larger limbs or at least the branches. In the remainder of this chapter, we shall follow him only as far as logic.

Logic: criteria, signs and proofs

As Sextus presents it, the main task of logic is to explain the nature of truth, and to explain how we may reliably distinguish it from what is false. The latter, epistemological topic, is by far the most prominent in both *M* 7–8 (*Against the Logicians*) and the parallel text, *PH* 2. So in both, texts, criteria, signs and proofs are central topics.[9] Before turning to some characteristic arguments against each of these, we must note that Sextus distinguishes criteria and signs that are sceptically acceptable from those that are not (see Figure 5). No kind of proof is sceptically acceptable since proof is a rational means of establishing the truth of some proposition. However, this does not preclude the sceptic from using proofs in his characteristically therapeutic manner, that is, without personally approving of the normative force of logical inference.

Criteria of action versus criteria of truth

The initial distinction is between a criterion of action and a criterion of truth. A criterion of action is merely an appearance, although it need not be limited to sensory appearances. For example, the honey might appear good to eat. This appearance, along with the sceptic's hunger, will explain why he ate the honey rather than a napkin. Unlike a criterion of truth, such appearances provide no justification

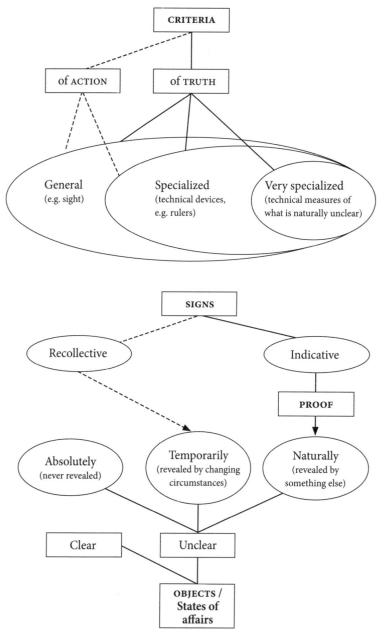

Figure 5. Criteria, signs and proof (*PH* 2; *M* 7–8)

or defence. These guiding appearances tell us nothing about whether the agent should have performed the action, in either the moral or prudential sense of "should". And they are supposed to guide the sceptic without compromising his *epochē* (we shall consider in Chapter 9 whether and how this might be so).

A criterion of truth, on the other hand, is the measure or standard one applies in moving beyond the appearance to the underlying reality, however that may be understood. There are three different types: general, specialized and very specialized. The general include sight, hearing and taste, among the others. The specialized include technical means of measure such as scales, ruler and compass. This group appears to be a subset of the general in so far as such criteria are extensions of our senses. Furthermore, if we cannot rely on sensations, the general criteria, then we cannot rely on the measurements we read from our technical instruments, the specialized criteria.

Sextus has no complaint against either of these as long as they are employed in the sceptical fashion, that is, for the sake of acting and not for the sake of assenting to truth. He characterizes them as ordinary or everyday standards in contrast with the very specialized type (*PH* 2.15). This set also appears to be a subset of the specialized in so far as the criteria are technical. The crucial differentiating feature is that very specialized criteria are meant to reveal unclear or non-evident matters. Sextus proposes to deal principally with these since, unlike the other two, they are the tools of dogmatic philosophers. (We shall return to the sceptic's reliance on appearances in Chapter 9.)

He further divides the very specialized criteria into three kinds (*PH* 2.16; *M* 7.35–37; not indicated in Figure 5) in order to systematically refute the most famous and plausible accounts available (*PH* 2.22–79; *M* 7.89–438). Here again he illustrates his point by way of a metaphor:

> … the human being, "by whom" the judgment occurs, is like the weigher or carpenter; sense-perception and thought, "through which" the judgment occurs, are like the scales and ruler; and the impact of the appearance, in virtue of which

the human being undertakes to judge, is like the state of the
aforementioned tools.   (*M* 7.37)

In terms of the metaphor, these three aspects are inextricably connected. If a carpenter is unreliable or unskilled, it does not matter
how accurate his sense-perceptions may be and how finely tuned
his tools are since he will not be able to reliably use them to get the
desired outcome. Similarly, even if the carpenter is skilled he will be
hampered by either unreliable perceptions or faulty tools.

The metaphor is limited, however, since there is no controversy
regarding what a carpenter is. In the analogous case there is no end
to the philosophical disputes regarding human nature. Sextus claims
that if we cannot resolve these disputes and make human nature
intelligible, we cannot appeal to it as the criterion by which something is judged to be true.

But even if we were able to make human nature intelligible, we
must notice that the judgement that human beings are the criterion
by which something is judged to be true is made *by* a human being.
So, in a manner reminiscent of Aenesidemus' ten modes, the judge
is party to the dispute. Furthermore, to grant this judgement presupposes that human beings are the criterion by which something
is judged to be true, which is the very issue at question.

And even if we grant that human beings are the criterion by
which something is judged to be true, we must then determine
which ones to trust, for human beings are particularly prone
to disagreement.[10] Now the problem will be that if one lacks the
expertise to qualify as the criterion by which something is judged
to be true, he will be unqualified to settle the disputes about which
human being is the criterion. As Cicero puts the point, it will be
the job of a sage to determine who is a sage (*Ac.* 2.9). On the other
hand, if he claims to be a sage himself, either he merely asserts this
or he backs it up with some proof. The sceptic will not be swayed
by mere assertion, but will hold the dogmatist to his own standard
and demand some rational justification. This in turn will lead to
a demand for a criterion by which, through which or in virtue of
which he may assess the proof. But in seeking to justify himself as

the criterion by which truth is revealed, the dogmatist is party to the dispute.

Moving to the criterion through which something is judged to be true, Sextus notes that only two faculties have been proposed: the senses and the intellect. This produces three possible accounts: we discern the truth through the senses alone, through the intellect alone or through both. If we suppose it is through the senses alone, how shall we decide the dispute among those who say the senses are always reliable, never reliable or only sometimes reliable? We cannot settle the matter by appeal to the senses since this would beg the question at issue. And if it must be decided by appealing to something else, we will have to reject the assumption that we discern the truth through the senses alone.

Similarly, if we suppose it is through the intellect alone, how shall we decide the dispute among those who arrive at incompatible views by the application of the intellect? We cannot settle the matter by appeal to the intellect since this would beg the question at issue. And again, if it must be decided by appealing to something else, we will have to reject the assumption that we discern the truth through the intellect alone.

Sextus next rejects the possibility that it is through both on the grounds that it will still be through one or the other in each case (assuming the two do not blend into some third, distinct type of faculty). So the previous considerations will still apply. And we will have to certify the reliability of both the senses and the intellect either through the senses or through the intellect. This will call for the reciprocal mode since either the senses or the intellect must first be certified before it can certify the other.

Finally, Sextus considers appearances as the criterion in virtue of which truth is discerned. Since an appearance is only the affection of our sense organs, it is generally thought to be different from the external object that gives rise to it. As Sextus puts it, "honey is not the same thing as my being affected sweetly" (*PH* 2.72); nor is a picture of Socrates the same as Socrates himself. This leads to Sextus' version of what we now typically call the "veil of perception". If our only access to the true nature of external objects or states of affairs is through the way they affect us, we may never confirm whether the appearances are accurate; we will never know whether the picture of Socrates is accurate since we can never meet Socrates himself (*PH* 2.74–75).

And even if we grant that we can grasp the underlying nature of things in virtue of the way they appear, we will have to determine whether every appearance is the criterion, or only some appearances. The first option leads directly to self-refutation since it appears to some that not every appearance is the criterion. So from the claim that every appearance is the criterion it would follow that not every appearance is the criterion.

The second option requires us to explain the basis on which we can make such a judgement. If we must rely on some other appearance, then the sceptic will set us off on an infinite regress and we will never finish justifying the initial appearances. It is more promising to claim, as the Stoics do, that certain appearances are self-evidently true, at least to those who have acquired the proper mental dispositions. After setting out the Stoic arguments in support of these kataleptic impressions (*M* 7.227–60), Sextus tries to lead his readers to equipollence by reporting the Academic arguments against them (*M* 7.402–35; see Chapter 4).

It remains possible that someone may discover a novel account of the criterion. What Sextus thinks he has shown is that for the most promising contenders available the arguments in support are as convincing as the arguments opposed.

Signs and proofs

Loosely speaking, signs and proofs are just different varieties of criteria since they are all supposed to explain how we are able to move from ignorance to knowledge. The Stoic account of signs and proofs, which is Sextus' principal target, is more narrowly logical (in our sense of the word). Stoics define a sign as the antecedent proposition in a sound conditional that is capable of uncovering the consequent (a sound conditional being one in which if the antecedent is true, the consequent is true; *M* 8.244–56; *PH* 2.104). These propositions articulate the content of a rational impression (*M* 8.70). Proofs, as we shall see, are a kind of sign since the conjunction of the premises can be understood as a sign of the truth of the conclusion (*M* 8.277, 299; *PH* 2.134).

The requirement that a sign (or proof) is capable of uncovering or revealing the truth of the consequent (or conclusion) is crucial since not every antecedent of a sound conditional uncovers the truth of the consequent. As an example, Sextus offers this: if it is day, it is light. In this conditional, if they are true, both antecedent and consequent are grasped independently of one another, by means of their own manifest character. This is not a terribly helpful example, however, since Sextus does not tell us what we would attend to (other than the fact that it is light) in grasping that it is day. Nevertheless, the point is that in some sound conditionals, the truth of the antecedent is not causally or even conceptually related to the truth of the consequent and hence does not reveal that truth.

Consider this conditional by contrast: if a woman is lactating, she has conceived. Here the antecedent shows that the consequent is true. It is supposedly *because* we apprehend that a woman is lactating that we apprehend she has conceived.

Since signs and proofs are necessarily revelatory, the consequents or conclusions must be initially unclear. Before considering two of Sextus' basic strategies for refuting signs and proofs, we must consider some important dogmatic distinctions Sextus reports between clear and unclear objects:

> Of the unclear, some are unclear once and for all [absolutely], some are unclear for the moment [temporarily], and some are unclear by nature [naturally]. What comes of itself to our knowledge, they say, is clear (e.g. that it is day); what does not have a nature such as to fall under our apprehension is unclear once and for all (e.g. that the stars are even in number); what has an evident nature but is made unclear for us for the moment by certain external circumstances is unclear for the moment (e.g. for me now, the city of the Athenians); and what does not have a nature such as to fall under our evident grasp is unclear by nature (e.g. imperceptible pores – for these are never apparent of themselves

but would be deemed to be apprehended, if at all, by way of
something else, e.g. by sweating …).

(*PH* 2.97–99; see *M* 8.145–50)

Things that are clear need no sign. As long as these are restricted
to appearances, Sextus will not object, for in that case there will be
no dispute about them. Similarly, no one bothers to argue that the
number of stars is odd (or even) since this is absolutely and permanently unclear:

> But things unclear for the moment and things unclear by
> nature are apprehended through signs – but not through
> the same signs: things unclear for the moment are appre-
> hended through recollective signs, things unclear by nature
> through indicative signs. … They call a sign recollective if,
> having been observed evidently together with the thing it
> signifies, at the same time as it makes an impression on
> us – and while the other thing remains unclear – it leads
> us to recall the thing which has been observed together
> with it and is not now making an evident impression on us
> (as in the case of smoke and fire). A sign is indicative they
> say, if it signifies that of which it is a sign not by having
> been observed evidently together with the thing it signi-
> fies but from its proper nature and constitution (as bodily
> movements are signs of the soul).
>
> (*PH* 2.99–101; see *M* 8.151–55)

The crucial difference is that indicative signs reveal something that
cannot be immediately grasped. The two objects or events linked by
recollective signs are both potentially observable. Since I can never
experience the soul directly, it can only be revealed by way of an
indicative sign.

Sextus has no problem with recollective signs. They are part and
parcel of our everyday activity, inspired by what Hume later refers
to as our inescapable expectation that the future will resemble the
past.[11] Sextus sees himself as the champion of common sense in

mounting his attack on the dogmatists' private fiction of indicative signs.

One of his central strategies for arguing against both indicative signs and proofs is to derive a contradiction from two features that the dogmatists claim are essential to both. Signs and proofs are both (i) relative to something. Signs are relative to the thing signified, and proofs are relative to the conclusion proved. But, signs and proofs are also both (ii) revelatory.

Now suppose A is a sign of B. On the Stoics' own account of things that are relative, A and B must be apprehended together. For:

> just as what is to the right cannot be apprehended as being to the right of what is to the left before what is to the left has been apprehended … so signs cannot be apprehended as signs of what is signified before what is signified has been apprehended. (PH 2.117)

Sextus' point is that we cannot grasp that A is true and that it is a sign of B without having already grasped that B is true. One might grasp that A is true without thereby grasping that it is a sign of B, but that is beside the point. Consider a red traffic light. In order for me to grasp it as a sign to stop, I must see it at one and the same time as a physical sign and as the command to stop.

However, if A and B must be apprehended simultaneously, A cannot be revelatory of B, because that would require that A be apprehended before B. Otherwise we cannot say that we were led to apprehend B because of A. In other words, for A to reveal the truth of B, there must be a moment in which we apprehend the truth of A followed by a moment in which we apprehend what was previously unclear, namely the truth of B. But again, this cannot happen if we must grasp the truth of what is signified simultaneously with the sign.

The second, more familiar sceptical strategy is to invoke the modes. Some say that indicative signs exist and others deny it:

> Now anyone who says that there are indicative signs will speak either simply and without proof, making a mere

assertion, or else with proof. But if he makes a mere assertion he will be unconvincing, and if he wants to give a proof he will take for granted the matter under investigation. For since proof is said to be a species of sign, then as it is controversial whether there are any signs or not, there will be controversy too as to whether there are any proofs or not – just as, if you are investigating, say, whether there are any animals, you are also investigating whether there are any humans … it is absurd to try to prove what is under investigation through what is equally under investigation or through itself ….

(*PH* 2.121–2)

Any proposed account of criteria, signs or proofs will be disputed. But there appears to be no way to provide a non-arbitrary, or non-question-begging, resolution of such disputes, and we cannot provide an infinite series of justifications. Sextus summarizes the application of the trilemma as follows:

In order for the dispute that has arisen about criteria to be decided, we must possess an agreed criterion through which we can judge it; and in order for us to possess an agreed criterion, the dispute about criteria must already have been decided. Thus the argument falls into the reciprocal mode and the discovery of a criterion is blocked – for we do not allow them to assume a criterion by hypothesis, and if they want to judge the criterion by a criterion we throw them into an infinite regress. (*PH* 2.20)

So it seems we currently possess no means by which to reveal what is not already apparent or cannot become apparent through everyday sorts of practice and observation. Thus dogmatic epistemology is stymied. All of the arguments in support of criteria, signs or proofs are met with equally powerful arguments in opposition.

Conclusion

Pyrrhonian Scepticism is only a challenge to those who believe it is important to resolve these persistent philosophical problems with some non-question-begging arguments that show why one side is rationally preferable. If you do not think this is important, then you will have no motivation to adopt and defend a position. In order for the Pyrrhonist's sceptical challenge to be effective, he must show that you have failed to abide by your own epistemic principles. If you are not committed to these principles, you will not be concerned with any failure to abide by them. But if we accept the challenge, there appears to be little hope of meeting it. The sceptic's arsenal is impressive.

NINE

The (ordinary) life of a Pyrrhonist

The most persistent objection to Pyrrhonian Scepticism is that life is not possible without beliefs. This may be applied to the practice of scepticism as well as ordinary, day-to-day activities. So while the sceptic goes shopping, makes breakfast or argues against dogmatists, she is deluded if she thinks she has no beliefs. According to the objection, all intentional, purposeful action presupposes some sort of belief.

There are two different types of response the sceptic might make, or that we might make on her behalf. First, we can deny that action presupposes belief. If so, the sceptic is able to act without holding any beliefs, and the scope of *epochē* may be unrestricted. Secondly, we can agree that action presupposes belief and claim that this is not a problem because the sceptic has the sort of belief necessary for the relevant action. In this case, the scope of *epochē* is limited: the sceptic does not suspend judgement about *everything*.[1] I shall follow Gail Fine (1996) in referring to these options as the "no-belief view" and the "some-belief view" respectively.[2]

Whether Sextus offers a no-belief view or a some-belief view remains controversial. The versatility of the concept of belief complicates the issue further by allowing for variations within each camp. One attractive hypothesis is that versions of both views appear in Sextus' work, reflecting competing strands in the history of Pyrrhonism. Unfortunately, this would saddle Sextus with two incompatible sceptical practices: one cannot, in practice, believe nothing and something. While I think it is nonetheless likely that both views show up in Sextus' work, I also think the no-belief view makes the stronger appearance. In this chapter I shall argue that the Pyrrhonist's reliance on appearances in her sceptical practice as well as in ordinary and skilful activities commits her to no beliefs.

To believe or not to believe

The equally compelling force of opposed arguments or appearances leads the sceptic to suspend judgement. In order to oppose arguments or appearances, they must refer to the same thing. If it is not the same tower that appears now round and now square, the appearances are not really opposed. Similarly, if two people use a key term, such as justice, to mean different things, they may have no real disagreement. To genuinely disagree with one another we have to be talking about the same things.

Appearances and arguments are easily opposed for the dogmatists in so far as he takes them to refer to, and ideally to reveal, some objective state of affairs. Dogmatists investigate whatever appears to be the case in order to determine whether it really is the case. The sceptic, however, does not investigate what is apparent, but rather what is said about what is apparent (*PH* 1.19–20). What the dogmatist typically says is that some appearance is true for such and such reasons. He is not content to merely say that this is how it seems. Thus the object of sceptical investigation is not the appearance "that *p*", but the appearance "that *p* is true" (*PH* 1.22) and, more precisely, what is said about, and in support of, the appearance that *p* is true. Sextus remarks that the sceptic will merely take the appearance "that *p*" for granted (*PH* 1.9).

The problem is to determine precisely what the sceptic is doing when she takes an appearance for granted. In particular, does she believe what she takes for granted or not? In what follows I will assume the standard analysis of belief: if *S* believes *p*, then *S* assents to the proposition that *p* is true.

If what the sceptic finds objectionable about dogmatism is its insistence that things *are* as they appear in some cases, then the no-belief view is correct. For in that case, the sceptic will never claim that things are as they appear. In other words, she will never assent to any appearance "that *p* is true". Consequently, given the standard analysis of belief, she will never believe that *p*.

The some-belief view and judgemental appearances

On the other hand, if what the sceptic finds objectionable about dogmatism is its insistence that things are as they appear *for the reasons advanced*, then the some-belief view will be correct. For in that case, the sceptic does not object to assenting to the appearance "that *p* is true"; she objects only to assenting on the basis of some rational considerations. So she may believe that *p* is true as long as this belief is not based on reasons; for if it is based on reasons, she will be inclined by her sceptical disposition to argue against it in order to achieve equipollence and be rid of the belief.

Accordingly, the some-belief view emphasizes the fact that Sextus explicitly offers his Pyrrhonian therapy to dogmatists (e.g. *PH* 3.280). The disturbances that scepticism can cure are all bred of dogmatic ambitions to reveal the hidden nature of things. If we leave such matters alone, we will not be disturbed, and we may continue to believe in the manner ordinary people do regarding ordinary things, exclusively on the basis of how they seem without any rational justification. Ordinarily, people do not invoke metaphysical, epistemological or scientific theories to support the belief that the cat is on the mat. And they would probably be at a complete loss if one were to challenge them to provide such weighty support for what they find perfectly evident. Since there appears to be no immediate practical benefit in finding rational support for what already works and is already clear, most people have no interest in doing so. It is only when things break down, contradictions arise or incoherence creeps in that people begin to call into question what is evidently the case. Thus begins the pursuit of truth, leading to the disturbing dogmatic beliefs that Sextus' sceptical therapy is supposed to eliminate.

Sceptically acceptable beliefs, on the other hand, are unavoidable, and ineliminable. I do not choose to believe, for example, that the book is green, that honey tastes sweet or that I am being affected in whatever way I am being affected. Such adventitious beliefs may be what Sextus has in mind when he remarks that sceptics "assent to the feelings forced upon them by appearances – for example, they would not say, when heated or chilled, 'I think I am not heated (or: chilled)'" (*PH* 1.13). What they resist is assenting to any unclear object of scientific investigation. Since what is disputed is whether or not some proposition is true, and specifically whether the reasons advanced in support establish this truth, the sceptic only needs to avoid accepting that something is true *based on rational considerations*.

If Sextus is using the term "assent" in something like the Stoic sense, there must be some proposition closely linked with the feelings forced on the sceptic. Otherwise, the feeling or appearance she receives will not be "saying" anything with which she might agree. And in order to capture the immediate and involuntary nature of the assent, we may think of the appearance she receives as *judgemental*: it will contain or imply the judgement that some proposition articulating the content of the appearance is true. But what is the propositional content of such appearances?

The appearance that the book is green may be articulated by two distinct propositions:

The book is green.
The appearance of the book is green.

The subject of the first proposition is an object in the world: the book. The subject of the second proposition is a mental state: the appearance of the book. This proposition refers to the way one is affected, while the first refers to what is causing the affection.

We should note the difference between what would have to be the case in order for each of these propositions to be true. The first one would be true, on a standard, correspondence theory of truth, just in case the book is green. The second one would be true, again on a correspondence theory, just in case the book appears green. The first proposition corresponds with a fact about the world that is external to the agent while the second proposition corresponds with the mental state one has when the book appears green.

Let us consider each of these in turn. First, does the sceptic believe that the book is green in accordance with the appearance? On at least one occasion, Sextus seems to say that he judges how perceptible things are on the basis of how they appear:

> Nothing is of a nature to be grasped by means of itself; everything is grasped by means of an effect, which is other than what produces it, the thing that appears. For when honey has been brought to me and I have been sweetened, I *guess* that the externally existing honey is sweet, and when fire has been brought to me and I have been warmed, I *take* the condition in me as a sign that the externally existing fire is warm, and the same argument applies in the case of other perceptible things. (*M* 7.365, emphasis added)

By "guessing" that honey is sweet and by "taking" the fire to be warm, Sextus seems to be saying that the sceptic believes these things.

If so, this could help us understand the sense in which Sextus champions ordinary life (*bios*; e.g. *PH* 2.244–6, 2.254, 2.258, 3.235). If we ordinarily take the way things appear to indicate the way they are, the business of ordinary life will be conducted in accordance with judgemental appearances. This applies not only to simple sensations, but also to evaluative judgements and predictions: it seems, and we believe, that hurting innocent people is wrong, that running red lights is dangerous and that a window will shatter when hit by a rock.

Our ability to make accurate predictions is a crucial element of everyday life. As we have seen, Sextus describes this in terms of recollective signs, which "lead us to recall the thing which has been observed together with it and is not now making an evident impression on us (as in the case of smoke and fire)" (*PH* 2.100). A recollective sign may be understood as a judgemental appearance: when I see smoke, I also receive the appearance that there is some fire there. The sceptic will register her tentative belief by saying, "there appears to be a fire". Obviously this is not a matter of actually seeing the fire, but rather it seeming to her that there is some fire causing the smoke.

Of course it remains possible that things are not what they appear to be. The sceptic can easily acknowledge this by holding her beliefs with the appropriate modesty. She only tentatively believes the appearances forced on her and she is entirely open to the possibility that things may not be as they seem. In any case, she is just as ready as any other Pyrrhonist to dispute dogmatic claims about non-evident matters.

While there is more that can be said in support of this view, there are powerful objections to be raised. First, on at least two occasions Sextus says that sceptics affirm nothing about external objects, which he explicitly contrasts with what is apparent and with the way the sceptic feels (*PH* 1.15, 1.208). In reporting how she feels then she is not saying anything about the external objects. And, more generally, Sextus insists that whenever he talks about things he should be understood as talking about how they appear (see especially Sextus' introductory remark at *PH* 1.4).

Secondly, the persistence of the *apraxia* objection strongly suggests that the Sceptics' opponents dug in their heals on precisely this point: action is impossible for one who has no beliefs. If the Sceptics actually claimed to assent to the truth of propositions about the external world implicit in appearances, they would have had a simple and conclusive response: action is possible for us because we have all the ordinary beliefs that everyone else has. But we have no evidence that any Pyrrhonist offered this response. So it seems that at least some Pyrrhonists were recommending a life without belief in the ordinary sense.

Let us turn to the second kind of proposition to which the sceptic might assent. Does the sceptic believe that the appearance of the book is green? If so, her belief is solely about the mental state she is in at that moment and not about the external object that is supposedly the cause of her experience. This may be what Sextus has in mind when he identifies passive and unwilled feelings as the standard according to which the sceptic guides her actions (*PH* 1.22, 1.13). As with the first version of this view, the appearance that the book is green carries with it a judgement – but in this case, it is the judgement that the book appears green, or that one is affected greenly. We may apply this interpretation to the sceptic's reliance on recollective signs as well. Having observed a scar, she says that a wound was inflicted, or "there appears to have been a wound here". She might mean that she cannot help but to think of wounds when she sees scars. If so, she is simply reporting how the observation affects her. Similarly, we may say that smoke serves as a sign only in drawing the mind on to expect another sort of appearance.

An advantage of this version of the some-belief view is that it allows us to explain why the Sceptics' opponents continued to raise the spectre of *apraxia*. If the objection is that action requires belief about external objects, it will continue to apply to those who claim not to have such beliefs. This view also allows us to understand how the sceptical reply might go. Sextus would be claiming that although the sceptic lacks beliefs about external objects, she nonetheless has beliefs (about her own mental states) that are sufficient for action.

Another advantage is that it reveals just how strange a character the sceptic is. This is fitting, since Sextus sometimes presents himself as the champion of scepticism in opposition to ordinary life as well as dogmatism. Sceptics are indifferent to the opinion of the many (*M* 1.5); indeed, Pyrrho is a model of sceptical eccentricity. More importantly, ordinary people are only marginally less likely to be disturbed than philosophers (e.g. *PH* 1.30). Interminable controversy is not the exclusive domain of intellectuals (*PH* 1.165). Ordinary people disagree about: which gods exist; whether health, wealth or wisdom is the greatest good (*M* 11.49), unless it is sex, gluttony, drunkenness or gambling (*PH* 3.180); and even whether apparent things are intelligible or perceptible (*M* 8.355). The point is that the divide between ordinary people and dogmatists is not nearly as wide as the one between them and the Sceptics. The Sceptic's refusal to believe anything about external objects helps to explain this divide.

There is, however, a fundamental problem with this view. When Sextus discusses the question of whether sceptics hold beliefs, he remarks that "if you hold beliefs, then you posit as real the things you are said to hold beliefs about" (*PH* 1.14). It follows immediately that if the sceptic holds beliefs about her mental states, she posits mental states as real. But clearly the sceptic should avoid such dogmatic commitments.

Mental states are theoretical entities that are hotly disputed by philosophers. Understood as objective features of the world, about which propositions may be true or false, they are not identical to perceptual awareness, understood from the first-person perspective. While some deny the very existence of mental states, no one sincerely denies that she feels as she does. So if the belief that she is being perceptually sweetened commits the sceptic to the existence of mental states (or some other supposedly real entity corresponding to the propositional content of her belief) then she should not have such beliefs.

A similar problem arises if we ask the some-belief sceptic why she believes she is perceptually sweetened when she tastes honey. There are two kinds of response she can make, neither of which are sceptically suitable. Clearly she will not respond with an account of the rational grounds in support of her belief; as we have seen, she would only do that in order to balance the psychological force of the considerations in support of the opposing view. But neither should she offer a purely causal account showing how she could not help believing as she does. If she appeals to the supposed fact that she could not resist believing that the honey appears sweet, she will once again move beyond what is immediately apparent and stray into the dogmatic territory of unclear and disputed matters.

The no-belief view and phenomenological appearances

On the other hand, if the sceptic has no beliefs she will not have to answer any questions about why she believes as she does. In order to see how this is possible we will need to articulate a non-cognitive, *phenomenological* view of appearances. According to this view, appearances contain or imply no propositions either about external objects or even about mental states. When the sceptic reports on the apparent sweetness of honey, she is only telling us about the way things are currently affecting her. She will be using language not to express some fact but rather simply to convey how she is feeling. It will still be possible to articulate some proposition to correspond to the content of her feeling. But if the phenomenological account is correct, it is not necessary for her to do so. Such articulation is a cognitive operation that is distinct from being passively affected by the way things appear. If she articulates the proposition and assents to it she will have moved beyond what is evident and taken a stand on what is really the case, regardless of whether she has any rational grounds for that stand. But again, such a step is not necessary; simple organisms, for example, are affected by the world without articulating any propositional content.

If the phenomenological view of appearances is correct, no beliefs are unavoidable and inelimenable, and no belief is immune from sceptical challenges. It will still be the case that I cannot help feeling pain when I do or tasting sweetness when I do, but I am never compelled to believe anything *about* these feelings. On the phenomenological view, appearances do not come bundled with judgements. Once I take the cognitive attitude that some part of the world is determinately one way rather than another, that is, that p is true, I must acknowledge the possibility that the contradictory claim not-p is true. And once these propositions have been opposed, I will be led by the sceptic to see, regardless of whether I currently have any rational grounds for my belief that p, that there is as much to be said in support of the one as for the other.

To avoid such problems, the Pyrrhonist should hold no beliefs. The phenomenological account of appearance shows how she may avoid doing so while nonetheless passively acquiescing, that is, not resisting, the natural push and pull of appearances.

This view enjoys the advantages I have attributed to the last, some-belief, interpretation: it shows just how strange a character the Pyrrhonist is; it explains the persistence of the *apraxia* objection; and it preserves the radical nature of Pyrrhonism. It also preserves the apparently universal reach of the Pyrrhonist's arguments, and allows us to take Sextus at his word when he repeatedly insists that the sceptic suspends judgement about everything.

External world scepticism

To consistently maintain this view, we will have to admit that radical scepticism challenges beliefs about the very existence of the external world, along with things such as mental states and causal laws. At M 7.366, Sextus argues that *all* external things are unclear and unknown to us. If we interpret this quite broadly it will include not only the properties of things, but also their very existence.[3] If the external world is permanently and irrevocably unclear, what entitles us to think that it exists in the first place?

Sextus attributes to the Cyrenaics the view that everyone is infallible with respect to the way things affect them. One cannot be mistaken that she is affected greenly, or sweetly, but it is impossible to ever know whether the cause of the affection is green or sweet:[4] "For the effect that happens in us reveals to us nothing more than itself. Hence … only the effect is apparent to us; the external thing productive of the effect is perhaps a being, but it is not apparent to us" (M 7.194). Sextus differentiates the sceptic from the Cyrenaic on precisely this key point: "We suspend judgment (as far as the argument goes) about external existing things, while the Cyrenaics assert that they have an inapprehensible nature" (*PH* 1.215). As Fine (1996: 281) points out, we may take the sceptic here to be suspending judgement only about the essential properties of things, or more broadly about whether they even exist.

The sceptic's *epochē* regarding the external world poses no particular problem provided we remember that it is not the same as Cartesian doubt. The Pyrrhonist does not hypothetically entertain, or worry about, the possibility that nothing exists except her mental states. Nor does she invoke the distinction between appearance and reality in order to claim that appearances reveal only themselves, as the Cyrenaics do. It may be the case that from the third-person perspective, we need some distinction between reality and appearance to make sense of the very idea of phenomenological, or even judgemental, appearances. But the sceptic does not need to make sense out of the ontological status of the psychological entity she is assenting to. She does not, and need not, take a position on whether the phenomenological or judgemental view of appearance is the right one. Being moved by the way things appear requires no commitment to the nature of mental states, or the mechanics of human perception and behaviour, as long as she does not take it to be true that she is so affected.

So, on one hand, the Pyrrhonist will not be sceptical about the existence of the external world in so far as that presupposes an ontological distinction between appearance and reality. External world scepticism, understood as solipsism, denies that certain kinds of entities exist: mind-independent objects and agents. It is a kind of negative dogmatism. By contrast, the Pyrrhonist will suspend judgement about whether some object really exists in so far as real existence is supposed to be something beyond what is apparent.

But even if we grant that the sceptic can navigate through the world by relying on phenomenological appearances, it is not so easy to see how she can conduct her argumentative practice without holding any beliefs. And even if we can show that the sceptic is indeed able to do everything she claims to be able to do without any beliefs, we should still wonder whether such a life is even remotely desirable. How, for example, can the sceptic ever acquire any moral virtues without evaluative commitments? How can she develop any practical skills? And how can she learn anything if she refuses to believe?

The fourfold observances

In order to answer these questions, and further develop the no-belief view, we shall examine Sextus' fourfold observances:

> Attending to what is apparent, we live in accordance with everyday observances, without holding opinions – for we

are not able to be utterly inactive. These everyday observances seem to be fourfold, and to consist in [i] guidance by nature, [ii] necessitation by feelings, [iii] handing down of laws and customs, and [iv] teaching of kinds of expertise. By nature's guidance we are naturally capable of perceiving and thinking. By the necessitation of feelings, hunger conducts us to food and thirst to drink. By the handing down of customs and laws, we accept, from an everyday point of view, that piety is good and impiety bad. By teaching of kinds of expertise we are not inactive in those which we accept.

(PH 1.23–4)

It is possible to interpret these observances as action in accordance with the tentative, sorts of beliefs countenanced on the some-belief views. We could say that someone seeks food because he feels, and thus believes, he is hungry. And we could say that someone obeys the laws because it seems to him, and thus he believes, it is right or at least prudential to do so.

On the other hand, it is also possible to interpret these observances as action in accordance with the sceptic's dispositions, without appealing to any beliefs. The plausibility of such interpretations, to be developed below, along with the objections to the some-belief view outlined above, should weigh in favour of the no-belief view.

Sceptical assent and pathological detachment: (i) nature's guidance and (ii) the necessitation of feelings

The feeling of thirst leads us to seek something to drink and hunger to food, just as pain leads a dog to remove the thorn from its paw (*PH* 1.238). The necessity is just a matter of natural reflex. Clearly a dog does not need beliefs about thorns and pain to behave this way. And similarly, one does not need beliefs about food and drink to seek them out.

Sextus' examples of the necessitation of feeling all deal with actions we have in common with non-rational animals. Such actions are rooted in our natures: a dog does not need to be trained to favour an injured leg, nor do human beings need to be taught to seek food and shelter. Similarly, we do not need to be taught to perceive sensible qualities; by our nature we are able to see the colour white, to taste sweet or to feel heat (*M* 8.203).

Obviously we are far more complex than this. In accordance with the first observance, our nature guides us not only to perceive, but also to think. And here we confront a problem: how can we continue to suspend judgement while nature guides us to think? Belief appears to be an essential part of thinking, both as cause and as effect. Thinking leads us to believe some things and reject others. And beliefs in turn inspire thought. To sever the connection between thinking and believing seems to undermine both.

The sceptic does not need to sever this connection, however, since it is not necessary to think about one's *own* beliefs to be thinking. One may have all sorts of thoughts about what others believe. I might reflect on the beliefs of Chaldean astrologers without accepting any of those odd claims myself. Merely thinking about these things does not necessarily entail belief – again on the standard view of belief – as long as I do not have the additional thought that the astrological claims are true or false. Furthermore, the sceptic will not accept that the purpose of thinking is to improve one's stock of beliefs. She will have no beliefs about why we think, or why we should think; she merely finds herself capable of thought, just as she finds herself capable of perception. But being aware of the flow of thoughts does not require her to commit to the truth or falsity of any of them; hence sceptical thinking occurs without believing.

Even granting this response, there is still one problematic difference between thinking and perceiving. It makes sense to say, "It seems to me that there is a puddle of water on the road, but I suspend judgement as to whether it is really there". In this and other familiar scenarios, we suffer no cognitive dissonance in entertaining a perception without assenting to it. But the same analysis does not seem to hold for thinking, or for statements of how things seem to us intellectually.[5]

Sextus insists that such intellectual seemings should be understood merely as feelings rather than positive assertions. Once again he is only reporting how he is currently affected, this time by the arguments:

> When Sceptics say "I determine nothing", what they say is this: "I now feel in such a way as neither to posit dogmatically nor to reject any of the things falling under this investigation". When they say this they are saying what is apparent to them about the subject proposed – not dogmatically making a confident assertion, but describing and reporting how they feel.   (*PH* 1.197; see also 1.7, 15, 193, 198, 200)

These passages all refer to a specifically intellectual feeling, which leads the sceptic to suspend judgement, or rather prevents her from making a judgement. Consider the Pyrrhonist's remark that it seems to me that opposed to every account is an equally powerful one, but I suspend judgement as to whether this is really the case (*PH* 1.202–5).

How can that be? How can it seem to the sceptic that, for example, honesty is the best policy while she nonetheless suspends judgement about whether it is the best policy? What can the seeming amount to in such cases if not believing? More to the point, how can such assertions as "I determine nothing" and "opposed to every claim is an equally powerful one" guide the sceptic's argumentative practice unless she believes them?

According to this objection, in order for me to truthfully deny that I believe what seems to be the case, I would have to be schizophrenic. I would literally have to be of two minds: it could then seem to one of my minds that honesty is the best policy, and to another of my minds that I have no belief on the matter since the arguments for and against are equally balanced. If so the sceptic can continue to suspend judgement about what seems, intellectually, to be the case only at the cost of a pathological detachment from her own mental states. Tranquillity would come at the cost of serious mental illness. So while it might be possible to carry on that way, no one in his right mind would.

We may try to meet this objection, on behalf of the sceptic, by appealing once again to phenomenological appearances and intellectual dispositions. The objection arises from the assumption that when it seems (intellectually) to me that *p*, I represent this as *my appearance*. So when it appears to me that honesty is the best policy I am not merely disposed to honest behaviour, I am also consciously aware of the fact that I am so disposed, perhaps by articulating the proposition corresponding to the appearance. If so, the judgemental view of appearances has crept into the account. For now, when the sceptic acknowledges the intellectual appearance that honesty is the best policy, she also assents to the fact that she is cognitively disposed in this way.

But the sceptic may be caught up in the flow of thoughts to such an extent that she does not become aware of any of these intellectual appearances as her own. This is a familiar experience: when we are totally engaged in some project, all we are aware of are the thoughts themselves, and not our rational or conscious relation to those thoughts. The conscious agent becomes wholly engrossed in the activity.

We can find this line of thought in the story about the painter Apelles (*PH* 1.28; see Chapter 7). As long as he struggles to get the desired effect of foam on the horse's mouth, he is frustrated. The dogmatic use of reason similarly leads to frustration, while the sceptical practice yields tranquillity. What Apelles and the sceptic have in common is that they get their desired results in unexpected ways; success comes on its own, indirectly. This suggests a similarity with Zen meditation. Consciously struggling to clear the mind is counterproductive. Success only comes by way of a different sort of effort. Rather than actively striving, we must simply allow the desired result to occur. This is not a matter of completely giving up, but rather putting oneself in the right condition to allow the desired result to occur. And that in turn requires first developing the right sorts of dispositions through practice.

If the Pyrrhonist suspends judgement in response to an argument that she has not yet managed to counterbalance, she need not consciously invoke the principle that opposed to every account is an equally powerful one. The accomplished sceptic will have no need to refer to such principles, just as a grandmaster would never interrupt his game to consult a rulebook. When Sextus discusses the sceptical phrases, he offers them as *descriptions* of sceptical practice from the outside, as it were.

This solution shows how it can seem to the sceptic that *p*, without her believing that *p*. Rather than radically dissociating herself from her own mental states, she will be totally engrossed in them. Indeed, the very notion of dissociation presupposes that the agent distances herself under one description from her self under a different description; and that in turn requires at least implicitly that she identify the relevant mental state as her own. If this is correct, it emphasizes again just how extraordinary the sceptic's mental life will be while still allowing for what looks like ordinary behaviour.

Sceptical virtue: (iii) laws and customs

Another serious objection to the no-belief view targets the sceptic's moral character. Many people find a lack of moral conviction to be highly suspect; it suggests a frightening degree of flexibility. Aristocles raises this spectre when he asks us to consider:

> What sort of citizen or judge or adviser or friend would he [the sceptic] be? What sort of person in general would he be? What evil thing would he not dare to do, thinking that nothing is really evil or shameful, just or unjust? One can't even say that the sceptics are afraid of laws and penalties. How could they be when they are, as they claim, unaffected and tranquil? (*Praep. Ev.* 14.18.18)

According to this objection, which we have already encountered many times, the sceptic is not only incapable of virtuous action, she is more likely to behave in vicious ways. She will have no moral beliefs to guide her. She will be unable and unwilling to justify any of her actions, or even her motivations and intentions. She might still try to prevent innocent suffering, but not because she believes it is bad. Then again, she might just as well inflict innocent suffering since she does not believe it is bad.

But Sextus claims that the sceptic is not only able to live, but to live correctly, "where correctly is understood not only with regard to virtue but more generally" (*PH* 1.17). It is crucial to point out that Sextus says only that the sceptic *is able* to live correctly, not that she *will*. In response to the objection, then, I will explain how it is possible for the sceptic to live virtuously; in other words, I will explain the kind of virtue that is compatible with the sceptic's lack of moral conviction.

To this end, we shall consider the sceptic's brand of piety. Sextus remarks that from an everyday point of view the sceptic deems piety to be good and impiety bad (*PH* 1.24, quoted above). And, "following ordinary life without opinions, we say that there are gods and we are pious towards the gods and say that they are provident" (*PH* 3.2). The sceptic even engages in religious ceremony, performing acts that contribute to the reverence and worship of the gods (*M* 9.49).

Even so, Sextus is keenly aware of the radical differences among religious rituals: some throw the dead for the fishes or dogs or vultures to eat, others pelt the body with stones until it is completely covered, and some even sacrifice people over sixty and eat them themselves. The sceptic's awareness of these apparently undecidable disputes does nothing to prevent her from participating in her religion's rituals. Having no belief as to whether they are any better or worse, more or less pleasing to the gods, she simply carries on.

Piety, like the other virtues, seems to require the proper intentional state. If the sceptic has no belief about whether God exists or not, it is hard to see what significance there could be in her reverence. She might just as well be preparing a meal, or spinning aimlessly in circles. Her conformity to local religious custom appears to be a caricature of piety.

The charge that the sceptic's piety is hypocritical or insincere, however, is not fair. In engaging in religious rituals, the sceptic is not trying to advance her own self-interest, or deceive anyone about her intentions. Nor is she trying to belittle her fellow worshippers. Such insincerity or duplicity would require her to conceal her real motives and beliefs; but she has nothing to conceal.

Nevertheless, sceptical piety may still seem to be an unintentional parody of the genuine article. This impression is unavoidable from the dogmatic believer's standpoint. If genuine piety requires having the right theological beliefs, then the sceptic cannot be pious. But from the sceptic's perspective there is really very little separating her religious observances from the dogmatic believer's. The dogmatist will have to agree that his sincere piety is based not just on any old belief, but rather on justified belief. If true piety were simply a matter of believing *something* about god, we would have to contend with an embarrassing wealth of incompatible pieties.[6]

But it seems to the sceptic that no one is able to justify the beliefs that might be supposed to be essential to genuine piety. If so, all that really differentiates the pious sceptic from the pious dogmatist is that the one acts on the basis of unjustified beliefs (which he takes to be justified), while the other acts in accordance with the fourfold observances and habitual dispositions. All piety is thus reduced to certain kinds of conventional behaviour along with the relevant dispositions. Belief or lack of belief is no longer essential.

Moral and political conformism

Morality often requires us to go against conventional norms. Nearly all of us would like to think that we would not have condoned slavery in the early nineteenth century, or the burning of "witches" in the seventeenth century. Such speculations are practically worthless in so far as we would not be the same people under such radically different conditions. Nonetheless, it is worth trying to understand what motivates people to do such things. A large part of their justification, or at least explanation, would probably have been in terms of accepted customs and conventions. Our willingness to obey authority, whether in the person of white-coated scientists, charismatic leaders or accepted conventions, is the dark side of our social nature. Such conformism is the breeding ground for what Hannah Arendt has aptly named the banality of evil. Viciousness can come to seem quite ordinary and acceptable given the right conditions.

An important part of the dogmatic attitude towards reason is the notion that the autonomous application of critical reason is the most potent antidote to this unfortunate tendency. The proper use of reason can improve not only our characters as individuals, but also the character of a people or society. The few brave individuals who first stood up to past injustices were able to see how unfair and ultimately irrational these accepted practices are. An initial step in righting these wrongs is to expose the flaws in the arguments that are supposed to warrant unjust actions.

While the sceptic would be happy to deconstruct such arguments, she would not do so for the sake of establishing the contradictory conclusion. In fact, it seems she would be willing to argue both for and against the injustice of slavery, for example. As a result she neither believes nor disbelieves that slavery is unjust, that it is wrong to cause innocent suffering, that all human beings deserve to be treated the same under the law, or any other moral proposition that most of us find indisputably true.

Furthermore, she neither believes nor disbelieves that careful rational scrutiny of our social and political institutions will produce any improvements. Indeed, in so far as the fundamental issue of what counts as an improvement is itself disputed, the sceptic suspends judgement on this point as well. Lacking any belief about how to make the world a better place is hardly a recipe for social activism, or even for self-improvement.

The sceptic's inability to denounce even such obviously unjust institutions as slavery is objectionable. But it does not follow from this either that she would or would not condone slavery in practice. When it comes to combating social injustice, public proclamations are usually far less effective than action. The sceptic might work just as hard as a dogmatist in seeking an end to slavery, although she will be far less likely to do so if she happens to be born into a family of slave-traders in the eighteenth century. On the other hand, it is also unlikely that a dogmatist born into a family of slave-traders would be an abolitionist. In either case, the decisive factor would be an unusual event, or series of events, that gives rise to the moral conviction that slavery is unjust (for the dogmatist) or to the disposition to treat enslaved people with the same consideration and respect that every other human being deserves (for the sceptic).

In general, the best response to the complacency objection is to show that the sceptic is not in fact more easily corrupted or more willing to commit moral atrocities than those who have firm convictions.

Suppose, for example, a tyrant has demanded that you must either help seize and kill an innocent person or be killed yourself. Sextus mentions this example in order to combat the objection that the sceptic's choice will reveal her true moral commitments (*M* 11.164–6; see DL 9.108). His response is simply that the sceptic acts in accordance with ancestral laws and customs without taking a stand on whether the action is really, in its nature, morally good or bad.

Although Sextus does not draw this point from the tyrant example, we should note that there is no obviously correct solution available to anyone. We can find arguments to support either course of action, but in the end there may simply be no good choice, there might not even be a lesser of two evils. If there are such genuine moral dilemmas, reason will not help us out. We must simply choose and then deal with the consequences. Sextus claims the sceptic will be able to bear these harsh realities more easily than the dogmatist who feels that he must rationally determine the proper course. Even if the dogmatist convinces himself that he has made the morally better choice, he will probably suffer painful doubts on future reflection.

From the sceptic's perspective, dilemmas are not exceptional; any situation requiring a moral judgement presents us with a rationally irresolvable problem, or at least this has always been the sceptic's experience. Reason fails us not only when tyrants make unacceptable demands but whenever we have to choose a course of action with significant consequences. If Sextus is right about our inability (so far) to rationally justify even the most seemingly obvious moral principles, then those with moral convictions are really no better off than the sceptic. The same is true with respect to our ability to revise our priorities or make progress towards becoming virtuous. If moral progress presupposes the efficacy of reason in determining the proper ends, and if the sceptic's attack on rational justification is successful, we can never be confident that we are moving in the right direction.

Teaching and learning: (iv) technical expertise
Sextus does, however, rely on a distinction between what is beneficial and harmful in everyday life. This distinction arises from our

ordinary experience of the world. Everyone agrees that what is good is beneficial. And even though we disagree vehemently about the nature of the good, there is a great deal of consensus that certain arts or kinds of expertise (*technē*) are beneficial. The cobbler's art provides us with shoes (*M* 1.294), navigation makes international commerce possible (*M* 1.51), herdsmen keep our flocks safe (*M* 2.20), astronomy predicts the weather (*M* 5.2; at least, its meteorological successor does), music is able to distract us from unpleasant tasks and make them easier to perform (*M* 6.21), and Sextus' own technical expertise, medicine, heals the sick (*M* 2.49).

In so far as there are no disputes about the utility of good shoes, we may take the beneficial nature of the cobbler's art as evident. For the most part, everyone would rather have good shoes, safe transportation, accurate weather predictions, pleasantly distracting music and good health than their opposites. It is only when we see these benefits as properly modest that we find consensus. Everyone agrees that well-made shoes are good for walking and protecting the feet, navigation is good for getting somewhere safely and knowing what the weather is likely to be is good for planning one's day, and so on. So what is harmful and beneficial in everyday life is a matter of what we all immediately recognize as *instrumentally* good or bad. Experience is enough to show us that well-made products and expert services are good for accomplishing our further ends.

Plato captures this modest spirit in his reflections on the skilful navigator's attitude towards his art (*Gorg.* 511d–512a). Having safely transported his passengers, along with their possessions, it is not clear to the navigator whether he has really benefited them, that is, whether they are better off as a result of having been transported safely. After all, the passengers are no different with respect to body or soul than when the journey began. The navigator has done them a valuable service, but he refuses to speculate as to whether the change of location is beneficial in some deep, or non-evident, manner. For all the modest navigator knows, some passengers may have been better off if their ship had not come in.

By contrast, the masters of the liberal arts that Sextus targets for refutation in *M* 1–6, exhibit an arrogance proportional to the disutility of their "art". Chaldean astrologers, for example, adorn themselves with important titles and try to support their predictions on the basis of elaborate theories linking the motion of the stars to what happens on earth (M 5). Some musicians claim their art is necessary for happiness since it harmonizes the soul and produces the proper dispositions (M 6). Grammarians also claim their art is necessary for happiness since only they can provide the correct interpretations of the wise sayings of the poets (M 1.270–71). And the claims of Pythagorean arithmeticians are inherently immodest, if not outrageous: the number ten, being the result of adding one, two, three and four, is the most perfect number and the source of the eternal roots of nature since the account of the structure of all things lies within it (M 4.3).

The paradigm for all of these is the expertise in living, promoted most enthusiastically by the Stoics. The good, the bad and indifferent are the basic concepts applied by practitioners of this art. But since, Sextus claims, he has shown that these concepts are incoherent, and thus correspond to nothing real, the art of living is unreal as well (PH 3.239; M 11.168–80). But we must remember that these refutations are offered to counterbalance the Stoic arguments in support. The proper sceptical attitude is to neither believe nor disbelieve that there is an art of living.

We find the same approach in his arguments against the liberal arts. For example, Sextus argues that points, lines and planes do not exist since we cannot conceive of the geometers' definitions (e.g. M 3.29–30). A point is supposed to be a sign without dimensions, and line is length without breadth. But we really have no idea what we are talking about when we utter these words: the point I can conceive has dimensions and the line I can conceive has breadth.[7] If the geometers' definitions fail to identify anything that really exists, then their expertise is unreal as well. Counterbalancing such considerations against the geometers' reasons in support of their expertise should lead us to suspend judgement.

The sceptic's basic argument against all forms of immodest expertise is that they lack the epistemic foundations they claim to have; note that the modest forms do not claim any such foundations. So we can see Sextus' attack on the liberal arts as an extension of his general sceptical agenda. In fact, in his introductory remarks, he claims that the sceptic initially undertakes the study of the liberal arts just as he did philosophy with the desire to discover the truth (*M* 1.6). But he is similarly frustrated and discovers only equipollent conflict and dispute. His study of the liberal arts thus ends like his study of philosophy, at least for the time being, in *epochē*.

Given this context, we should interpret all of his seemingly dogmatic claims that such-and-such an art does not exist as one side of the equipollent conflict. This interpretation, however, is complicated by Sextus' appropriation of arguments from Epicurus, who "took the position that the liberal arts are no help in perfecting wisdom" (*M* 1.1). What motivates Epicurus' arguments is his own positive conception of wisdom. Not sharing this conception, Sextus can only retail these arguments to combat the professors' claim that their arts are beneficial if not essential for attaining virtue and happiness.

Nevertheless, Sextus' reliance on both Epicurus and previous Sceptics gives the impression of two discordant voices in *M* 1–6 (Barnes 1988). According to the first, moderate, Epicurean voice, some arts are useless and others are useful. The useful studies are based on everyday observation and make no pretence of uncovering the hidden nature of things. According to the second, radically sceptical, voice, there are no arts at all; rather, we must suspend judgement regarding the existence of the arts, whether useful or useless.

But as long as the sceptical practitioner of useful arts refuses to justify his practice by appealing to some theory, nothing prevents him from acknowledging and advertising his expertise. He does not need to believe anything about the objects and principles of his art. We do not need a theory of numbers in order to count them, or of lines and shapes in order to design and build things, or of musical notes and temporal intervals in order to play an instrument. The sceptic may learn and practise any art in so far as it is merely a collection and arrangement of observed regularities, that is, recollective rather than indicative signs (*PH* 2.102; *M* 8.156–58). In doing so, he will make use of the two sorts of criteria of action that Sextus approves of: the senses, and technical devices such as ruler and compass (*PH* 2.14–15). All of this can be brought under the heading of the fourth type of observance: the teaching (and learning) of kinds of expertise.

The sort of teaching and learning available to the sceptic cannot be a matter of transferring true beliefs from teacher to student. It is a matter of learning how to do something rather than learning that something is true, like an apprentice imitating the master.[8]

The sceptic physician

The sceptic who studies medicine, for example, will not end up with medical knowledge, but rather a medical disposition (see *M* 11.188, 255). Although Sextus grants that both the common person and the skilled physician perform actions that restore health, the physician does so in an observably medical fashion: quickly, painlessly and in an orderly manner (*M* 11.204). The disposition from which these actions arise is not itself observable, but the features that differentiate his actions from the ordinary person's are. So we may distinguish the expert from the non-expert in the same way that ordinary people do: on the basis of their actions.

Furthermore, the sceptic physician performs these skilful actions without any reference to unobservable, theoretical features of human physiology. In fact, he will not provide any sort of causal explanation for the patient's condition. Instead, he will be guided exclusively by the phenomena, that is, his observation of events and conditions.

This is the approach taken by medical empiricists. Empiricism arose in response to the apparent failure of rationalist theories about physiology and the hidden causes of illness. None of the theories produced significantly better results and, like the Sceptics, the empiricists doubted that these theoretical disputes could be resolved. According to this view, medical theories provide no better guidance than experience: they are practically useless.

The rationalists countered, arguing that experience by itself cannot account for observed regularities. We have to rely on reason to discern the underlying principles and structures that regulate the body. So reason is necessary to establish and expand medical knowledge. But according to Galen, the dispute gradually became irrel-

THE (ORDINARY) LIFE OF A PYRRHONIST

evant, at least from a practical standpoint, since both rationalist and empiricist physicians tended to agree on the appropriate treatment. In the end they merely disagreed about how the correct diagnoses and prescriptions are arrived at (Walzer & Frede 1985).

Sextus' name indicates that he was a member of the empiricist school. And although there is a striking similarity with Pyrrhonian Scepticism, Sextus insists that they are not the same in so far as empiricists make affirmations about the inapprehensibility of unclear matters (*PH* 1.236). In other words, they are negatively dogmatic in insisting that the rationalists could not possibly get the knowledge they aimed at. The proper sceptical attitude is to suspend judgement as to whether the body is composed of theoretical entities such as atoms and invisible pores and as to whether we could ever know this.

Rather than reading this as a complete abandonment of empiricism, it is more likely that Sextus is only criticizing one version of empiricism. In responding to the rationalists, some empiricists probably presented their side as an alternative epistemological theory, one that relies dogmatically on experience as a kind of justification. But since Sextus argues against all forms of justification, experience is no more acceptable than reason. The objectionable kind of empiricism would be both negatively dogmatic in denying the rationalists' claims, and positively dogmatic in supporting their own.

What the sceptic needs is not a theory to underwrite his expertise, but rather an explanation of how he is able to learn and practice it without unwittingly acquiring dogmatic beliefs. We can see this in Sextus' praise for a third school, methodism (*PH* 1.236, 238). In agreement with empiricism, the methodists rejected the dogmatic view that we must rely on unobservable, theoretical entities in searching for and justifying medical knowledge. However, they disagree with empiricism in so far as it leads to the negatively dogmatic conclusion that we can never uncover the hidden causes and underlying natures of things relating to health and disease. In contrast to both, methodists considered irrelevant the causal history of the disease along with facts about the patient's age, habits and previous condition. Direct observation of the patient's current condition is sufficient to indicate the proper treatment (Edelstein 1967).

Sextus compares the methodist's practice to the second observance: necessitation of feelings. Being chilled, we feel compelled to seek warmth; so too when the sceptic physician observes that part of the body is constricted, he will try to loosen or expand it (*PH* 1.238). In so far as such treatments restore and preserve health, he will continue to use them. The idea is that expertise is a disposition to respond in appropriate and effective ways. Just as nature gives us the disposition to seek warmth when cold, experience that is properly informed by a desire to heal gives us medical expertise.

One last point in favour of methodism is that it reduced the extensive and costly course of medical training to six months. This effectively opened up the field of medicine to a much wider stratum of society while undermining the notion that medicine is an extremely difficult and abstruse art. In his role as champion of ordinary life, Sextus may well have been attracted by this attempt to reveal the pretensions of medical theories. But despite his sympathy for methodism, Sextus would not have adopted it as the right theory, because, again, the sceptic has no need for theories, and in fact rejects them all.

The sceptic's philanthropy

There is no difference in kind between sceptical philosophy and sceptical medicine. They are both therapeutic practices developed over time on the basis of experience. They are both aimed at relieving the patient of physical disease or mental disturbance on the basis of observable conditions of the body or mind. The former are revealed to the physician by direct observation and the latter are revealed to the sceptic by means of the patient's statement of his beliefs and the kinds of rational considerations he finds persuasive. Both of these practices proceed from developed dispositions but without any reference to guiding beliefs, principles or rational judgements. So Sextus' philanthropy may be revealed either through his attempt to cure the conceit and rashness of the dogmatists (*PH* 3.280), or through his attempt to alleviate the physical suffering of his patients.

But there is at least one important disanalogy that can serve as an objection to the sceptic's dialectical practice. The philosophical dogmatist is, typically, not like a medical patient seeking help from a physician. The patient is often quite sure he has a problem and he trusts that his physician can help. These two become engaged in the same project, and work together to accomplish their shared goal. The dogmatist, by contrast, will probably see the sceptic as the one with the problem. At the very least, he will be reluctant to concede to the sceptic's arguments. So, from a psychological standpoint, the sceptic's benevolence will probably be met with resistance, if not hostility. This will be exacerbated if the dogmatist understands that they are engaged in two quite different projects. The sceptic aims at eliminating beliefs, the dogmatist at acquiring or improving them.

Alternatively, we might say that from the sceptical perspective the dogmatist is like a mental patient who is not aware that he needs therapy. This preserves the medical analogy, but it also reveals just how insulting the sceptic's view is from the dogmatist's perspective. It also emphasizes the fact that they are engaged in very different projects, arising from very different attitudes towards reason.

Although the Pyrrhonist sees himself as a philanthropist, the dogmatist, if aware of what the sceptic is up to, will see him as a duplicitous sneak. The dogmatist is engaged in a project that the sceptic is trying to get him to give up. This makes for an odd relationship; the dogmatist might mistakenly think he is arguing against his opponent, and trying to get her to see the rational superiority of his position, but his sceptical opponent has no position to defend, and does not feel bound by the same rational, normative principles.

I can think of no response that would satisfy the dogmatist on this point. As long as he is engaged in the project of seeking the most rationally defensible view, he will find the sceptic's offer of therapy insulting: indeed, he should. But from the sceptic's perspective, this is just what we would expect from "mad" dogmatists who have been captivated by the alluring promise of reason.

But even if the dogmatist rejects the offer of therapy, he will have a strong incentive to engage the sceptic in argument. He does not need to see the proceedings as therapeutic. He should see it, in accordance with his acceptance of the obligations of rational agency, as an opportunity to put his position to the test. Refusing to debate the sceptic, the dogmatist abandons his own rational standards.

Conclusion

Unlike ordinary people, the sceptic has no beliefs. It is hard to imagine what such a life would be like from the inside. However, I have argued that it can be coherently described and defended from the outside.

If Sextus' self-purging attack on rationality is successful, we must conclude that none of the things we typically think of as constituting progress are the fruit of reason. Every virtuous action, every technically skilful action, and every socially beneficial action proceeds from certain sorts of dispositions. And we have no good grounds on which to think reason, as employed by epistemically optimistic dogmatists, is better able to produce these dispositions than environmental or other non-rational forces. Consequently, we are no better off than the sceptic with regard to our ability to live happy, fulfilling and even virtuous lives. And as long as we are unable to meet the sceptical challenge, we are far more prone to suffer unnecessary disturbances.

Notes

1. Introduction

1. The distinction between ancient and modern forms of scepticism is a very controversial topic. M. F. Burnyeat, "The Sceptic in his Place and Time", in *Philosophy in History: Essays on the Historiography of Philosophy*, R. Rorty, J. B. Schneewind & Q. Skinner (eds), 225–54 (Cambridge: Cambridge University Press, 1984) introduces and explores the metaphor of insulation to describe the practice of separating philosophical arguments and their conclusions from the activity of ordinary life. See also J. Annas, "Doing Without Objective Values: Ancient and Modern Strategies", in *The Norms of Nature: Studies in Hellenistic Ethics*, M. Schofield & G. Striker (eds), 3–29 (Cambridge: Cambridge University Press, 1986) and "Scepticism, Old and New", in *Rationality in Greek Thought*. M. Frede & G. Striker (eds), 239–54 (Oxford: Oxford University Press, 1996), and R. Bett, "Scepticism and Everyday Attitudes in Ancient and Modern Philosophy", *Metaphilosophy* 24 (1993), 363–81, especially for discussion of the practice of insulation with regard to ethical issues.
2. Compare DL 1.16, 9.69 and *PH* 1.7, and see L. Floridi, *Sextus Empiricus: The Transmission and Rediscovery of Pyrrhonism* (Oxford: Oxford University Press, 2002), 103–4.
3. The term translated as "apprehend", *comprehendi*, is the Latin translation of the technical Stoic term *katalēpton* (*Ac.* 2.18). This is not surprising as both the Academic and Pyrrhonian views develop in close dialectical contact with Stoicism, and especially their account of how we are able to grasp the truth with certainty. See Chapter 3 for more detail on Stoic epistemology.
4. Translations of Sextus' *Outlines of Pyrrhonism* [*PH*] throughout this book are taken from J. Annas & J. Barnes, *Outlines of Scepticism* (Cambridge: Cambridge University Press, 2000), with slight modifications.

5. Unless otherwise indicated, all subsequent translations of Cicero's *Academica* [*Ac.*] are from C. Brittain, *Cicero, On Academic Scepticism* (Indianapolis, IN: Hackett, 2006), with slight modifications.

6. The view I attribute to Cicero in Chapter 5 is perhaps the most controversial of all the interpretations I offer in this book. However, it is very similar to the view that Charles Brittain attributes to Philo of Larissa in his supposedly middle period, that is, between his initial endorsement of the scepticism of Clitomachus and Carneades and his later dogmatic view in his Roman books (*Philo of Larissa: The Last of the Academic Sceptics* [Oxford: Oxford University Press, 2001]). Those who are unconvinced by my account of Cicero may thus prefer to read it as an exposition of Philo's middle period. However, see the extensive and critical review of Brittain in J. Glucker, "The Philonian/Metrodorians: Problems of Method in Ancient Philosophy", *Elenchos* 25 (2004), 99–152.

7. See E. Spinelli, "Sextus Empiricus, the Neighbouring Philosophies and the Sceptical Tradition (Again on *Pyr.* I 220–225)", in *Ancient Scepticism and the Sceptical Tradition*, J. Sihvola (ed.), *Acta Philosophica Fennica* 66, 36–61 (Helsinki: Philosophical Society of Finland, 2000) for discussion of how Sextus differentiates his Pyrrhonism from "neighbouring" philosophies, with which it appears to have something in common (*PH* 1.210–241). I discuss Aenesidemus' puzzling relationship with Heraclitus in Chapter 6.

8. On the dangers and pitfalls of working with the fragmentary evidence for ancient Scepticism and Hellenistic philosophy, see R. Sharples, "The Problem of Sources", in *A Companion to Ancient Philosophy*, M. L. Gill & P. Pellegrin (eds), 430–47 (Oxford: Blackwell, 2006), and J. Mansfeld, "Sources", in *The Cambridge History of Hellenistic Philosophy*, K. Algra, J. Barnes, J. Mansfeld & M. Schofield (eds), 3–30 (Cambridge: Cambridge University Press, 1999). For illuminating discussions on the nature and purpose of historical approaches to philosophy in general, see Rorty *et al.*, *Philosophy in History*, and M. Frede, *Essays in Ancient Philosophy* (Minneapolis, MN: University of Minnesota Press, 1987), ix–xxvii.

2. Pyrrho and Timon: the origin of Pyrrhonian Scepticism

1. J. Brunschwig, "Introduction: The Beginnings of Hellenistic Epistemology", in Algra *et al.*, *The Cambridge History of Hellenistic Philosophy*, 241 n.36, provides a list of eight different types of interpretation of Pyrrho with bibliographic details for examples of each.

2. The "since" in this translation is the result of an emendation to the text that requires only a very slight change and makes excellent grammatical sense. Consequently, it is widely agreed that the issue can only be resolved on the basis of what Timon means. R. Bett, *Pyrrho, his Antecedents, and his Legacy* (New York: Oxford University Press, 2000), 25–7, summarizes the issue, and argues against the emendation. The insertion of the adverb "consistently" is a

plausible, though disputed, interpretation of the sense of Timon's statement, but there is no corresponding Greek adverb in the text. In defence of the insertion, see M. R. Stopper, "Schizzi Pirroniani", *Phronesis* **28** (1983), 265–97 and T. Brennan, "Pyrrho on the Criterion", *Ancient Philosophy* **18**(2) (1998), 417–34, and opposed, Bett, *Pyrrho, his Antecedents, and his Legacy*, 22–3, 60–62.

3. Anaxarchus may have derived his moral conventionalism from an interpretation of the atomism of his teacher Democritus; see J. Warren, *Epicurus and Democritean Ethics: An Archaeology of* Ataraxia (Cambridge: Cambridge University Press, 2002).

4. In *Met.* 4.4–5, Aristotle deals with those who maintain that it is possible for a thing to have both of a pair of contradictory properties (see *Met.* 4.3, 1005b19–20). One consequence of this is that everything would be indefinite, or indeterminate (*Met.* 4.4, 1007b27). And when we examine what the defender of this view means, we find there is nothing to examine, since he neither says something is so, or not so, but both so and not so, and then again he even denies these very assertions so as to say nothing definite at all (*Met.* 4.4, 1008b30–35). While this view has some similarities with Pyrrho's, there is no good reason to suppose that Aristotle was arguing against him. In fact, there is no evidence that Aristotle even knew of Pyrrho. For more detail, see Bett, *Pyrrho, his Antecedents, and his Legacy*, 179–82.

5. There are in all of this some striking similarities to the attitude promoted in Zen Buddhism. The notions that we must escape from desire and opinion and that the things people generally care about have no real value are common to both. There are also some similarities between the types of utterances forbidden on both views. These observations, along with the tantalizing remark about Pyrrho's journeys (DL 9.61), have encouraged the speculation that his view was in some way influenced by the Indian "gymnosophists". It appears, however, that what are supposed to be distinctively Buddhist elements are discernible in earlier Greek philosophers as well. So although the hypothesis of Buddhist influence cannot be ruled out, it is not required by the evidence we have. See E. Flintoff, "Pyrrho and India", *Phronesis* **25** (1980), 88–108, and § "Later Pyrrhonism and Indian philosophy" in the Guide to Further Reading.

3. Arcesilaus: the origin of Academic Scepticism

1. For a detailed exploration of the evidence for the development of the early Academy, see H. Cherniss, *The Riddle of the Early Academy* (Berkeley, CA: University of California Press, 1945); J. Dillon, *The Heirs of Plato: A Study of the Old Academy (347–274 BC)* (Oxford: Oxford University Press, 2003); and E. Watts, "Creating the Academy: Historical Discourse and the Shape of the Community in the Old Academy", *Journal of Hellenic Studies* **127** (2007), 106–22.

2 Characterizing the dialogues as dialectical simply means that the investigation proceeds by articulating views and developing objections and replies.

3. Although we normally think of propositions or positions as the only sorts of things that can be refuted, in the Socratic sense a person is refuted when he contradicts himself or gives an incoherent account of what he believes. See T. Brickhouse & N. Smith, *Plato's Socrates* (New York: Oxford University Press, 1994), esp. 12–14.

4. Given the diverse variety of his intellectual influences, we cannot be sure that this is the actual origin of Arcesilaus' scepticism. It is at least possible that he discovered his scepticism in Plato's dialogues after his conversion.

5. It is not clear exactly what Arcesilaus would have said about the many apparently dogmatic passages in Plato's dialogues, especially those deemed middle and late by many commentators. For the most influential chronological arrangement of Plato's dialogues, see G. Vlastos, *Socrates, Ironist and Moral Philosopher* (Ithaca, NY: Cornell University Press, 1991). J. Annas, "Plato the Sceptic", in *The Socratic Movement*, P. Vander Waerdt (ed.), 309–40 (Ithaca, NY: Cornell University Press, 1994) argues that the sceptical reading of Plato's Socrates requires severing his positive, dogmatic convictions from his negative argumentative practice. In this way, Arcesilaus could claim that Socrates' arguments never proceed from his own convictions, but rather exclusively from those of his interlocutors. C. Shields, "Socrates Among the Sceptics", in Vander Waerdt, *The Socratic Movement*, 341–66, argues that although we do not find Arcesilaus' scepticism practised even by the Socrates of Plato's early dialogues, his claim to carrying on the Socratic mantle is at least as defensible as that of the Stoics.

6. Like Socrates, Arcesilaus left no writings. According to one account, he wrote nothing because of his universal *epochē* (DL 4.32). But it is reasonable to suppose that both Arcesilaus and Socrates were so intent on refuting live interlocutors that literary endeavours paled by comparison (see *Ap.* 38a). Reading arguments against one's own view is simply not as effective as having to defend those views against a live Socrates.

7. There is scant evidence for the view that Arcesilaus was secretly dogmatic, testing his students with sceptical dialectic before deciding to reveal Platonic doctrine to them in private (*PH* 1.234). But even Numenius, who is generally quite hostile to the sceptical Academy, rejects the idea that Arcesilaus' *epochē* is merely a facade (*Praep. Ev.* 14.6.6).

8. Cicero includes Democritus, Anaxagoras, Empedocles and nearly all the old philosophers among those who claim that truth is beyond our comprehension owing to the limits of our senses, the feebleness of our minds and the brevity of life (*Ac.* 1.44). Protagoras similarly attributes his agnosticism to the obscurity of the question and the shortness of life (DL 9.51).

9. The merely human wisdom that Socrates allows himself (*Ap.* 20d–e, 21d, 23a–b) – the awareness of his own ignorance – is not the wisdom he seeks. Being humanly wise is a matter of not having any misplaced confidence about the status of one's beliefs. So it is consistent with saying that Socrates, like the rest of the Athenians, lacks virtue.

10. The influence of Pyrrho is also evident in the description of Arcesilaus by a contemporary Stoic, Ariston, as a philosophical chimera composed of Plato in front, Pyrrho behind and the dialectician Diodorus Cronus in the middle (DL 4.33). It is not clear exactly what Ariston meant to convey about the relative importance or relation of these "parts"; however, D. N. Sedley, "The Protagonists", in *Doubt and Dogmatism*, M. Schofield, M. Burnyeat & J. Barnes (eds) (Oxford: Oxford University Press, 1980), 11, offers a plausible account.

11. For more on the relation between Stoic ethics and other parts of the Stoic system, see the dispute between J. Cooper, "Eudaimonism and the Appeal to Nature in the Morality of Happiness: Comments on Julia Annas, *The Morality of Happiness*", and J. Annas, "Reply to Cooper", *Philosophy and Phenomenological Research* 55(3) (1995), 587–98, 599–610.

12. See B. Reed, "The Stoics' Account of the Cognitive Impression", *Oxford Studies in Ancient Philosophy* 23 (2002), 147–80, for a different assessment.

13. Diogenes (7.177, LS 40F) records an amusing anecdote about a Stoic being deceived by a bowl of wax pomegranates. His response was that he had not assented to the false impression that they were real pomegranates; rather, he had assented to the true impression that it was reasonable that they were pomegranates – for discussion, see T. Brennan, "Reasonable Impressions in Stoicism", *Phronesis* 41 (1996), 318–34.

14. For more detail on the Stoic psychology of human action, see LS 57 and B. Inwood, *Ethics and Human Action in Early Stoicism* (Oxford: Oxford University Press, 1985). According to the Stoics, both human and non-human animals are born with a natural impulse towards self-preservation (a sort of proprietary affection towards themselves). But only human beings are capable of moral action, in accordance with our distinctively rational capacity for self-governance.

15. Plato sometimes has Socrates refute characteristically Socratic theses as defended by his interlocutors. For example, in the *Laches* (194d–199e), Nicias unsuccessfully defends the Socratic claim that courage is a kind of knowledge, and in the *Charmides* (164d–172a), Critias unsuccessfully defends the Socratic claim that temperance is a kind of knowledge.

4. Carneades

1. For more on the sorites see T. Williamson, *Vagueness* (London: Routledge, 1994).

2. For more on the Stoic response see J. Barnes, "Medicine, Experience and Logic", in *Science and Speculation: Studies in Hellenistic Theory and Practice*, J. Barnes, J. Brunschwig, M. Burnyeat & M. Schofield (eds), 24–68 (Cambridge: Cambridge University Press, 1982); M. Mignucci, "The Stoic Analysis of the Sorites", *Proceedings of the Aristotelian Society* 93 (1993), 231–45.

3. Carneades' division is somewhat clumsy with regard to Epicurean ethics since Epicurus argues that it is not possible to live pleasantly (i.e. to consistently

attain pleasure) without living virtuously and vice versa (*Fin.* 1.57). If he is right, the distinctions between (1) and (4), and similarly between (2) and (5), would vanish.

4. This and all subsequent translations of Sextus' *Against the Logicians* [= *M* 7–8] are from R. Bett, *Sextus Empiricus, Against the Logicians* (Cambridge: Cambridge University Press, 2005).

5. Cicero does not explicitly credit this argument to Carneades, and Sextus' report of a very similar argument seems to have already worried Chrysippus, so it is probably not Carneades' invention. Nevertheless, given his attachment to the sorites (see above, and *Ac.* 2.91–4) it is likely that he employed it against the Stoics.

6. More sophisticated developments of this line of thought can be found in externalist epistemological theories. The defining feature of such theories is the denial of the so called KK thesis: in order to have knowledge, one must know that he has knowledge. According to the KK thesis, in order to know that one's belief p is true, one must be aware of the reasons that establish, reveal, entail or justify that p is true. Externalists, by contrast, often provide causal accounts of justification that do not require the agent to be aware of the justifying grounds. If my belief is formed in the right way then I can be said to know it. I need not be aware of how my belief was formed: the justification is a matter of the external relationship between my belief and the world. The internalist, however, would object that this relationship determines whether or not the belief is true, but not whether it is justified. See W. Alston, *Epistemic Justification: Essays in the Theory of Knowledge* (Ithaca, NY: Cornell University Press, 1989); H. Kornblith, *Epistemology: Internalism and Externalism* (Cambridge, MA: MIT Press, 2001). For problems with the notion that the Stoics eventually develop an externalist epistemology, see Reed, "The Stoics' Account of the Cognitive Impression".

7. An influential defence of the purely sceptical or dialectical Carneades is M. Burnyeat, "Carneades was no Probabilist," (unpublished). See also: J. Allen, "Academic Probabilism and Stoic Epistemology", *Classical Quarterly* 44 (1994), 85–113, and "Carneadean Argument in Cicero's *Academic Books*", in *Assent and Argument: Studies in Cicero's Academic Books, Proceedings of the Seventh Symposium Hellenisticum*, B. Inwood & J. Mansfeld (eds), 2117–56 (Leiden: Brill, 1997); R. Bett, "Carneades' *Pithanon*: A Reappraisal of its Role and Status", *Oxford Studies in Ancient Philosophy* 7 (1989), 59–94, and "Carneades' Distinction between Assent and Approval", *Monist* 73 (1990), 3–20; M. Frede, "The Sceptic's Two Kinds of Assent and the Question of the Possibility of Knowledge", in Rorty *et al.*, *Philosophy in History*, 255–78; and G. Striker, "Sceptical Strategies", in Schofield *et al.*, *Doubt and Dogmatism*, 54–83, and "Uber den Unterschied zwischen den Pyrrhoneern und den Akademikern", *Phronesis* 26 (1981), 153–71 [reprinted in English as "On the Difference Between the Pyrrhonists and the Academics", in her *Essays on Hellenistic Epistemology and Ethics*, 135–49 (Cambridge: Cambridge University Press, 1996)]. Suzanne

Obdrzalek, "Living in Doubt: Carneades' *Pithanon* Reconsidered", *Oxford Studies in Ancient Philosophy* **31** (2006), 243–80, provides a convincing defence of the fallibilist interpretation of Carneades' criterion, but without taking a position on whether Carneades himself endorses it.

8. As we shall see in Chapter 5, after Carneades' death there was some disagreement in the Academy about how to understand the great Sceptic. So it is possible that Sextus takes this remark from a later, controversial account of Carneades. On the other hand, it is also the kind of softening of an originally uncompromising sceptical stance that we may expect to result from many years of intense dialectical battle with the Stoics.

5. Cicero: the end of the sceptical Academy

1. In contemporary epistemology we tend to talk more of knowledge than wisdom. So the analogous question in contemporary discussions is whether it is possible to know *p* and yet not have conclusive grounds for believing *p*; see, for example, M. Steup, *An Introduction to Contemporary Epistemology* (Upper Saddle River, NJ: Prentice Hall, 1996). Most contemporary epistemologists are not sceptics since they defend some account of fallible knowledge. That is, they wish to show that one can be fully justified in believing *p*, and hence know that *p*, while still having good rational grounds to doubt that *p* is true; see B. Reed, "How to Think About Fallibilism", *Philosophical Studies* **107** (2002), 143–57. By contrast, the view under examination in this chapter is a form of scepticism since it is an attempt to show how wisdom, not knowledge, is compatible with fallibility. According to the mitigated scepticism described here, knowledge has been shown to be neither possible nor impossible.

2. The only possible, although crucial, exception to this is that by arguing dialectically for and against the existence of kataleptic impressions, Carneades may have judged that it is probable that nothing can be grasped with certainty (*Ac.* 2.109–10). If Carneades had made this judgement it would have served as an important precedent for the later development of Academic fallibilism, but it is by no means necessary to think Carneades was the first to make this move.

3. For other interpretations of Philo's Roman books, see especially Brittain, *Philo of Larissa*, 129–68; J. Glucker, *Antiochus and the Late Academy* (Göttingen: Vandenhoeck & Ruprecht, 1978); and H. Tarrant, "Agreement and the Self-Evident in Philo of Larissa", *Dionysius* **5** (1981), 66–97.

4. His earliest published work, which dates back to 81 BCE, also expresses this same Academic outlook. In fact, W. Görler, "Cicero's Philosophical Stance in the *Lucullus*", in Inwood & Mansfeld, *Assent and Argument*, 36–57, argues that Cicero's philosophical allegiance remained constant throughout his life. The apparently dogmatic tone of his dialogues dealing with political philosophy (written between 55 and c.51 BCE) simply expresses his more epistemically optimistic side.

5. Brittain, *Philo of Larissa*, has argued that Philo's movement away from Clitomachus' view occurred in two stages. Philo supposedly endorsed three distinct positions throughout his career: first, a radical Clitomachean scepticism that holds firmly to *epochē*; secondly, a mitigated scepticism that preserves the rejection of Stoic epistemology but allows for fallible beliefs (including philosophical judgements); and thirdly, the novel dogmatic view of the Roman books. For reasons that would take us too far from the main themes of the introductory account offered here, I reject the thesis that Philo defended the second of these three positions. Although he may have made some modifications to Clitomachus' view – augmenting or adding to them – I believe his one dramatic shift is from scepticism to the dogmatism of his Roman books. In his extensive review of Brittain, Glucker, "The Philonian/Metrodorians", offers a number of serious, and I think convincing, objections. See also my "Radical and Mitigated Scepticism in Cicero's *Academica*", in *Cicero's Practical Philosophy*, W. Nicgorski (ed.) (Notre Dame, IL: University of Notre Dame Press, forthcoming).

6. For a defence of the view that Cicero is the first to apply the Academic method for these positive aims see W. Görler, "Ältere Pyrrhonismus, Jüngere Akademie, Antiochos aus Askalon", in *Grundriss der Geschichte der Philosophie, Die Philosophie der Antike*, Bd. 4. *Die hellenistische Philosphie* (Basel: Schwabe, 1994).

7. Cicero frequently singles out this freedom as the most definitive and attractive feature of the Academics' philosophical practice; see, for example, *Inv.* 2.9–10; *Div.* 2.150; *Tusc.* 5.83; *Off.* 3.20.

8. Cicero often berates others for their obstinacy (*pertinacia*; e.g. *Ac.* 2.7, 65; *Fin.* 1.27). Interestingly, he also acknowledges the difficulty in clearly differentiating *pertinacia* from *perseverantia* (*Top.* 87; see also *Inv.* 2.165, where he notes that the latter borders on the former).

6. Aenesidemus: the Pyrrhonian revival

1. Although we have no certain evidence in support of Aenesidemus' membership in Philo's sceptical Academy, this is the most plausible interpretation of Photius' report that Aenesidemus dedicates his books to a certain fellow-member of the Academy, Lucius Tubero; see J. Mansfeld, "Aenesidemus and the Academics", in *The Passionate Intellect*, L. Ayres (ed.), 235–48 (New Brunswick, NJ: Transaction, 1995) in opposition to the view set forth by F. Decleva Caizzi, "Aenesidemus and the Academy", *Classical Quarterly* 42(1) (1992), 176–89.

2. *Praep. Ev.* 14.18.29. It is puzzling that Cicero never mentions Aenesidemus, especially since the *Pyrrhonist Discourses* are dedicated to Cicero's lifelong friend, Lucius Tubero. Cicero and Tubero had grown up together, were connected by marriage and had devoted themselves to the same studies (Cicero, *Pro Ligario* 21). Given his devotion to the Academy, it is unlikely that Cicero was unaware of Aenesidemus' radical faction, especially if his close friend

had been a member. The most reasonable hypothesis is that Cicero's neglect is an intentional snub, consistent with his generally dismissive attitude to the historical Pyrrho; see Glucker, *Antiochus and the Late Academy*.

3. Other references to Aenesidemus' *Pyrrhonist Discourses* are found at DL 9.78, 106–7, 116; *M* 8.215. Sextus is probably drawing extensively from this work also in his presentation of Aenesidemus' Ten Modes (*PH* 1.36–163, on which see below), but it is not clear how strictly he keeps to this text. Diogenes refers to two other works, *Against Wisdom* and *On Inquiry*, about which we know only that they repeat Aenesidemus' contention that Pyrrho determines nothing dogmatically but guides himself by what is apparent (DL 9.107).

4. The reference to "self-evident cognition" in this passage suggests that his primary target is Philo's Roman view. Numenius remarks that Philo abandoned *epochē* because of the clarity and consistency of his experience (*Praep. Ev.* 14.9.2); see Tarrant, "Agreement and the Self-Evident", 72; Glucker, *Antiochus and the Late Academy*, 1–83; and Brittain, *Philo of Larissa*, 133 n.6.

5. There are plausible externalist replies one might make. Of course I can be mistaken in claiming to know something. But it need not follow from this that the idea of fallible knowledge is untenable. The externalist can argue that we are fallible about what we know and do not know. Our knowledge is secured by being in the right causal relationship with the world whether or not we are aware of this fact. More generally, one might simply discard the assumption that only conclusive justification is genuine justification. This is the approach taken by most contemporary epistemologists (Reed, "How to Think About Fallibilism").

6. Photius reports that the aim of the *Pyrrhonist Discourses* "is to establish firmly [*bebaiōsai*] that there is nothing firm [*bebaion*] to be grasped" (*Bib.* 169b18–19). It is not clear whether this formulation is actually Aenesidemus' or whether it is Photius' own ironic jab. In either case, it pointedly recalls the ambiguity between epistemological and metaphysical readings of Pyrrho.

7. The author of *On Drunkenness* (*De Ebr.*) is Philo of Alexandria, a Jewish philosopher and political leader who flourished around the first century CE. I refer to him below simply as Philo, but he should not be confused with the Academic, Philo of Larissa.

8. For a detailed defence, see Bett, *Pyrrho, his Antecedents, and his Legacy*; S. Gaukroger, "The Ten Modes of Aenesidemus and the Myth of Ancient Scepticism", *British Journal for the History of Philosophy* 3 (1995), 371–87; and P. Woodruff, "Aporetic Pyrrhonism", *Oxford Studies in Ancient Philosophy* 6 (1988), 139–68. Although Woodruff argues for a negatively dogmatic interpretation of Aenesidemus, he attributes only a semantic, rather than ontological, relativism to him. In other words, the restrictions on what the Pyrrhonist may say and believe do not entail any claims about how things are, but only about the appropriate use of language: to say, for example, that honey is sweet *means* that honey is sweet relative to certain conditions. This sort of relativism leaves it entirely open as to whether honey is or is not sweet by nature; M. Schofield, "Aenesidemus: Pyrrhonist and Heraclitean", in *Pyrrhonists, Patri-*

cians, *Platonizers: Hellenistic Philosophy in the Period 155–86 BC. Proccedings of the Tenth Symposium Hellenisticum*, A. M. Ioppolo & D. N. Sedley (eds), 269–338 (Naples: Bibliopolis, 2007).

9. I follow Sextus' enumeration of the modes in what follows. Diogenes numbers the ten modes differently, and Philo, who includes only eight in his account, does not number them at all.

10. The interpretation of these passages, and the general issue of ethical relativism within Pyrrhonian scepticism, is explored in Schofield, "Aenesidemus: Pyrrhonist and Heraclitean"; R. J. Hankinson, "Values, Objectivity and Dialectic; The Sceptical Attack on Ethics: Its Methods, Aims, and Success", *Phronesis* **39**(1) (1994), 45–68; Bett, *Pyrrho, his Antecedents, and his Legacy*; Annas, "Doing Without Objective Values".

11. J. Annas & J. Barnes, *The Modes of Scepticism* (Cambridge: Cambridge University Press, 1985), 143–5, hypothesize that Sextus imports the later Agrippan relativity mode (*PH* 1.167) into his account of Aenesidemus' relativity mode (*PH* 1.135–40). In both discussions, he says that objects appear relative to the judging subject and to the things observed together. This explains a number of otherwise very puzzling aspects of Sextus' text: for example, unlike the other nine modes, there are no examples drawing on traditional observations, and instead we find a series of highly abstract arguments much more characteristic of Agrippa's modes.

12. In the following account I rely on Schofield's resolution (in "Aenesidemus: Pyrrhonist and Heraclitean") of this long-standing "scholarly headache". Among the many details I leave out of consideration, it is important to note Schofield's contention that Aenesidemus is motivated, at least in part, by a desire to undermine the Stoic appropriation of Heraclitus as an authoritative precursor. See also the detailed study in R. Polito, *The Sceptical Road: Aenesidemus' Appropriation of Heraclitus* (Leiden: Brill, 2004), and J. Rist, "The Heracliteanism of Aenesidemus", *Phoenix* **24**(4) (1970), 309–19.

13. See Schofield, "Aenesidemus: Pyrrhonist and Heraclitean", for discussion of the awkward expression Sextus frequently uses to introduce these interpretations: "Aenesidemus' followers' interpretation of Heraclitus", or "Heraclitus according to Aenesidemus". The views expressed are regarding the nature of the intellect (*M* 7.350), the relation of part to whole (*M* 9.337), time (*M* 10.216, 233; *PH* 3.138) and motion (*M* 10.83). In his translation of the text, Bett, *Sextus Empiricus, Against the Logicians*, deletes the words "and Heraclitus" at *M* 8.8.

14. See Bett, *Pyrrho, his Antecedents, and his Legacy*, 114–23, for a more positive view about the role of opposing appearances in Pyrrho's view.

7. Sextus Empiricus: the consistency of Pyrrhonian Scepticism

1. Diogenes' genealogical list also contains a number of prominent empiricist physicians. This close connection with medical empiricism indicates that the

development of Pyrrhonism is tied up with emerging debates on the methodology and epistemology of medicine; see M. Frede, "The Method of the So-Called Methodical School of Medicine", in Barnes *et al.*, *Science and Speculation*, 1–23; J. Allen, "Pyrrhonism and Medical Empiricism", *Aufstieg und Niedergang der Römischen Welt*, II 37(1) (1993), 646–90.

2. Jonathan Barnes succinctly lays out the relevant evidence in the introduction to Annas & Barnes, *The Modes of Scepticism*. D. House, "The Life of Sextus Empiricus", *Classical Quarterly* 30 (1980), 227–38, goes into greater detail, but see also Floridi, *Sextus Empiricus*, who suggests that House is overly cautious about the possibility of reaching firmer conclusions regarding the life of Sextus.

3. There is a good deal of controversy regarding the chronology of these texts. Some maintain that *PH* is an earlier version of the material that Sextus later reworked as the *Sceptical Commentaries*: notably K. Janáček, *Prolegomena to Sextus Empiricus* "Acta Universitatis Palackianae Olomucensis" No. 4 (Olomoue: Nákladem Palackého University, 1948). Others argue that *PH* is a more sophisticated abridgement that strengthens the earlier version of the *Sceptical Commentaries*: most notably R. Bett, *Sextus Empiricus, Against the Ethicists* (Oxford: Clarendon Press, 1997) and *Sextus Empiricus, Against the Logicians*. Yet others argue that if Sextus' purpose is therapeutic, then what may be effective for one reader (or patient) may not be effective for another. Thus one Sceptical text may be better suited to treat one person and another text better suited to treat another person. In that case, we can sensibly talk about better or worse Sceptical texts only relative to the particular needs of the Sceptic's dogmatic patients.

4. The following references are not exhaustive: *PH* 1.8, 1.78, 1.121, 1.128, 1.129, 1.134, 1.163, 2.95, 3.65; *M* 9.436, 10.168.

5. *PH* 1.31, 1.35, 1.36, 1.79. 1.87, 1.99, 1.117, 1.123; *M* 8.2, 8.160, 9.191, 10.6. The notion that *epochē* follows (*akolouthei*) equipollence (*PH* 1.167; *M* 9.194; cf. DL 9.79) is particularly significant since Sextus uses the same verb (*akolouthei*) to describe the fortuitous attendance of *ataraxia* on *epochē* (*PH* 1.26, 29, 31).

6. *PH* 1.61, 1.140, 1.163, 1.170, 1.175, 2.192, 3.6, 3.29; *M* 7.380, 8.177, 8.259, 8.380, 8.401.

7. *M* 8.346, 8.428; cf. *M* 8.380, 8.477, 11.168, which also suggest that *epochē* is the result of a conscious, deliberate decision.

8. Note how similar [I] is to W. K. Clifford's famous assertion that "It is wrong always, everywhere, and for anyone, to believe anything upon insufficient evidence" (*The Ethics of Belief and Other Essays* [Amherst, NY: Prometheus, [1877] 1999).

9. The problem is that the existence of moral and natural evils seems incompatible with the existence of a God who is both and able and willing to prevent innocent suffering.

10. See J. Brunschwig, "Once Again on Eusebius on Aristocles on Timon on Pyrrho", in his *Papers in Hellenistic Philosophy*, 190–211 (Cambridge: Cambridge University Press, 1994) for a detailed analysis of the expression "as far as the argument goes".

11. Contrary to J. Barnes, "Introduction", in Annas & Barnes, *The Modes of Scepticism*, xxvii–xxix, I think we must admit that the sceptic as therapist might knowingly apply invalid or incoherent arguments. But all that this can mean is that such arguments appear weak to him. It cannot be construed as an attempt to deceive or mislead the "patient". The thought that a therapeutically effective, but invalid, argument is deceptive or misleading presupposes that one *should* not argue this way. But the philanthropic sceptic will have no such scruples. Furthermore, the only time it would make sense to knowingly offer an invalid argument would be when a valid argument with the same conclusion would not be as convincing. While it is true that fallacious reasoning can be quite convincing to those unfamiliar with logic, those in need of sceptical therapy will probably be better served with coherent, valid arguments. But again, the therapeutic sceptic's preference for valid arguments cannot be due to any epistemic advantage such arguments are supposed to offer.

12. However, the Stoics insist that tranquillity itself is not the *summum bonum* but rather a welcome by-product (see *Ac.* 2.138).

13. Another explanation is that the physiology of belief accounts for its disturbance. M. McPherran, "*Ataraxia* and *Eudaimonia* in Ancient Pyrrhonism: Is the Sceptic Really Happy?", *Proceedings of the Boston Area Colloquium in Ancient Philosophy* 5 (1989), 135–71, esp. 158, notes that both the Stoics and Sextus describe reason as an active faculty that is itself in motion when it assents, and that such a goal-directed motion is just what it is to experience the disturbance of belief. Suspension of judgement eliminates the disturbing psychic motion and leaves a relatively untroubled, smooth motion.

8. Pyrrhonian arguments

1. For the persistence of the challenge provided by Pyrrhonian Scepticism, see R. Fogelin, R. *Pyrrhonian Reflections on Knowledge and Justification* (New York: Oxford University Press, 1994).

2. My discussion of the sceptical modes in this chapter is heavily indebted to J. Barnes, *The Toils of Scepticism* (Cambridge: Cambridge University Press, 1990).

3. Diogenes attributes these same modes to Agrippa and his school (DL 9.88). This is virtually all we know about Agrippa.

4. See P. D. Klein, "Human Knowledge and the Infinite Regress of Reasons", *Philosophical Perspectives* 13 (1999), 297–325, for a defence of infinitism.

5. Aristotle frequently makes this distinction: for example, *NE* 1.3, 1095a2–4; *De Anima* 2.1, 413a11–12; *Met.* 7.3, 1029b3–12.

6. A more plausible response to the charge of circularity is to embrace it. Contemporary epistemologists have developed a variety of coherence theories that do just that. Perhaps the most difficult problem with coherence theories is to explain why the coherence among a set of propositions makes them more

likely to be true than an equally coherent set of incompatible propositions; see
L. Bonjour, *The Structure of Empirical Knowledge* (Cambridge, MA: Harvard
University Press, 1985).

7. Sextus offers a different, and incompatible solution in *M* 8.333a. We cannot
decide which among competing conceptions of soul (for example) is the right
one to begin with; but we cannot really enquire into the nature of the soul
until we settle this issue, so enquiry cannot even get started. See J. Brunschwig,
"Sextus Empiricus on the Kriterion: The Sceptic as Conceptual Legatee", in
The Question of "Eclecticism": Studies in Later Greek Philosophy, J. M. Dillon &
A. A. Long (eds), 145–75 (Berkeley, CA: University of California Press, 1988).

8. We can begin to get a sense of the boundaries of these sub-fields by considering the Greek words from which their names are derived: *ēthos, physis and
logos*. Ethics deals with normative and evaluative concepts, applied to human
beings individually and collectively, so it includes moral and political philosophy; physics deals with nature, including metaphysical as well as scientific
questions, both about human beings as well as the earth and the universe;
and logic deals with the many uses of language and reason, including formal
methods of inference along with rhetorical and epistemological topics.

9. At *M* 7.25 Sextus says that a criterion is the mark of an immediately observable,
or self-evident, truth, while signs and proofs provide us with a way of discerning the truth of things that are not immediately evident. Given the variety of
ways Sextus' dogmatic opponents used such epistemological notions, however,
it is not surprising that he does not keep strictly to this distinction; see G.
Striker, "*Kritêrion tês alêtheias*", *Nachrichten der Akademie der Wissenschaften
zu Göttingen* I. Phil.-hist. Klasse 2 (1974), 48–110.

10. Sextus does not at this point consider Protagoras' view that every human being
is the criterion by which something is judged to be true, because he counts
him among those who do away with the criterion. If we allow that whatever
appears to be the case is the case for me at this moment, then we effectively do
away with truth as typically conceived, and thus have no need of a criterion.
Sextus also briefly refers to Plato's "exquisite argument" (*Tht.* 171a): "if every
appearance is true, then even *not* every appearance's being true, since it takes
the form of an appearance, will be true" (*M* 7.390).

11. The nature of the sceptic's reliance on recollective signs, and especially whether
it presupposes some form of belief, is discussed in Chapter 9.

9. The (ordinary) life of a Pyrrhonist

1. These options are examined and developed in an influential set of essays in M.
F. Burnyeat & M. Frede (eds), *The Original Sceptics: A Controversy* (Indianapolis, IN: Hackett, 1997).

2. The terms more frequently used, adopted from Barnes, who takes them from
Galen, are "rustic" and "urbane". Fine points out that these terms, as usually

applied, do not exhaust the relevant logical space, whereas her terms do. In particular, it is possible to reject more kinds of belief than the urbane sceptic does (as urbanity is variously interpreted), and yet to stop short of a complete ban on belief. G. Fine, "Scepticism, Existence, and Belief", *Oxford Studies in Ancient Philosophy* 14 (1996), 286 n.25, refers to this excluded middle, neither urbane nor rustic, as "suburban scepticism".

3. See G. Fine, "Sextus and External World Scepticism", *Oxford Studies in Ancient Philosophy* 24 (2003), 341–85, for discussion of whether Sextus' Pyrrhonism includes some form of external world scepticism.

4. See V. Tsouna, *The Epistemology of the Cyrenaic School* (Cambridge: Cambridge University Press, 1998) for a detailed examination of Cyrenaic epistemology.

5. I take the following objection from M. F. Burnyeat, "Can the Sceptic Live His Scepticism?", in Schofield *et al.*, *Doubt and Dogmatism*, 20–53. The response is further elaborated in my "Is the Examined Life Worth Living? A Pyrrhonian Alternative", *Apeiron* 36(3) (2003), 229–49; see also B. C. Johnsen, "On the Coherence of Pyrrhonian Scepticism", *Philosophical Review* 110(4) (2001), 521–61, for a different response.

6. Defenders of fideism would argue that unjustified belief can be, and perhaps must be, the foundation for religious observances. See T. Penelhum, *God and Scepticism* (Boston, MA: Reidel, 1983) for more on the relation between varieties of scepticism and fideism.

7. Sextus mentions Aristotle's suggestion for making sense of the notion that a line is length without breadth. The dispute turns on what it means to conceive a line. If we must represent it visually then there can be no conception of line without breadth. But if conception occurs in some non-visual form of representation, the concept of line is perfectly coherent. But of course Sextus' argument need not be conclusive since he is only seeking to balance the competing claims. For more detail see I. Mueller, "Geometry and Scepticism", in Barnes *et al.*, *Science and Speculation*, 69–95.

8. J. Barnes, "Scepticism and the Arts", in *Method, Medicine and Metaphysics: Studies in the Philosophy of Ancient Science*, R. J. Hankinson (ed.), *Apeiron* 12(2) (1988), 53–77, esp. 61, marks this distinction in terms of formal and informal teaching. Although Sextus never draws this distinction himself, it is at the very least suggested by the distinction between a criterion of action and a criterion of truth, along with the sceptic's reliance on teaching of forms of expertise. There is no other way to make sense of how the sceptic could learn any form of expertise except by imitation. See also D. L. Blank, *Sextus Empiricus, Against the Grammarians* (Oxford: Clarendon Press, 1998), xxxiv.

Guide to further reading

1. Introduction

Translations and collections of texts and fragments

The relevant ancient texts are widely scattered. A good place to start is A. A. Long & D. N. Sedley (eds), *The Hellenistic Philosophers*, 2 vols (Cambridge: Cambridge University Press, 1987) [= LS]. Volume 1 contains selections of texts translated into English followed by commentary. Volume 2 contains the original Greek and Latin texts along with critical notes and bibliography. Another good point of entry is B. Inwood & L. P. Gerson, *Hellenistic Philosophy: Introductory Readings*, 2nd edn (Indianapolis, IN: Hackett, 1997) [= IG]. In many cases I have taken the translations of ancient texts from these volumes.

More detailed information on primary texts can be found below in the relevant sections of this guide.

A very efficient way to become familiar with what scholars consider most interesting, noteworthy or controversial is to read book reviews. Each of the following sections of this guide will include references in square brackets after some entries. Additionally, reliable and informative online reviews can be found at *Notre Dame Philosophical Reviews* (http://ndpr.nd.edu/) and at *Bryn Mawr Classical Review* (http://ccat.sas.upenn.edu/bmcr/).

Secondary literature

An excellent overview of the epistemological issues at the heart of ancient Scepticism is J. Brunschwig, "Introduction: The Beginnings of Hellenistic Epistemology", in *The Cambridge History of Hellenistic Philosophy*, K. Algra, J. Barnes, J. Mansfeld & M. Schofield (eds), 229–59 (Cambridge: Cambridge University Press, 1999). There are also very instructive chapters on Pyrrhonian and Academic Scepticism in M. L. Gill & P. Pellegrin (eds), *A Companion to Ancient Philosophy* (Oxford: Blackwell, 2006): C. Levy, "The New Academy and its Rivals", 448–64, and J. Brunschwig, "Pyrrhonism", 465–85. See also: D. N. Sedley, "The Motivation of Greek Scepticism", in *The Sceptical Tradition*, M. Burnyeat (ed.), 9–29 (Berkeley, CA: University of California Press, 1983); A. A. Long, *Hellenistic Philosophy*, 2nd edn (Berkeley, CA: University of California Press, 1986), 75–106; and R. W. Sharples, *Stoics, Epicureans and Sceptics* (London: Routledge, 1996).

The most comprehensive study is R. J. Hankinson, *The Sceptics* (London: Routledge, 1998) [REVIEWS: C. Brittain in *Philosophical Review* 106(4) (1997), 635–8; G. Fine, "Scepticism, Existence, and Belief", *Oxford Studies in Ancient Philosophy* 14 (1996), 273–90; D. W. Hamlyn in *Philosophical Investigations* 19(3) (1996), 270–74; C. Osborne in *Mind* 107 (1998), 478–82; P. K. Sakezles in *Ancient Philosophy* 18(1) (1998), 202–6]; an engaging study mostly aimed at defending Pyrrhonism is A. Bailey, *Sextus Empiricus and Pyrrhonean Scepticism* (Oxford: Oxford University Press, 2002) [REVIEWS: J. Barnes in *Mind* 112 (2003), 496–9; R. Bett in *Philosophical Review* 112(1) (2003), 100–102; M. McPherran in *Philosophical Quarterly* 54 (2004), 319–21]; a controversial interpretation linking ancient Scepticism with anti-realism is L. Groarke, *Greek Scepticism* (Montreal: McGill-Queen's University Press, 1990) [REVIEWS: C. Hookway in *Mind* 101 (1992), 145–8; R. Pierson in *Dialogue: Canadian Philosophical Review* 35 (1996), 183–5; A. Silverman in *Phoenix* 48(2) (1994), 165–70]; still valuable is the pioneering work of C. L. Stough, *Greek Scepticism* (Berkeley, CA: University of California Press, 1969) [REVIEWS: M. Frede in *Journal of Philosophy* 70 (1973), 805–10; A. A. Long in *Philosophy* 46 (1971), 77–8]. Also worth consulting is M. M. Patrick, *The Greek Sceptics* (New York: Columbia University Press, 1929). More book-length studies dealing with Pyrrhonian Scepticism are listed below in the section on Sextus Empiricus.

For readers of French, German or Italian: V. Brochard, *Les Sceptiques Grecs*, 2nd edn (Paris: Vrin, 1923); M. Dal Pra, *Lo scetticismo Greco*, 3rd edn (Bari: Laterza, 1989); L. Robin, *Pyrrhon et le Scepticisme Grec* (New York: Garland, 1980); A. Goedeckemeyer, *Die Geschichte des Griechischen Skeptizismus* (New York: Garland, 1987); R. Ricken, *Antike Skeptiker* (Munich: C. H. Beck, 1994).

Sceptical antecedents

(See also § "On the origins of the sceptical Academy", below.)

Bett, R. "On the Pre-history of Pyrrhonism", *Proceedings of the Boston Area Colloquium in Ancient Philosophy* 15 (1999), 137–66.

Brunschwig, J. "Le fragmente DK 70B 1 de Métrodore de Chio", in *Polyhistor: Studies in the History and Historiography of Ancient Philosophy*, K. A. Algra, P. W. van der Horst & D. T. Runia (eds), 21–38 (Leiden: Brill, 1996).

Lee, M.-K. *Epistemology After Protagoras: Responses to Relativism in Plato, Aristotle and Democritus* (Oxford: Clarendon Press, 2005) [REVIEWS: D. T. J. Bailey in *Mind* 115 (2006), 1151–3; L. Castagnoli in *Ancient Philosophy* 27(2) (2007), 405–18; J. Warren in *Classical Review* 56 (2006), 59–61].

Warren, J. *Epicurus and Democritean Ethics: An Archaeology of* Ataraxia (Cambridge: Cambridge University Press 2002) [REVIEWS: V. Tsouna in *Classical Philology* 99 (2004), 174–82; W. Englert in *Ancient Philosophy* 24 (2004), 496–500].

2. Pyrrho

Translations and collections of texts and fragments
Although Pyrrho wrote nothing, much has been written about him, starting with his student Timon. These testimonies are gathered in F. Decleva Caizzi, *Pirrone: Testimonianze* (Naples: Bibliopolis, 1981), which also contains translations and extensive commentary in Italian [REVIEWS: W. Görler in *Archiv für Geschichte der Philosophie* 67 (1985), 320–25; A. A. Long in *Classical Review* 34(2) (1984), 219–21]. LS 1–3 is a more selective collection of texts translated into English and followed by insightful commentary.

Eusebius, a bishop of Caesarea, records the Aristotelian philosopher Aristocles' polemical account of Pyrrho and his followers in *Praeparatio Evangelica*, Book 14, Chapter 18. The only complete English translation is E. H. Gifford (trans.), *Preparation for the Gospels*, 4 vols (Oxford: Clarendon Press, 1903). A thorough, scholarly treatment of the work of Aristocles can be found in M. L. Chiesara, *Aristocles of Messene, Testimonia and Fragments* (Oxford: Oxford University Press 2001) [REVIEW: G. Karamanolis in *Classical Review* 54(1) (2004), 57–9].

Diogenes Laertius' Lives of Pyrrho and Timon (DL 9.61–116) is a compressed account of the entire history of Pyrrhonian Scepticism containing many dubious yet entertaining anecdotes about the historical Pyrrho: R. Hicks (trans.), *Diogenes Laertius, Lives of Eminent Philosophers* (Cambridge, MA: Harvard University Press, 1972). This text is excerpted in IG III-22, 23.

Secondary literature
Ausland, H. "On the Moral Origin of the Pyrrhonian Philosophy", *Elenchos* 10 (1989), 359–434.
Barnes, J. "Diogenes Laertius IX 61–116: The Philosophy of Pyrrhonism", *Aufstieg und Niedergang der römischen Welt* II 36.6 (1992), 4241–301.
Bett, R. *Pyrrho, his Antecedents, and his Legacy* (Oxford: Oxford University Press, 2000) [REVIEWS: J. Barnes in *Mind* 110 (2001), 1043–6; L. Castagnoli in *Ancient Philosophy* 22(2) (2002), 443–58; R. Ferwerda in *Mnemosyne* 54(6) (2001), 743–6; A. M. Ioppolo in *Gnomon* 76 (2004) 114–19; P. Woodruff in *Review of Metaphysics* 55(2) (2001), 379–80].

Bett, R. "Aristocles on Timon on Pyrrho: The Text, its Logic and its Credibility", *Oxford Studies in Ancient Philosophy* 12 (1994), 137–81.

Bett, R. "What did Pyrrho think about 'The Nature of the Divine and the Good?'" *Phronesis* 34(3) (1994), 303–37.

Brennan, T. "Pyrrho on the Criterion", *Ancient Philosophy* 18(2) (1998), 417–34.

Brunschwig, J. "Once Again on Eusebius on Aristocles on Timon on Pyrrho", in his *Papers in Hellenistic Philosophy*, 190–211 (Cambridge: Cambridge University Press, 1994).

Brunschwig, J. "Le titre des 'Indalmoi' de Timon: d'Ulysse à Pyrrhon", *Recherches sur la philosophie et le langage* 12 (1990), 83–99. [Reprinted in English as "The title of Timon's *Indalmoi*: from Odysseus to Pyrrho", in his *Papers in Hellenistic Philosophy*, 212–23.]

Burnyeat, M. F. "Tranquility Without a Stop: Timon fr. 68", *Classical Quarterly* 30 (1980), 86–93.

DeLacy, P. "*Ou mallon* and the Antecedents of Ancient Scepticism", *Phronesis* 3 (1958), 59–71.

Lesses, G. "Pyrrho the Dogmatist", *Apeiron* 35(3) (2002), 255–71.

Long, A. A. "Timon of Phlius: Pyrrhonist and Satirist", *Proceedings of the Cambridge Philological Society* 24 (1978), 68–91.

Powers, N. "Fourth Century Flux Theory and the Origin of Pyrrhonism", *Apeiron* 34(1) (2001), 37–50.

Sakezles, P. "Pyrrhonian Indeterminacy: A Pragmatic Interpretation", *Apeiron* 26(2) (1993), 77–95.

Stopper, M. R. "Schizzi Pirroniani", *Phronesis* 28 (1983), 265–97.

Svavarsson, S. H. "Pyrrho's Undecidable Nature", *Oxford Studies in Ancient Philosophy* 27 (2004), 249–95.

Svavarsson, S. H. "Pyrrho's Dogmatic Nature", *Classical Quarterly* 52 (2002), 248–56.

Warren, J. "Aristocles' Refutations of Pyrrhonism", *Proceedings of the Cambridge Philological Society* 46 (2000), 140–64.

Pyrrho, later Pyrrhonism and Indian philosophy

Chatterjee, D. "Scepticism and Indian Philosophy", *Philosophy East and West* 27(2) (1977), 195–209.

Flintoff, E. "Pyrrho and India", *Phronesis* 25 (1980), 88–108.

Frenkian, A. M. "Sextus Empiricus and Indian Logic", *Philosophical Quarterly (India)* 30 (1957), 115–26.

McEvilley, T. 1982. "Pyrrhonism and Madhyamika", *Philosophy East and West* 32(1) (1982), 3–35.

3–5. Arcesilaus, Carneades, Cicero, (Philo and Antiochus)

Translations and collections of texts and fragments

The relevant texts for the study of the sceptical Academics are collected in H. J. Mette, "Zwei Akademiker heute: Krantor von Soloi und Arkesilaos von Pitane", *Lustrum* **26** (1984), 7–94; "Weitere Akademiker heute Von Lakydes bis zu Kleitomachos", *Lustrum* **27** (1985), 39–148; and "Philon von Larisa und Antiochos von Askalon", *Lustrum* **28–9** (1986–7), 9–63. Also, C. Brittain, *Philo of Larissa: The Last of the Academic Sceptics* (Oxford: Oxford University Press, 2001) has, in an appendix, collected and translated into English the testimonia on Philo of Larissa.

Cicero, Sextus and Diogenes Laertius are our richest sources of information on the sceptical Academy. Also important is the fragmentary *Index Academicorum* (*History of the Academy*) written by the Epicurean Philodemus: T. Dorandi (ed.), *Filodemo, Storia dei filosofi: Platone e l'Academia* (Naples: Bibliopolis 1991) [Greek text with Italian translation]. References to Sextus' texts are in § "7–9. Sextus Empiricus", below. In Book 4 of *Lives of Eminent Philosophers*, Diogenes presents brief biographies of the Academics from Plato's successor Speusippus up to Carneades' successor Clitomachus.

Of Cicero's philosophical dialogues, the *Academica* is by far the most important, but *De finibus*, *De natura deorum*, *De fato* and *De divinatione* also contain a great deal of Academic argumentation, and the *Tusculanarum Disputationes* and *De officiis* are essential for understanding Cicero's own views. For the *Academica*, there are excellent notes on the text along with commentary in J. S. Reid (ed.), *M. Tulli Ciceronis, Academica* (London: Macmillan, 1885). Cicero's dialogues are all available in Loeb Classical Library editions, with English translations facing Latin text (Cambridge, MA: Harvard University Press).

Here are some more recent and readable translations with useful introductions and notes:

Cicero, *On Academic Scepticism*, C. Brittain (trans.) (Indianapolis, IN: Hackett, 2006).
Cicero, *On Duties*, M. T. Griffin & E. M. Atkins (trans.) (Cambridge: Cambridge University Press, 1991).
Cicero, *On the Emotions, Tusculan Disputations 3 and 4*, M. Graver (trans. and comm.) (Chicago, IL: University of Chicago Press, 2002).
Cicero, *On the Ideal Orator*, J. M. May & J. Wisse (trans.) (Oxford: Oxford University Press, 2001).
Cicero, *On Moral Ends*, J. Annas (intro.), R. Woolf (trans.) (Cambridge: Cambridge University Press 2001).
Cicero, *The Nature of the Gods*, P. G. Walsh (trans.) (Oxford: Clarendon Press, 1997).

Secondary literature on the sceptical Academy (from Arcesilaus to Cicero)

Since so much Academic argument is aimed specifically at the Stoics, a good place to start is M. Frede, "Stoic Epistemology", followed by M. Schofield, "Academic Epistemology", both in Algra, *The Cambridge History of Hellenistic Philosophy*, 295–322 and 323–354. An excellent collection of essays dealing with the sceptical Academy is B. Inwood & J. Mansfeld (eds), *Assent and Argument* (Leiden: Brill, 1997).

Allen, J. "Academic Probabilism and Stoic Epistemology", *Classical Quarterly* **44** (1994), 85–113.

Barnes, J. "Antiochus of Ascalon", in *Philosophia Togata: Essays on Philosophy and Roman Society*, M. Griffin & J. Barnes (eds), 51–96 (Oxford: Oxford University Press, 1989).

Bett, R. "Carneades' *Pithanon*: A Reappraisal of its Role and Status", *Oxford Studies in Ancient Philosophy* **7** (1989), 59–94.

Bett, R. "Carneades' Distinction between Assent and Approval", *Monist* **73** (1990), 3–20.

Brennan, T. "Reasonable Impressions in Stoicism", *Phronesis* **41** (1996), 318–34.

Brittain, C. *Philo of Larissa: The Last of the Academic Sceptics* (Oxford: Oxford University Press, 2001) [REVIEWS: J. Glucker, "The Philonian/Metrodorians: Problems of Method in Ancient Philosophy", *Elenchos* **25** (2004), 99–152; J. C. Laursen in *Journal of the History of Philosophy* **40**(1) (2002), 116–18, in A. A. Long, *Classical Review* **53**(2) (2003), 314–16].

Burnyeat, M. "Gods and Heaps", in *Language and Logos: Studies in Ancient Greek Philosophy presented to G. E. L. Owen*, M. Schofield & M. Nussbaum (eds), 315–38 (Cambridge: Cambridge University Press, 1982).

Cooper, J. "Arcesilaus: Socratic and Sceptic", in his *Knowledge, Nature, and the Good, Essays on Ancient Philosophy*, 81–103 (Princeton, NJ: Princeton University Press, 2004).

Couissin, P. "Le Stoicisme de la nouvelle Academie", *Revue d'historie de la philosophie* **3** (1929), 241–76. [Reprinted in English as "The Stoicism of the New Academy", in Burnyeat, *The Sceptical Tradition*, 31–63.]

De Lacy, P. "Plutarch and the Academic Sceptics", *Classical Journal* **49**(2) (1953), 79–85.

Frede, D. "How Sceptical were the Academic Sceptics?", in *Scepticism in the History of Philosophy*, R. H. Popkin (ed.), 1–26 (Dordrecht: Kluwer, 1996).

Frede, M. "The Sceptic's Two Kinds of Assent and the Question of the Possibility of Knowledge", in *Philosophy in History: Essays on the Historiography of Philosophy*, R. Rorty, J. B. Schneewind & Q. Skinner (eds), 255–78 (Cambridge: Cambridge University Press, 1984). [Reprinted in his *Essays in Ancient Philosophy*, 201–24 (Minneapolis, MN: University of Minnesota Press, 1987).]

Frede, M. "Stoics and Sceptics on Clear and Distinct Impressions" in Burnyeat, *The Sceptical Tradition*, 65–94.

Glucker, J. *Antiochus and the Late Academy* (Göttingen: Vandenhoeck & Ruprecht, 1978) [REVIEWS: J. Dillon in *Classical Review* 31(1) (1981), 60–62; H. Tarrant, "Academics and Platonics", *Prudentia* 12(2) (1980), 109–18].

Hankinson, R. J. "A Purely Verbal Dispute? Galen on Stoic and Academic Epistemology", *Revue Internationale de Philosophie* 45 (1991), 267–300.

Hankinson, R. J. 1997. "Natural Criteria and the Transparency of Judgment: Antiochus, Philo and Galen on Epistemological Justification". In Inwood & Mansfeld, *Assent and Argument*, 161–216.

Inwood, B. "*Rhetorica Diputatio:* The strategy of *De Finibus* II", in *The Poetics of Therapy*, M. Nussbaum (ed.), *Apeiron* 23(4) (1990), 143–64.

Johnson, O. "Mitigated Scepticism", *Ratio* 18 (1976), 73–84.

Long, A. A. "Diogenes Laertius, the Life of Arcesilaus", *Elenchos* 7 (1986) 429–49.

Long, A. A. "Stoa and Sceptical Academy: Origins and Growth of a Tradition", *Liverpool Classical Monthly* 5 (1980), 161–74.

Long, A. A. "Carneades and the Stoic *telos*", *Phronesis* 12 (1967), 59–90.

MacKendrick, P. *The Philosophical Books of Cicero* (London: Duckworth, 1989).

Maconi, H. "Nova Non Philosophandi Philosophia", *Oxford Studies in Ancient Philosophy* 6 (1988), 231–53.

Meador, P. A. "Sceptic Theory of Perception: A Philosophical Antecedent to Ciceronian Probability", *Quarterly Journal of Speech* 54 (1968), 340–51.

Niiniluoto, I. "Scepticism, Fallibilism, and Verisimilitude", in *Ancient Scepticism and the Sceptical Tradition*, J. Sihvola (ed.), *Acta Philosophica Fennica* 66 (2000), 145–69.

Obdrzalek, S. "Living in Doubt: Carneades' *Pithanon* Reconsidered", *Oxford Studies in Ancient Philosophy* 31 (2006), 243–80.

Perin, C. "Academic Arguments for the Indiscernibility Thesis", *Pacific Philosophical Quarterly* 86(4) (2005), 493–517.

Powell, J. G. F. (ed.) *Cicero the Philosopher: Twelve Papers* (Oxford: Oxford University Press, 1995).

Reed, B. "The Stoics' Account of the Cognitive Impression", *Oxford Studies in Ancient Philosophy* 23 (2002), 147–80.

Reinhardt, T. "Rhetoric in the Fourth Academy", *Classical Quarterly* 50(2) (2000), 531–47.

Striker, G. "Sceptical Strategies", in *Doubt and Dogmatism*, M. Schofield, M. Burnyeat & J. Barnes (eds), 54–83 (Oxford: Oxford University Press, 1980). [Reprinted in her *Essays on Hellenistic Epistemology and Ethics*, 92–115 (Cambridge: Cambridge University Press, 1996).]

Striker, G. "Uber den Unterschied zwischen den Pyrrhoneern und den Akademikern", *Phronesis* 26 (1981), 153–71. [Reprinted in English as "On the Difference Between the Pyrrhonists and the Academics", in her *Essays on Hellenistic Epistemology and Ethics*, 135–49.]

Striker, G. "Cicero and Greek Philosophy", *Harvard Studies in Classical Philology* 97 (1995), 53–61.

Tarrant, H. *Scepticism or Platonism? The Philosophy of the Fourth Academy* (Cambridge: Cambridge University Press, 1985) [REVIEWS: J. Annas in *Canadian Philosophical Reviews* 6(1) (1986), 33–5; J. Rist in *Phoenix* 40(4) (1986), 467–9].

Tarrant, H. "Agreement and the Self-Evident in Philo of Larissa", *Dionysius* 5 (1981), 66–97.

Wilkerson, K. E. "Carneades at Rome: a Problem of Sceptical Rhetoric", *Philosophy and Rhetoric* 21 (1988), 131–44.

On the origins of the sceptical Academy

Annas, J. "Plato the Sceptic", in *The Socratic Movement*, P. Vander Waerdt (ed.), 309–40 (Ithaca, NY: Cornell University Press, 1994).

Annas, J. "The Heirs of Socrates", *Phronesis* 23(1) (1988), 100-12.

Brittain, C. & J. Palmer, "The New Academy's Appeals to the Presocratics", *Phronesis* 46(1) (2001), 38–72.

Dillon, J. *The Heirs of Plato: A Study of the Old Academy (347–274 BC)* (Oxford: Oxford University Press, 2003) [REVIEWS: G. Boys-Stone in *American Journal of Philology* 125 (2004), 459–62; L. P. Gerson in *Mind* 113 (2004), 168–71; C. Steel in *Journal of the History of Philosophy* 43(2) (2005), 204–5].

Long, A. A. "Socrates in Hellenistic Philosophy", *Classical Quarterly* 38(1) (1988), 150–71.

Sedley, D. "The End of the Academy", *Phronesis* 26 (1981), 67–75.

Shields, C. "Socrates Among the Sceptics", in Vander Waerdt, *The Socratic Movement*, 341–66.

Tarrant, H. "Socratic *Synousia*: A Post-Platonic Myth?", *Journal of the History of Philosophy* 43(2) (2005), 131–55.

Warren, J. "Socratic Scepticism in Plutarch's *Adversus Colotem*", *Elenchos* 23(2) (2002), 333–56.

Woodruff, P. "The Sceptical Side of Plato's Method", *Revue Internationale de Philosophie* 40 (1986), 22–37

6. Aenesidemus

Translations and collections of texts and fragments

In addition to Sextus, the main sources for the views of Aenesidemus are Diogenes Laertius, Philo of Alexandria and Photius. Many of the relevant texts are assembled in LS 71–2, IG III-25, 35. Texts bearing specifically on the ten modes are assembled, along with illuminating commentary in J. Annas & J. Barnes, *The Modes of Scepticism* (Cambridge: Cambridge University Press, 1985).

The Greek text of Photius' summary of Aenesidemus with facing French translation can be found in R. Henry (ed.), *Photius, Biliothèque, Tome III* (Paris: Société d'édition "Les Belles Lettres", 1962). For more on Photius and an English translation of the summary see N. G. Wilson, *The Bibliotheca: A Selection*, (London: Duckworth, 1994).

Secondary literature

Decleva Caizzin, F. "Aenesidemus and the Academy", *Classical Quarterly* 42(1) (1992), 176–89.

Gaukroger, S. "The Ten Modes of Aenesidemus and the Myth of Ancient Scepticism", *British Journal for the History of Philosophy* 3 (1995), 371–87.

Mansfeld, J. "Aenesidemus and the Academics", in *The Passionate Intellect*, L. Ayres (ed.), 235–48 (New Brunswick, NJ: Transaction, 1995).

Polito, R. *The Sceptical Road: Aenesidemus' Appropriation of Heraclitus* (Leiden: Brill, 2004) [REVIEWS: D. Machuca in *British Journal for the History of Philosophy* 14(1) (2006), 160–64; M. Schofield in *Journal of Hellenic Studies* 126 (2006), 215–16; A. Tigani in *Rhizai* 2(2) (2005), 293–300].

Rist, J. M. "The Heracliteanism of Aenesidemus", *Phoenix* 24(4) (1970), 309–19.

Romanalcala, R. "Aenesidemus: The Recuperation of Greek Sceptic Tradition", *Pensamiento* 52 (1996) 383–402.

Woodruff, P. "Aporetic Pyrrhonism", *Oxford Studies in Ancient Philosophy* 6 (1988), 139–68.

Schofield, M. "Aenesidemus: Pyrrhonist and Heraclitean". In *Pyrrhonists, Patricians, Platonizers*, A. M. Ioppolo & D. N. Sedley (eds), 269–338 (Naples: Bibliopolis, 2007).

Striker, G. "The Ten Tropes of Aenesidemus", in Burnyeat, *The Sceptical Tradition*, 95–115. [Reprinted in her *Essays on Hellenistic Epistemology and Ethics*, 116–34.]

7–9. Sextus Empiricus

Translations and texts

Sextus' extant texts are available in four volumes of the Loeb series, all translated by R. G. Bury: vol. 1, *Outlines of Pyrrhonism* [= *PH*]; vol. 2, *Against the Logicians* [= *M* 7–8], vol. 3, *Against the Physicists, Against the Ethicists* [= *M* 9–11]; vol. 4, *Against the Professors* [= *M* 1–6]; (Cambridge, MA: Harvard University Press, 1933–49). The Greek text alone is available in H. Mutschmann & J. Mau (eds), *Sexti Empirici Opera*, 3 vols (Leipzig: Teubner, 1954–58).

Large portions of the *Outlines of Pyrrhonism* are excerpted in IG III 26-51 along with other relevant texts. Also, many passages from Sextus' works are translated in LS, but only as evidence for the views of other philosophers. Translations of selected texts can also be found in S. G. Etheridge, *Sextus Empiricus, Selections from the Major Writings on Scepticism Man and God* (Indianapolis, IN: Hackett, 1985).

The following are recent and reliable translations, many of which include helpful introductions, notes and commentaries:

Sextus Empiricus, *Outlines of Scepticism*, 2nd edn. J. Annas & J. Barnes (trans.) (Cambridge: Cambridge University Press, 2000).

Sextus Empiricus, *Against the Logicians*, R. Bett (trans.) (Cambridge: Cambridge University Press, 2005).

Sextus Empiricus, *Against the Ethicists*, R. Bett (trans.) (Oxford: Clarendon Press, 1997).

Sextus Empiricus, *The Sceptic Way, Sextus Empiricus' Outlines of Pyrrhonism*, B. Mates (trans.) (Oxford: Oxford University Press, 1996).

Sextus Empiricus, *Against the Grammarians* [= *M* 1], D. L. Blank (trans.) (Oxford: Clarendon Press, 1998).

Sextus Empiricus, *Against the Musicians* [= *M* 6], D. D. Greaves (trans.) (Lincoln, NE: University of Nebraska Press, 1986).

Secondary literature

Annas, J. "Sextus Empiricus and the Peripatetics", *Elenchos* **13** (1992), 201–31.

Barnes, J. *The Toils of Scepticism* (Cambridge: Cambridge University Press, 1990) [REVIEWS: R. Bett in *Journal of Hellenic Studies* **113** (1993), 199–200; N. Denyer, "Symbolic Scepticism", *Phronesis* **36**(3) (1991), 313–18; C. Hookway in *Mind* **101** (1992), 145–8; A. Silverman in *Phoenix* **48**(2) (1994), 168–70].

Barnes, J. "Scepticism and Relativity", *Philosophical Studies* **32** (1988–90), 1–31.

Barnes, J. "Pyrrhonism, Belief and Causation: Observations on the Scepticism of Sextus Empiricus", *Aufstieg und Niedergang der Römischen Welt* II 36(4) (1990), 2608–95.

Barnes, J. "Ancient Scepticism and Causation", in Burnyeat, *The Sceptical Tradition*, 149–204.

Barnes, J. "Proof Destroyed", in Schofield *et al.*, *Doubt and Dogmatism*, 161–81.

Bett, R. "Sextus' *Against the Ethicists*: Scepticism, Relativism or Both?", *Apeiron* **27** (1994), 123–61.

Brennan, T. *Ethics and Epistemology in Sextus Empiricus* (London: Routledge, 1999) [REVIEW: M. Matthen in *Philosophy in Review* **21** (2001), 237–9].

Brunschwig, J. "Proof Defined", in Schofield *et al.*, *Doubt and Dogmatism*, 125–60.

Brunschwig, J. "La Formule *hoson epi tō logō* chez Sextus Empiricus", in *Le Scepticisme antique, Cahiers de la Revue de Théologie et de Philosophie*, A. J. Voelke (ed.), 107–21 (Geneva: Revue de Théologie et de Philosophie, 1990). [Reprinted as "The *hoson epi tō logō* Formula in Sextus Empiricus", in his *Papers in Hellenistic Philosophy*, 244–58.]

Ebert, T. "The Origin of the Stoic Theory of Signs in Sextus Empiricus", *Oxford Studies in Ancient Philosophy* **5** (1987), 83–126.

Everson, S. "The Objective Appearances of Pyrrhonism", in *Pyschology*, S. Everson (ed.), 121–47 (Cambridge: Cambridge University Press, 1991).

Fine, G. "Sextus and External World Scepticism", *Oxford Studies in Ancient Philosophy* **24** (2003), 341–85.

Fine, G. "Sceptical Dogmata, *Outlines of Pyrrhonism* 1.13", *Methexis* **13** (2000), 81–105.

Glidden, D. "Sceptic Semiotics", *Phronesis* **28** (1983), 213–55.

Hankinson, R. J. "Values, Objectivity and Dialectic; The Sceptical Attack on Ethics: Its Methods, Aims, and Success", *Phronesis* **39**(1) (1994), 45–68.

Harte, V. & M. Lane, "Pyrrhonism and Protagoreanism: Catching Sextus Out?", *Logical Analysis and History of Philosophy* **2** (1999), 157–72.

House, D. "The Life of Sextus Empiricus", *Classical Quarterly* **30** (1980), 227–38.

Janáček, K. *Prolegomena to Sextus Empiricus* "Acta Universitatis Palackianae Olomucensis" No. 4 (Olomoue: Nákladem Palackého University, 1948).

Janáček, K. *Sextus Empiricus' Sceptical Methods* (Praha: Universita Karlova, 1972).

La Sala, R. *Die Züge des Skeptikers: Die dialektische Charakter von Sextus Empiricus' Werk* (Götingen: Vandenhoeck & Ruprecht, 2005).

Lammenranta, M. "The Pyrrhonian Problematic", in *The Oxford Handbook of Scepticism*, J. Greco (ed.), 9–33 (Oxford: Oxford University Press, 2008).

Long, A. A. "Sextus Empiricus on the Criterion of Truth", *Bulletin of the Institute of Classical Studies of the University of London* **25** (1978), 35–49.

McPherran, M. "Pyrrhonism's Arguments Against Value", *Philosophical Studies* **60** (1990), 127–42.

Palmer, J. A. "Sceptical Investigation", *Ancient Philosophy* **20** (2000), 351–75.

Perin, C. "Pyrrhonian Scepticism and the Search for Truth," *Oxford Studies in Ancient Philosophy* **30** (2006), 337–60.

Sedley, D. N. "Sextus Empiricus and the Atomist Criteria of Truth", *Elenchos* **13** (1992), 19–56.

Shields, C. "The Truth Evaluability of Stoic *Phantasiai*: *Adversus Mathematicos* 7.242–46", *Journal of the History of Philosophy* **31**(3) (1993), 325–47.

Spinelli, E. "Sceptics and Language: *Phonai* and *Logai* in Sextus Empiricus", *Histoire, Épistémologie, Langage* **13**(2) (1991), 57–70.

Stough, C. "Sextus Empiricus on Non-assertion", *Phronesis* **29** (1984), 137–64.

Wlodarczyk, M. A. *Pyrrhonian Inquiry* (Cambridge: Cambridge Philological Society, 2000).

Pyrrhonism and self-refutation

Bailey, A. "Pyrrhonean Scepticism and the Self-Refutation Argument", *Philosophical Quarterly* **40** (1990), 27–44.

Brunschwig, J. "Sextus Empiricus on the Kriterion: The Sceptic as Conceptual Legatee," in *The Question of "Eclecticism": Studies in Later Greek Philosophy*, J. M. Dillon & A. A. Long (eds), 145–75 (Berkeley, CA: University of California Press, 1988).

Burnyeat, M. F. "Protagoras and Self-Refutation in Later Greek Philosophy", *Philosophical Review* **135** (1976), 44–69.

Castagnoli, L. "Self-bracketing Pyrrhonism", *Oxford Studies in Ancient Philosophy* **18** (2000), 263–328.

Hankinson, R. J. "The End of Scepticism", *Kriterion* **38** (1997), 7–32.

Johnsen, B. C. "On the Coherence of Pyrrhonian Scepticism", *Philosophical Review* **110** (2001), 521–61.

McPherran, M. "Sceptical Homeopathy and Self-refutation", *Phronesis* **32** (1987), 290–328.

Pyrrhonism as a way of life, tranquillity and the sceptic's beliefs

Five very influential papers dealing with these topics are collected in M. Burnyeat & M. Frede (eds), *The Original Sceptics: A Controversy* (Indianapolis, IN: Hackett, 1997).

Barney, R. "Appearances and Impressions", *Phronesis* **37**(3) (1992), 283–313.

Bett, R. "Scepticism as a Way of Life and Scepticism as 'Pure Theory'", in *Homo Viator: Classical Essays for John Bramble*, M. Whitby & P. Hardie (eds), 49–57 (Oak Park, IL: Bristol Classical Press, 1987).

Cohen, A. "Sextus Empiricus: Scepticism as a Therapy", *Philosophical Forum* **15**(4) (1984), 405–24.

Frede, M. "Des Skeptikers Meinungen", *Neue Hefte für Philosophie, Aktualität der Antike* **15/16** (1979), 102–29. [Reprinted as "The Sceptic's Beliefs", W. Mann (trans.), in his *Essays in Ancient Philosophy*, 179–200.]

Garner, D. "Scepticism, Ordinary Language, and Zen Buddhism", *Philosophy East and West* **27**(2) (1977), 165–81.

Machuca, D. "The Pyrrhonist's *Ataraxia* and *Philanthropia*", *Ancient Philosophy* **26** (2006), 111–39.

McPherran, M. "*Ataraxia* and *Eudaimonia* in Ancient Pyrrhonism: Is the Sceptic Really Happy?" *Proceedings of the Boston Area Colloquium in Ancient Philosophy* **5** (1989), 135–71.

Moller, D. "The Pyrrhonian Sceptic's *Telos*", *Ancient Philosophy* **24** (2004), 425–41.

Morrison, D. "The Ancient Sceptic's Way of Life", *Metaphilosophy* **21**(3) (1990), 204–22.

Nussbaum, M. "Sceptic Purgatives: Therapeutic Arguments in Ancient Scepticism", *Journal of the History of Philosophy* **19** (1991), 1–33.

Riberio, B. "Is Pyrrhonism Psychologically Possible?", *Ancient Philosophy* **22**(2) (2002), 319–31.

Striker, G. "*Ataraxia*: Happiness as Tranquility", *Monist* **73** (1990), 97–100 [Reprinted in her *Essays on Hellenistic Epistemology and Ethics*, 183–95.

Thorsrud, H. "Is the Examined Life Worth Living? A Pyrrhonian Alternative", *Apeiron* **36**(3) (2003), 229–49.

Trowbridge, J. "Scepticism as a Way of Living: Sextus Empiricus and Zhuangzi", *Journal of Chinese Philosophy* **33**(2) (2006), 249–65.

Tsouna-McKirahan, V. "Conservatism and Pyrrhonian Scepticism", *Syllecta Classica* **6** (1995), 69–86.

Wientraub, R. "The Sceptical Life", *Dialectica* **50**(3) (1996), 225–33.

Pyrrhonism and technical expertise

Allen, J. "Pyrrhonism and Medical Empiricism", *Aufstieg und Niedergang der Römischen Welt*, II **37**(1) (1993), 646–90.

Allen, J. *Inference from Signs: Ancient Debates about the Nature of Evidence* (Oxford: Clarendon Press, 2001), 87–146.

Barnes, J. "Scepticism and the Arts", in *Method, Medicine and Metaphysics: Studies in the Philosophy of Ancient Science*, R. J. Hankinson (ed.), *Apeiron* 12(2) (1988), 53–77.

Barnes, J. "Medicine, Experience and Logic", in *Science and Speculation: Studies in Hellenistic Theory and Practice*, J. Barnes, J. Brunschwig, M. Burnyeat & M. Schofield (eds), 24–68 (Cambridge: Cambridge University Press, 1982).

Blank, D. L. "Introduction", in *Sextus Empiricus, Against the Grammarians*, xiii–lv.

Edelstein, L. "Empiricism and Scepticism in the Teaching of the Greek Empiricist School", in his *Ancient Medicine*, 195–204 (Baltimore, MD: Johns Hopkins University Press, 1967).

Edelstein, L. "The Methodists", in his *Ancient Medicine*, 173–91.

Frede, M. "The Method of the So-Called Methodical School of Medicine", in Barnes *et al.*, *Science and Speculation*, 1–23. [Reprinted in his *Essays in Ancient Philosophy*, 261–78.]

Hankinson, R. J. *Cause and Explanation in Ancient Greek Thought* (Oxford: Clarendon Press, 1998), 268–322.

Krentz, E. "Philosophic Concerns in Sextus Empiricus, *Adversus Mathematicos* I", *Phronesis* 7 (1962), 152–60.

Walzer, R. & M. Frede (eds), *Galen, Three Treatises on the Nature of Science* (Indianapolis, IN: Hackett, 1985).

The legacy of ancient Scepticism

A great deal has been written on this topic. The following is only a small sample:

Ainslie, D. C. "Hume's Scepticism and Ancient Scepticisms", in *Hellenistic and Early Modern Philosophy*, J. Miller & B. Inwood (eds), 251–73 (Cambridge: Cambridge University Press, 2003).

Annas, J. "Hume and Ancient Scepticism", in Sihvola, *Ancient Scepticism and the Sceptical Tradition*, 271–85.

Annas, J. "Doing Without Objective Values: Ancient and Modern Strategies", in *The Norms of Nature: Studies in Hellenistic Ethics*, M. Schofield & G. Striker (eds), 3–29 (Cambridge: Cambridge University Press, 1986).

Annas, J. "Scepticism, Old and New", in *Rationality in Greek Thought*, M. Frede & G. Striker (eds), 239–54 (Oxford: Clarendon Press, 1996).

Bett, R. "Scepticism and Everyday Attitudes in Ancient and Modern Philosophy", *Metaphilosophy* 24 (1993), 363–81.

Burnyeat, M. F. "The Sceptic in his Place and Time," in Rorty *et al.*, *Philosophy in History*, 225–54.

Burnyeat, M. F. "Idealism in Greek Philosophy: What Descartes Saw and Berkeley Missed", *Philosophical Review* 91(1) (1982), 3–40.

Curley, A. J. *Augustine's Critique of Scepticism: A Study of* Contra Academicos (New York: Peter Lang, 1996).

Dillon, J. *The Middle Platonists: A Study of Platonism 80 BC to AD 200* (London: Duckworth, 1977).

Doty, R. "Carneades, a Forerunner of William James's Pragmatism", *Journal of the History of Ideas* 47 (1986), 133–8.

Fine, G. "Subjectivity Ancient and Modern: The Cyrenaics, Sextus, and Descartes," in Miller & Inwood, *Hellenistic and Early Modern Philosophy*, 192–231.

Floridi, L. *Sextus Empiricus: The Transmission and Rediscovery of Pyrrhonism* (Oxford: Oxford University Press, 2002).

Floridi, L. "*Cupiditas Veri Videndi:* Pierre de Villemandy's Dogmatic vs. Cicero's Sceptical Interpretation of 'Man's Desire to Know'", *British Journal for the History of Philosophy* 3(1) (1995), 29–56.

Hiley, D. R. *Philosophy in Question: Essays on a Pyrrhonian Theme* (Chicago, IL: University of Chicago Press, 1988) [REVIEW: C. Guignon in *Review of Metaphysics* 43(1) (1989), 168].

Hookway, C. *Scepticism* (London: Routledge, 1990) [REVIEWS: R. Fogelin in *Philosophy and Phenomenological Research* 53(1) (1993), 215–20; J. Thomas in *Philosophical Quarterly* 42 (1992), 499–501].

Laursen, J. C. *The Politics of Scepticism in the Ancients, Montaigne, Hume and Kant* (Leiden: Brill, 1992).

Loeb, L. "Sextus, Descartes, Hume, and Peirce: On Securing Settled Doxastic States", *Noûs* 32 (1998), 205–30.

Lom, P. *The Limits of Doubt: the Moral and Political Implications of Scepticism* (Albany, NY: SUNY Press, 2001).

Luper, S. (ed.) *The Sceptics: Contemporary Essays* (Aldershot: Ashgate, 2003).

Maia Neto, J. R. "Academic Scepticism in Early Modern Philosophy", *Journal of the History of Ideas* 58(2) (1997), 199–220.

Musgrave, A. *Common Sense, Science and Scepticism: A Historical Introduction to the Theory of Knowledge* (Cambridge: Cambridge University Press 1993).

Naess, A. *Scepticism* (New York: Humanities Press, 1969) [REVIEW: B. Stroud in *Philosophical Review* 80(2) (1971), 235–56].

Opsomer, J. *In Search of the Truth: Academic Tendencies in Middle Platonism* (Brussels: Verhandelingen van de Koninklijke Academie voor Wetenschappen, 1998).

Penelhum, T. *God and Scepticism* (Boston, MA: Reidel, 1983).

Popkin, R. H. *The History of Scepticism from Erasmus to Spinoza*, 2nd edition (Berkeley, CA: University of California Press, 1979).

Popkin, R. H. *The High Road to Pyrrhonism*, R. A. Watson & J. E. Force (eds) (Indianapolis, IN: Hackett, 1993).

Price, J. V. "Sceptics in Cicero and Hume", *Journal of the History of Ideas* 25(1) (1964), 97–106.

Schmitt, C. B. *Cicero Scepticus: A Study of the Influence of the* Academica *in the Renaissance* (The Hague: Martinus Nijhoff, 1972).

Sinnott-Armstrong, W. (ed.) *Pyrrhonian Scepticism* (New York: Oxford University Press, 2004).

Contemporary Pyrrhonism

Although I do not discuss Robert Fogelin's contemporary version of Pyrrhonian Scepticism in this book, a few bibliographical notes are worth making: see first, his *Pyrrhonian Reflections on Knowledge and Justification* (New York: Oxford University Press, 1994) [REVIEWS: L. Floridi in *Philosophical Quarterly* 47 (1997), 406–8; J. Greco in *International Philosophical Quarterly* 37(1) (1997), 115–19; C. Hookway in *European Journal of Philosophy* 5(1) (1997), 93–7; B. Stroud in *Journal of Philosophy* 92 (1995), 662–5]. He develops this further in *Walking the Tightrope of Reason* (New York: Oxford University Press, 2003).

For a summary of the work see his "Précis of *Pyrrhonian Reflections on Knowledge and Justification*", *Philosophy and Phenomenological Research* 57(2) (1997), 395–400. The précis opens a Book Symposium, which includes: P. K. Moser, "The Relativity of Scepticism", 401–6; F. Dretske, "So Do We Know or Don't We?", 407–9; B. Stroud, "Unpurged Pyrrhonism", 410–16; and R. Fogelin, "What Does a Pyrrhonist Know?", 417–25.

References

Algra, K. 1997. "Chrysippus, Carneades, Cicero: The Ethical *Divisions* in Cicero's *Lucullus*". See Inwood & Mansfeld (1997), 107–39.

Algra, K., J. Barnes, J. Mansfeld & M. Schofield (eds) 1999. *The Cambridge History of Hellenistic Philosophy*. Cambridge: Cambridge University Press.

Allen, J. 1993. "Pyrrhonism and Medical Empiricism". *Aufstieg und Niedergang der Römischen Welt*, II 37(1): 646–90.

Allen, J. 1994. "Academic Probabilism and Stoic Epistemology". *Classical Quarterly* 44: 85–113.

Allen, J. 1997. "Carneadean Argument in Cicero's *Academic* Books". See Inwood & Mansfeld (1997), 217–56.

Alston, W. 1989. *Epistemic Justification: Essays in the Theory of Knowledge*. Ithaca, NY: Cornell University Press.

Annas, J. 1986. "Doing Without Objective Values: Ancient and Modern Strategies". In *The Norms of Nature: Studies in Hellenistic Ethics*, M. Schofield & G. Striker (eds), 3–29. Cambridge: Cambridge University Press.

Annas, J. 1993. *The Morality of Happiness*. New York: Oxford University Press.

Annas, J. 1994. "Plato the Sceptic". In *The Socratic Movement*, P. Vander Waerdt (ed.), 309–40. Ithaca, NY: Cornell University Press.

Annas, J. 1995. "Reply to Cooper". *Philosophy and Phenomenological Research* 55(3): 599–610.

Annas, J. 1996. "Scepticism, Old and New". In *Rationality in Greek Thought*. M. Frede & G. Striker (eds), 239–54. Oxford: Oxford University Press.

Annas, J. 1999. *Platonic Ethics Old and New*. Ithaca, NY: Cornell University Press.

Annas, J. 2001. "Introduction". In *Cicero, On Moral Ends*, R. Woolf (trans.), ix–xxvii. Cambridge: Cambridge University Press.

Annas, J. 2007. "Carneades' Classification of Ethical Theories". In *Pyrrhonists, Patricians, Platonizers: Hellenistic Philosophy in the Period 155–86 BC. Proccedings of the Tenth Symposium Hellenisticum*, A. M. Ioppolo & D. N. Sedley (eds), 187–224. Naples: Bibliopolis.

Annas, J. & J. Barnes 1985. *The Modes of Scepticism*. Cambridge: Cambridge University Press.

Annas, J. & J. Barnes 2000. *Outlines of Scepticism*. Cambridge: Cambridge University Press.

Barnes, J. 1982a. "Medicine, Experience and Logic". See Barnes *et al.* (1982), 24–68.

Barnes, J. 1982b. "The Beliefs of a Pyrrhonist". *Proceedings of the Cambridge Philological Society* **28**: 1–29. Reprinted in *The Original Sceptics: A Controversy*, M. Burnyeat & M. Frede (eds), 58–91 (Indianapolis, IN: Hackett, 1997).

Barnes, J. 1988. "Scepticism and the Arts". In *Method, Medicine and Metaphysics: Studies in the Philosophy of Ancient Science*, R. J. Hankinson (ed.), *Apeiron* **12**(2): 53–77.

Barnes, J. 1990. *The Toils of Scepticism*. Cambridge: Cambridge University Press.

Barnes, J., J. Brunschwig, M. Burnyeat & M. Schofield (eds) 1982. *Science and Speculation: Studies in Hellenistic Theory and Practice*. Cambridge: Cambridge University Press.

Bett, R. 1989. "Carneades' *Pithanon*: A Reappraisal of its Role and Status". *Oxford Studies in Ancient Philosophy* **7**: 59–94.

Bett, R. 1990. "Carneades' Distinction between Assent and Approval". *Monist* **73**, 3–20.

Bett, R. 1993. "Scepticism and Everyday Attitudes in Ancient and Modern Philosophy". *Metaphilosophy* **24**, 363–81.

Bett, R. 1997. *Sextus Empiricus, Against the Ethicists*. Oxford: Clarendon Press.

Bett, R. 2000. *Pyrrho, his Antecedents, and his Legacy*. New York: Oxford University Press.

Bett, R. 2005. *Sextus Empiricus, Against the Logicians*. Cambridge: Cambridge University Press.

Blank, D. L. 1998. *Sextus Empiricus, Against the Grammarians*. Oxford: Clarendon Press.

Bonjour, L. 1985. *The Structure of Empirical Knowledge*. Cambridge, MA: Harvard University Press.

Brennan, T. 1996. "Reasonable Impressions in Stoicism". *Phronesis* **41**: 318–34.

Brennan, T. 1998. "Pyrrho on the Criterion". *Ancient Philosophy* **18**(2): 417–34.

Brickhouse, T. & N. Smith 1994. *Plato's Socrates*. New York: Oxford University Press.

Brittain, C. 2001. *Philo of Larissa: The Last of the Academic Sceptics*. Oxford: Oxford University Press.

Brittain, C. 2006. *Cicero, On Academic Scepticism*. Indianapolis, IN: Hackett.

Brittain, C. & J. Palmer 2001. "The New Academy's Appeals to the Presocratics". *Phronesis* **46**(1): 38–72.

Brouwer, R. 2002. "Sagehood and the Stoics". *Oxford Studies in Ancient Philosophy* **23**: 181–224.

Brunschwig, J. 1988. "Sextus Empiricus on the Kriterion: The Sceptic as Conceptual Legatee". In *The Question of "Eclecticism": Studies in Later Greek Philosophy*, J. M. Dillon & A. A. Long (eds), 145–75. Berkeley, CA: University of California Press.

Brunschwig, J. 1994. "Once Again on Eusebius on Aristocles on Timon on Pyrrho". In his *Papers in Hellenistic Philosophy*, 190–211. Cambridge: Cambridge University Press.

Brunschwig, J. 1999. "Introduction: The Beginnings of Hellenistic Epistemology". See Algra *et al.* (1999), 229–59.

Burnyeat, M. F. 1976. "Protagoras and Self-Refutation in Later Greek Philosophy". *Philosophical Review* 135: 44–69.

Burnyeat, M. F. 1980. "Can the Sceptic Live His Scepticism?". See Schofield *et al.* (1980), 20–53. Reprinted in *The Original Sceptics: A Controversy*, M. Burnyeat & M. Frede (eds), 25–57 (Indianapolis, IN: Hackett, 1997).

Burnyeat, M. F. 1982a. "Idealism in Greek Philosophy: What Descartes Saw and Berkeley Missed". *Philosophical Review* 91(1): 3–40.

Burnyeat, M. F. 1982b. "Gods and Heaps". In *Language and Logos: Studies in ancient Greek philosophy presented to G.E.L Owen*, Schofield and Nussbaum (eds), 315–38. Cambridge: Cambridge University Press.

Burnyeat, M. F. 1984. "The Sceptic in his Place and Time". In *Philosophy in History: Essays on the Historiography of Philosophy*, R. Rorty, J. B. Schneewind & Q. Skinner (eds), 225–54. Cambridge: Cambridge University Press.

Burnyeat, M. F. n.d. "Carneades was no Probabilist". Unpublished.

Burnyeat, M. F. & M. Frede (eds) 1997. *The Original Sceptics: A Controversy*. Indianapolis, IN: Hackett.

Cherniss, H. 1945. *The Riddle of the Early Academy*. Berkeley, CA: University of California Press.

Chiesara, M. L. 2001. *Aristocles of Messene, Testimonia and Fragments*. Oxford: Oxford University Press.

Clifford, W. K. [1877] 1999. *The Ethics of Belief and Other Essays*. Amherst, NY: Prometheus.

Cooper, J. 1995. "Eudaimonism and the Appeal to Nature in the Morality of Happiness: Comments on Julia Annas, *The Morality of Happiness*". *Philosophy and Phenomenological Research* 55(3), 587–98.

Cooper, J. 2004. "Arcesilaus: Socratic and Sceptic". In his *Knowledge, Nature, and the Good, Essays on Ancient Philosophy*, 81–103. Princeton, NJ: Princeton University Press.

Cottingham, J. (ed.) 1986. *René Descartes, Meditations on First Philosophy*. Cambridge: Cambridge University Press.

Decleva Caizzi, F. 1992. "Aenesidemus and the Academy". *Classical Quarterly* 42(1): 176–89.

DeLacy, P. 1958. "*Ou mallon* and the Antecedents of Ancient Scepticism". *Phronesis* 3, 59–71.

Dillon, J. 2003. *The Heirs of Plato: A Study of the Old Academy (347–274 BC)*. Oxford: Oxford University Press.

Dorandi, T. 1999. "Chronology". See Algra *et al.* (1999), 31–54.

Edelstein, L. 1967. "The Methodists". In his *Ancient Medicine*, O. Tempikin & C. L. Temkin (eds), 173–91. Baltimore, MD: Johns Hopkins University Press.

Fine, G. 1996. "Scepticism, Existence, and Belief". *Oxford Studies in Ancient Philosophy* 14: 273–90.

Fine, G. 2003. "Sextus and External World Scepticism". *Oxford Studies in Ancient Philosophy* 24: 341–85.

Flintoff, E. 1980. "Pyrrho and India". *Phronesis* 25: 88–108.

Floridi, L. 2002. *Sextus Empiricus: The Transmission and Rediscovery of Pyrrhonism.* Oxford: Oxford University Press.

Fogelin, R. 1994. *Pyrrhonian Reflections on Knowledge and Justification.* New York: Oxford University Press.

Frede, M. 1982. "The Method of the So-Called Methodical School of Medicine". See Barnes *et al.* (1982), 1–23. Reprinted in his *Essays in Ancient Philosophy*, 261–78.

Frede, M. 1984. "The Sceptic's Two Kinds of Assent and the Question of the Possibility of Knowledge". In *Philosophy in History: Essays on the Historiography of Philosophy*, R. Rorty, J. B. Schneewind & Q. Skinner (eds), 255–78. Cambridge: Cambridge University Press. Reprinted in his *Essays in Ancient Philosophy*, 201–24.

Frede, M. 1987. *Essays in Ancient Philosophy.* Minneapolis, MN: University of Minnesota Press.

Frede, M. 1999. "Stoic Epistemology". See Algra *et al.* (1999), 295–322.

Gaukroger, S. 1995. "The Ten Modes of Aenesidemus and the Myth of Ancient Scepticism". *British Journal for the History of Philosophy* 3: 371–87.

Glucker, J. 1978. *Antiochus and the Late Academy.* Göttingen: Vandenhoeck & Ruprecht.

Glucker, J. 1995. "*Probabile, Veri Simile*, and Related Terms". See Powell (1995), 115–44.

Glucker, J. 2004. "The Philonian/Metrodorians: Problems of Method in Ancient Philosophy". *Elenchos* 25: 99–152.

Görler, W. 1994. "Ältere Pyrrhonismus, Jüngere Akademie, Antiochos aus Askalon". In *Grundriss der Geschichte der Philosophie, Die Philosophie der Antike*, Bd. 4. *Die hellenistische Philosphie.* Basel: Schwabe.

Görler, W. 1997. "Cicero's Philosophical Stance in the *Lucullus*". See Inwood & Mansfeld (1997), 36–57.

Grube, G. M. A. 1997. *Crito.* In *Plato, Collected Works.* J. M. Cooper & D. S. Hutchinson (eds). Indianapolis, IN: Hackett.

Hadot, P. 1995. *Philosophy as a Way of Life: Spiritual Exercises from Socrates to Foucault*, M. Chase (trans.). Oxford: Blackwell.

Hadot, P. 2002. *What is Ancient Philosophy?*, M. Chase (trans.). Cambridge, MA: Harvard University Press.

Hankinson, R. J. 1994. "Values, Objectivity and Dialectic; The Sceptical Attack on Ethics: Its Methods, Aims, and Success". *Phronesis* 39(1): 45–68.

Hankinson, R. J. 1997a. "Natural Criteria and the Transparency of Judgment: Antiochus, Philo and Galen on Epistemological Justification". See Inwood & Mansfeld (1997), 161–216.

Hankinson, R. J. 1997b. "The End of Scepticism". *Kriterion* 38: 7–32.

Hankinson, R. J. 1998a. *The Sceptics*. London: Routledge.

Hankinson, R. J. 1998b. *Cause and Explanation in Ancient Greek Thought*. Oxford: Clarendon Press.

House, D. 1980. "The Life of Sextus Empiricus". *Classical Quarterly* 30: 227–38.

Inwood, B. 1985. *Ethics and Human Action in Early Stoicism*. Oxford: Oxford University Press.

Inwood, B. 1990. "*Rhetorica Diputatio*: The Strategy of *De Finibus* II". In *The Poetics of Therapy*, M. Nussbaum (ed.), *Apeiron* 23(4): 143–64.

Inwood B. & J. Mansfeld (eds) 1997. *Assent and Argument: Studies in Cicero's Academic Books, Proceedings of the Seventh Symposium Hellenisticum*. Leiden: Brill.

James, W. [1897] 1979. *The Will to Believe and Other Essays in Popular Philosophy*. Cambridge, MA: Harvard University Press.

Janáček, K. 1948. *Prolegomena to Sextus Empiricus* "Acta Universitatis Palackianae Olomucensis" No. 4. Olomoue: Nákladem Palackého University.

Johnsen, B. C. 2001. "On the Coherence of Pyrrhonian Scepticism". *Philosophical Review* 110(4): 521–61.

Klein, P. D. 1999. "Human Knowledge and the Infinite Regress of Reasons". *Philosophical Perspectives* 13: 297–325.

Kornblith, H. 2001. *Epistemology: Internalism and Externalism*. Cambridge, MA: MIT Press.

Long, A. A. 1988. "Socrates in Hellenistic Philosophy". *Classical Quarterly* 38(1): 150–71.

Long, A. A. 1990. "Scepticism about Gods in Hellenistic Philosophy". In *Cabinet of the Muses: Essays on Classical and Comparative Literature in Honor of Thomas G. Rosenmeyer*, M. Griffith & D. J. Mastronarde (eds), 279–91. Atlanta, GA: Scholars Press.

Long, A. A. 1995. "Cicero's Plato and Aristotle". See Powell (1995), 37–62.

Mansfeld, J. 1995. "Aenesidemus and the Academics". In *The Passionate Intellect*, L. Ayres (ed.), 235–48. New Brunswick, NJ: Transaction.

Mansfeld, J. 1999. "Sources". See Algra *et al.* (1999), 3–30.

May, J. M. & J. Wisse 2001. *Cicero, On the Ideal Orator*. Oxford: Oxford University Press.

McPherran, M. 1989. "*Ataraxia* and *Eudaimonia* in Ancient Pyrrhonism: Is the Sceptic Really Happy?". *Proceedings of the Boston Area Colloquium in Ancient Philosophy* 5: 135–71.

Mignucci, M. 1993. "The Stoic Analysis of the Sorites". *Proceedings of the Aristotelian Society* 93: 231–45.

Mueller, I. 1982. "Geometry and Scepticism". See Barnes *et al.* (1982), 69–95.

Obdrzalek, S. 2006. "Living in Doubt: Carneades' *Pithanon* Reconsidered". *Oxford Studies in Ancient Philosophy* 31: 243–80.

Palmer, J. A. 2000. "Sceptical Investigation". *Ancient Philosophy* **20**: 351–75.

Penelhum, T. 1983. *God and Scepticism*. Boston, MA: Reidel.

Polito, R. 2004. *The Sceptical Road: Aenesidemus' Appropriation of Heraclitus*. Leiden: Brill.

Popper, K. 1963. *Conjectures and Refutations: The Growth of Scientific Knowledge*. London: Routledge.

Powers, N. 2001. "Fourth Century Flux Theory and the Origin of Pyrrhonism". *Apeiron* **34**(1): 37–50.

Price, J. V. 1964. "Sceptics in Cicero and Hume". *Journal of the History of Ideas* **25**(1): 97–106.

Reed, B. 2002a. "How to Think About Fallibilism". *Philosophical Studies* **107**: 143–57.

Reed, B. 2002b. "The Stoics' Account of the Cognitive Impression", *Oxford Studies in Ancient Philosophy* **23**: 147–80.

Rist, J. 1970. "The Heracliteanism of Aenesidemus". *Phoenix* **24**(4): 309–19.

Rorty, R., J. B. Schneewind & Q. Skinner (eds) 1984. *Philosophy in History: Essays on the Historiography of Philosophy*. Cambridge: Cambridge University Press.

Schofield, M. 2007. "Aenesidemus: Pyrrhonist and Heraclitean". In *Pyrrhonists, Patricians, Platonizers: Hellenistic Philosophy in the Period 155–86 BC. Proccedings of the Tenth Symposium Hellenisticum*, A. M. Ioppolo & D. N. Sedley (eds), 269–338. Naples: Bibliopolis.

Schofield, M., M. Burnyeat & J. Barnes (eds) 1980. *Doubt and Dogmatism*. Oxford: Oxford University Press.

Sedley, D. N. 1980. "The Protagonists". See Schofield *et al.* (1980), 1–19.

Sharples, R. 2006. "The Problem of Sources". In *A Companion to Ancient Philosophy*, M. L. Gill & P. Pellegrin (eds), 430–47. Oxford: Blackwell.

Shields, C. 1994. "Socrates Among the Sceptics". In *The Socratic Movement*, P. Vander Waerdt (ed.), 341–66. Ithaca, NY: Cornell University Press.

Sihvola, J. (ed.) 2000. *Ancient Scepticism and the Sceptical Tradition. Acta Philosophica Fennica* **66**. Helsinki: Philosophical Society of Finland.

Spinelli, E. 2000. "Sextus Empiricus, the Neighbouring Philosophies and the Sceptical Tradition (Again on *Pyr.* I 220–225)". In *Ancient Scepticism and the Sceptical Tradition*, J. Sihvola (ed.), *Acta Philosophica Fennica* **66**: 36–61. Helsinki: Philosophical Society of Finland.

Steup, M. 1996. *An Introduction to Contemporary Epistemology*. Upper Saddle River, NJ: Prentice Hall.

Stopper, M. R. 1983. "Schizzi Pirroniani". *Phronesis* **28**: 265–97.

Striker, G. 1974. "*Kritêrion tês alêtheias*". *Nachrichten der Akademie der Wissenschaften zu Göttingen* I. Phil.-hist. Klasse, 2, 48–110. Reprinted in Striker (1996), 22–76.

Striker, G. 1980. "Sceptical Strategies". See Schofield *et al.* (1980), 54–83. Reprinted in Striker (1996), 92–115.

Striker, G. 1981. "Uber den Unterschied zwischen den Pyrrhoneern und den Akademikern". *Phronesis* **26**, 153–71. Reprinted in English as "On the Difference

Between the Pyrrhonists and the Academics". In her *Essays on Hellenistic Epistemology and Ethics*, 135–49 (Cambridge: Cambridge University Press, 1996).

Striker, G. 1983. "The Ten Tropes of Aenesidemus". In *The Sceptical Tradition*. M. Burnyeat (ed.), 95-116. Reprinted in Striker (1996), 116-34.

Striker, G. 1996. *Essays on Hellenistic Epistemology and Ethics*. Cambridge: Cambridge University Press.

Striker, G. 1997. "Academics Fighting Academics". See Inwood & Mansfeld (1997), 257–76.

Svavarsson, S. H. 2004. "Pyrrho's Undecidable Nature". *Oxford Studies in Ancient Philosophy* 27: 249–95.

Tarrant, H. 1981. "Agreement and the Self-Evident in Philo of Larissa". *Dionysius* 5: 66–97.

Thorsrud, H. 2003. "Is the Examined Life Worth Living? A Pyrrhonian Alternative". *Apeiron* 36(3): 229–49.

Thorsrud, H. forthcoming. "Radical and Mitigated Scepticism in Cicero's *Academica*". In *Cicero's Practical Philosophy*, W. Nicgorski (ed.). Notre Dame, IL: University of Notre Dame Press.

Tsouna, V. 1998. *The Epistemology of the Cyrenaic School*. Cambridge: Cambridge University Press.

Vlastos, G. 1991. *Socrates, Ironist and Moral Philosopher*. Ithaca, NY: Cornell University Press.

Walsh, P. G. 1997. *Cicero, The Nature of the Gods*. Oxford: Clarendon Press.

Walzer, R. and M. Frede 1985. *Galen, Three Treatises on the Nature of Science*. Indianapolis, IN: Hackett.

Warren, J. 2002. *Epicurus and Democritean Ethics: An Archaeology of Ataraxia*. Cambridge: Cambridge University Press.

Watts, E. 2007. "Creating the Academy: Historical Discourse and the Shape of the Community in the Old Academy". *Journal of Hellenic Studies* 127: 106–22.

White, S. 1995. "Cicero and the Therapists". See Powell (1995), 219–46.

Williamson, T. 1994. *Vagueness*. London: Routledge.

Wilson, N. G. 1994. *The Bibliotheca: A Selection*. London: Duckworth.

Woodruff, P. 1988. "Aporetic Pyrrhonism". *Oxford Studies in Ancient Philosophy* 6: 139–68.

Woodruff, P. 1999. "Rhetoric and Relativism: Protagoras and Gorgias". In *The Cambridge Companion to Early Greek Philosophy*. A. A. Long (ed.), 290–310. Cambridge: Cambridge University Press.

Index of passages

Index